# THE GREAT PURSUIT

THE MESSAGE FOR THOSE IN SEARCH OF GOD

# THE GREAT PURSUIT

THE MESSAGE TEXT BY EUGENE H. PETERSON

ADDITIONAL CONTENT BY RANDALL NILES

NAVPRESS®

BRINGING TRUTH TO LIFE

The Navigators is an international Christian organization. Our mission is to advance the gospel of Jesus and His kingdom into the nations through spiritual generations of laborers living and discipling among the lost. We see a vital movement of the gospel, fueled by prevailing prayer, flowing freely through relational networks and out into the nations where workers for the kingdom are next door to everywhere.

NavPress is the publishing ministry of The Navigators. The mission of NavPress is to reach, disciple, and equip people to know Christ and make Him known by publishing life-related materials that are biblically rooted and culturally relevant. Our vision is to stimulate spiritual transformation through every product we publish.

© 2007 by Eugene H. Peterson

All rights reserved. No part of this publication may be reproduced in any form without written permission from NavPress, P.O. Box 35001, Colorado Springs, CO 80935.
www.navpress.com

NAVPRESS, BRINGING TRUTH TO LIFE, and the NAVPRESS logo are registered trademarks of NavPress. Absence of ® in connection with marks of NavPress or other parties does not indicate an absence of registration of those marks.

ISBN 1-57683-939-7

Cover design by studiogearbox.com
Cover image by Craig Cameron Olson/Getty Images
Creative Team: Kent Wilson, John Blase, Darla Hightower, Arvid Wallen, Kathy Guist

Notes and Commentary by Randall Niles
Edited by John Blase

**Published in association with the literary agency of Alive Communications, Inc., 7680 Goddard St., Suite 200, Colorado Springs, CO 80920.**

Some of the anecdotal illustrations in this book are true to life and are included with the permission of the persons involved. All other illustrations are composites of real situations, and any resemblance to people living or dead is coincidental.

All Scripture quotations in this publication are taken from the *THE MESSAGE* (MSG). Copyright © 1993, 1994, 1995, 1996, 2000, 2001, 2002, 2005. Used by permission of NavPress Publishing Group.

Library of Congress Cataloging-in-Publication Data

Bible. English. Message. Selections. 2007.
   The great pursuit : the message for those in search of God / the message by Eugene H. Peterson ; notes and commentary by Randall Niles.
       p. cm.
   Includes bibliographical references.
   ISBN 1-57683-939-7
   1. Bible--Criticism, interpretation, etc. I. Peterson, Eugene H., 1932- II. Niles, Randall. III. Title.
BS195.M47 2007
220.5'209--dc22
                            2006029574

Printed in the United States of America

1 2 3 4 5 6 7 8 / 11 10 09 08 07

FOR A FREE CATALOG OF NAVPRESS BOOKS & BIBLE STUDIES,
CALL 1-800-366-7788 (USA) OR 1-800-839-4769 (CANADA)

# CONTENTS

# AN INTRODUCTION

We all pursue something.

Throughout the seasons of life, we churn through cycles of pursuit. Whether fame and power, peace and abundance, fun and pleasure, or healing and forgiveness, we actively seek something at every phase of existence.

Often, we enter dry periods where paying the mortgage is more important than contemplating the meaning of being—where self-sufficiency is more focal than selfless reflection.

And then it happens . . .

At some point in life, we catch a glimpse of the miraculous . . . maybe the mysterious. We contemplate our earthly origin or we grapple with our eternal destiny.

It could be the birth of a child, the death of a loved one, or a devastating divorce.

It could be the vision of a starving child digging through trash in a street-bound slum.

It could be the vision of a heroic soldier saving a child from the chaos of a street-side bomb.

It could be a massive, star-filled sky or a tiny hummingbird hovering nearby.

It may strike as a monumental epiphany, or it may sneak up as an inconsequential flash.

Regardless, it happens, and the deep questions of life return—if just for an instant. A passion to pursue ultimate purpose, meaning, and truth is reignited in our soul!

Who am I, *really*?

Why am I *really* here?

Where will I *really* be in 10,000 years?

And, most important, where does God fit into all of this?

Who is God, *really* . . . and how do I *really* pursue him?

Throughout the seasons of history, all of humanity has faced this same cycle of perplexity. Whether great thinkers or everyday peasants, our ancestors have all confronted the mystery of God. Some meet God and immediately walk away. Some meet God and embrace him eternally. Some pursue a relationship, while others retreat from possible engagement.

Yes, we all pursue something . . .

This is the story of mankind's pursuit of God . . .

. . . and God's pursuit of mankind.

# AN INVITATION

Life should be an honest quest.

The journey isn't easy, but at least it should be real.

Many pilgrims throughout history left us with authentic portrayals of their pursuits. They recorded the miraculous, mysterious, and spiritual, so we could share in their wonder. They exposed their questions, doubts, and fears, so we could share in their confusion.

Scientists, artists, poets, philosophers, kings, musicians. They wrote from their hearts as they experienced God and sought answers from him.

In this book, we've collected some of the timeless texts that reveal *The Great Pursuit* in all of us. Here are seven biblical accounts along with stories from our ancestors and contemporaries that consider the relationship between God and humanity.

We'll explore the musings of a mighty ruler, witness the trials of a wealthy businessman, hear the cries of an anointed prophet, and share the up-and-down battle of a shepherd-king. We'll peer into the mystical world of a crusty fisherman, walk the path of a loyal scribe, and watch as a simple man hears from God and makes a 180-degree turn in his life.

Like those who've gone before us, we invite you to open your mind, expose your heart, and embark on an authentic journey. We encourage you to dispense with your notions of religion, and just seek *God*.

Even if for a moment, leave your baggage behind.

Ponder. Struggle. Yell. Cry. Pour out your heart to God.

A meaningful search means exposing it all—the good, the bad, and the ugly.

A true pursuit of God requires honesty—honesty before God and honesty with ourselves.

Ask some tough questions, explore some long-held assumptions, and see where *The Great Pursuit* takes you.

# ECCLESIASTES

Unlike the animals, who seem quite content to simply be themselves, we humans are always looking for ways to be more than or other than what we find ourselves to be. We explore the countryside for excitement, search our souls for meaning, shop the world for pleasure. We try this. Then we try that. The usual fields of endeavor are money, sex, power, adventure, and knowledge.

Everything we try is so promising at first! But nothing ever seems to amount to very much. We intensify our efforts—but the harder we work at it, the less we get out of it. Some people give up early and settle for a humdrum life. Others never seem to learn, and so they flail away through a lifetime, becoming less and less human by the year, until by the time they die there is hardly enough humanity left to compose a corpse.

Ecclesiastes is a famous—maybe the world's most famous—witness to this experience of futility. The acerbic wit catches our attention. The stark honesty compels notice. And people do notice—oh, how they notice! Nonreligious and religious alike notice. Unbelievers and believers notice. More than a few of them are surprised to find this kind of thing in the Bible.

But it is most emphatically and necessarily in the Bible in order to call a halt to our various and futile attempts to make something of our lives, so that we can give our full attention to God—who God is and what he does to make something of us. Ecclesiastes actually doesn't say that much about God; the author leaves that to the other sixty-five books of the Bible. His task is to expose our total incapacity to find the meaning and completion of our lives on our own.

Ecclesiastes challenges the naive optimism that sets a goal that appeals to us and then goes after it with gusto, expecting the result to be a good life. The author's cool skepticism, a refreshing negation to the lush and seductive suggestions swirling around us, promising everything but delivering nothing, clears the air. And once the air is cleared, we are ready for reality—for God.

["Ecclesiastes" is a Greek word that is usually translated "the Preacher" or "the Teacher." Because of the experiential stance of the writing in this book, giving voice to what is so basic among men and women throughout history, I have translated it "the Quester."]

## The Quester

**01.** These are the words of the Quester, David's son and king in Jerusalem:

> Smoke, nothing but smoke. [That's what the Quester says.]
>> There's nothing to anything — it's all smoke.
> What's there to show for a lifetime of work,
>> a lifetime of working your fingers to the bone?
> One generation goes its way, the next one arrives,
>>> but nothing changes — it's business as usual for old
>>>> planet earth.
> The sun comes up and the sun goes down,
>> then does it again, and again — the same old round.
> The wind blows south, the wind blows north.
>> Around and around and around it blows,
>> blowing this way, then that — the whirling, erratic wind.
> All the rivers flow into the sea
>> but the sea never fills up.

The rivers keep flowing to the same old place,
    and then start all over and do it again.
Everything's boring, utterly boring —
    no one can find any meaning in it.
Boring to the eye,
    boring to the ear.
What was will be again,
    what happened will happen again.
There's nothing new on this earth.
    Year after year it's the same old thing.
Does someone call out, "Hey, *this* is new"?
    Don't get excited — it's the same old story.
Nobody remembers what happened yesterday.
    And the things that will happen tomorrow?
Nobody'll remember them either.
    Don't count on being remembered.

### I've Seen It All

Call me "the Quester." I've been king over Israel in Jerusalem. I looked most carefully into everything, searched out all that is done on this earth. And let me tell you, there's not much to write home about. God hasn't made it easy for us. I've seen it all and it's nothing but smoke — smoke, and spitting into the wind.

Life's a corkscrew that can't be straightened,
A minus that won't add up.

I said to myself, "I know more and I'm wiser than anyone before me in Jerusalem. I've stockpiled wisdom and knowledge." What I've finally concluded is that so-called wisdom and knowledge are mindless and witless — nothing but spitting into the wind.

Much learning earns you much trouble.
The more you know, the more you hurt.

The writer described himself as "David's son" and "king over Israel in Jerusalem." Thus, King Solomon is the traditional choice for the autobiographer of this reflective prose. Here's a king who had experienced it all—great wisdom and wealth, great power and pleasure. Yet, as he reflected on his life, the aging Quester now considered everything meaningless smoke—worthless trinkets in the puff of vapor called "life." Only here, at the end of his great pursuit, did the Quester understand and accept the ultimate truth concerning the vanity of a self-centered, world-focused existence.

**02.** I said to myself, "Let's go for it—experiment with pleasure, have a good time!" But there was nothing to it, nothing but smoke.

What do I think of the fun-filled life? Insane! Inane!
    My verdict on the pursuit of happiness? Who needs it?
With the help of a bottle of wine
    and all the wisdom I could muster,
I tried my level best
    to penetrate the absurdity of life.
I wanted to get a handle on anything useful we mortals might do
    during the years we spend on this earth.

**I Never Said No to Myself**

Oh, I did great things:
    built houses,
    planted vineyards,
    designed gardens and parks
        and planted a variety of fruit trees in them,
    made pools of water
        to irrigate the groves of trees.
I bought slaves, male and female,
        who had children, giving me even more slaves;
    then I acquired large herds and flocks,

larger than any before me in Jerusalem.
I piled up silver and gold,
    loot from kings and kingdoms.
I gathered a chorus of singers to entertain me with song,
    and — most exquisite of all pleasures —
    voluptuous maidens for my bed.

Oh, how I prospered! I left all my predecessors in Jerusalem far behind, left them behind in the dust. What's more, I kept a clear head through it all. Everything I wanted I took — I never said no to myself. I gave in to every impulse, held back nothing. I sucked the marrow of pleasure out of every task — my reward to myself for a hard day's work!

## I Hate Life

Then I took a good look at everything I'd done, looked at all the sweat and hard work. But when I looked, I saw nothing but smoke. Smoke and spitting into the wind. There was nothing to any of it. Nothing.

And then I took a hard look at what's smart and what's stupid. What's left to do after you've been king? That's a hard act to follow. You just do what you can, and that's it. But I did see that it's better to be smart than stupid, just as light is better than darkness. Even so, though the smart ones see where they're going and the stupid ones grope in the dark, they're all the same in the end. One fate for all — and that's it.

When I realized that my fate's the same as the fool's, I had to ask myself, "So why bother being wise?" It's all smoke, nothing but smoke. The smart and the stupid both disappear out of sight. In a day or two they're both forgotten. Yes, both the smart and the stupid die, and that's it.

I hate life. As far as I can see, what happens on earth is a bad business. It's smoke — and spitting into the wind.

And I hated everything I'd accomplished and accumulated on this earth. I can't take it with me — no, I have to leave it to whoever comes after me. Whether they're worthy or worthless — and who's to tell? — they'll take over the earthly results of my intense thinking and hard work. Smoke.

That's when I called it quits, gave up on anything that could be hoped for on this earth. What's the point of working your fingers to the bone if you hand over what you worked for to someone who never lifted a finger for it? Smoke, that's what it is. A bad business from start to finish. So what do you get from a life of hard labor? Pain and grief from dawn to dusk. Never a decent night's rest. Nothing but smoke.

The best you can do with your life is have a good time and get by the best you can. The way I see it, that's it — divine fate. Whether we feast or fast, it's up to God. God may give wisdom and knowledge and joy to his favorites, but sinners are assigned a life of hard labor, and end up turning their wages over to God's favorites. Nothing but smoke — and spitting into the wind.

---

▶ By the world's standards, the Quester had everything a man could desire—fame, charm, smarts, big money, women knocking at every door. Yet, in his twilight years, the wise teacher realized that "the big things in life" paled in comparison to the sovereign and eternal reality of God.

Regardless of our position, power, or prosperity, we have little control over the seasons of our existence. Without God, life's meaning wobbles on a world without an axis.

---

## There's a Right Time for Everything

**03.** There's an opportune time to do things, a right time for everything on the earth:

A right time for birth and another for death,
A right time to plant and another to reap,
A right time to kill and another to heal,
A right time to destroy and another to construct,

A right time to cry and another to laugh,
A right time to lament and another to cheer,
A right time to make love and another to abstain,
A right time to embrace and another to part,
A right time to search and another to count your losses,
A right time to hold on and another to let go,
A right time to rip out and another to mend,
A right time to shut up and another to speak up,
A right time to love and another to hate,
A right time to wage war and another to make peace.

But in the end, does it really make a difference what anyone does? I've had a good look at what God has given us to do—busywork, mostly. True, God made everything beautiful in itself and in its time—but he's left us in the dark, so we can never know what God is up to, whether he's coming or going. I've decided that there's nothing better to do than go ahead and have a good time and get the most we can out of life. That's it—eat, drink, and make the most of your job. It's God's gift.

---

### Turn! Turn! Turn!

To every thing, turn, turn, turn
There is a season, turn, turn, turn
And a time to every purpose under heaven
A time to be born, a time to die
A time to plant, a time to reap
A time to kill, a time to heal
A time to laugh, a time to weep

To every thing, turn, turn, turn
There is a season, turn, turn, turn
And a time for every purpose under heaven
A time to build up, a time to break down
A time to dance, a time to mourn
A time to cast away stones, a time to gather stones together

— Pete Seeger, 1966

---

I've also concluded that whatever God does, that's the way it's going to be, always. No addition, no subtraction. God's done it and that's it. That's so we'll quit asking questions and simply worship in holy fear.

Whatever was, is.
Whatever will be, is.
That's how it always is with God.

## God's Testing Us

I took another good look at what's going on: The very place of judgment — corrupt! The place of righteousness — corrupt! I said to myself, "God will judge righteous and wicked." There's a right time for every thing, every deed — and there's no getting around it. I said to myself regarding the human race, "God's testing the lot of us, showing us up as nothing but animals."

Humans and animals come to the same end — humans die, animals die. We all breathe the same air. So there's really no advantage in being human. None. Everything's smoke. We all end up in the same place — we all came from dust, we all end up as dust. Nobody knows for sure that the human spirit rises to heaven or that the animal spirit sinks into the earth. So I made up my mind that there's nothing better for us men and women than to have a good time in whatever we do — that's our lot. Who knows if there's anything else to life?

## Slow Suicide

04. Next I turned my attention to all the outrageous violence that takes place on this planet — the tears of the victims, no one to comfort them; the iron grip of oppressors, no one to rescue the victims from them. So I congratulated the dead who are already dead instead of the living who are still alive. But luckier than the

dead or the living is the person who has never even been, who has never seen the bad business that takes place on this earth.

Then I observed all the work and ambition motivated by envy. What a waste! Smoke. And spitting into the wind.

> The fool sits back and takes it easy,
> His sloth is slow suicide.

> One handful of peaceful repose
> Is better than two fistfuls of worried work —
> More spitting into the wind.

## Why Am I Working Like a Dog?

I turned my head and saw yet another wisp of smoke on its way to nothingness: a solitary person, completely alone — no children, no family, no friends — yet working obsessively late into the night, compulsively greedy for more and more, never bothering to ask, "Why am I working like a dog, never having any fun? And who cares?" More smoke. A bad business.

> It's better to have a partner than go it alone.
> Share the work, share the wealth.
> And if one falls down, the other helps,
> But if there's no one to help, tough!

> Two in a bed warm each other.
> Alone, you shiver all night.

> By yourself you're unprotected.
> With a friend you can face the worst.
> Can you round up a third?
> A three-stranded rope isn't easily snapped.

A poor youngster with some wisdom is better off than an old but foolish king who doesn't know which end is up. I saw a youth just like this start with nothing and go from rags to riches, and I saw everyone rally to the rule of this young successor to the king. Even so, the excitement died quickly, the throngs of people soon lost interest. Can't you see it's only smoke? And spitting into the wind?

## God's in Charge, Not You

**05.** Watch your step when you enter God's house.
Enter to learn. That's far better than mindlessly offering a
sacrifice,
Doing more harm than good.

Don't shoot off your mouth, or speak before you think.
Don't be too quick to tell God what you think he wants to hear.
God's in charge, not you — the less you speak, the better.

Overwork makes for restless sleep.
Overtalk shows you up as a fool.

When you tell God you'll do something, do it — now.
God takes no pleasure in foolish gabble. Vow it, then do it.
Far better not to vow in the first place than to vow and not
pay up.

Don't let your mouth make a total sinner of you.
When called to account, you won't get by with
"Sorry, I didn't mean it."
Why risk provoking God to angry retaliation?

But against all illusion and fantasy and empty talk
There's always this rock foundation: Fear God!

> The Quester understood the vanity of superficial and secularized religion. God's "house" was the first Jewish Temple in Jerusalem, which was created as a place for heartfelt worship and sacrifice. Within years of its completion, the religious bureaucracy took over. As a result, the people focused more on the ceremonial machine than the sincere pursuit of God. This has been humanity's timeless travesty—and it continues to this day.
>
> Although a pessimist on the surface, Quester is wise and willing to nudge us back on course. He reminds us that our pursuit of God has nothing to do with mindless religion—rule and ritual for the sake of ceremony. Simply, it is the fear of God that strips religion naked and exposes its misguided appendages. Rather than uttering alms, we should fall to our knees in utter awe.

## A Salary of Smoke

Don't be too upset when you see the poor kicked around, and justice and right violated all over the place. Exploitation filters down from one petty official to another. There's no end to it, and nothing can be done about it. But the good earth doesn't cheat anyone — even a bad king is honestly served by a field.

The one who loves money is never satisfied with money,
Nor the one who loves wealth with big profits. More smoke.

The more loot you get, the more looters show up.
And what fun is that — to be robbed in broad daylight?

Hard and honest work earns a good night's sleep,
Whether supper is beans or steak.
But a rich man's belly gives him insomnia.

Here's a piece of bad luck I've seen happen:
A man hoards far more wealth than is good for him
And then loses it all in a bad business deal.
He fathered a child but hasn't a cent left to give him.

He arrived naked from the womb of his mother;
He'll leave in the same condition — with nothing.
This is bad luck, for sure — naked he came, naked he went.
So what was the point of working for a salary of smoke?
All for a miserable life spent in the dark?

## Make the Most of What God Gives

After looking at the way things are on this earth, here's what I've decided is the best way to live: Take care of yourself, have a good time, and make the most of whatever job you have for as long as God gives you life. And that's about it. That's the human lot. Yes, we should make the most of what God gives, both the bounty and the capacity to enjoy it, accepting what's given and delighting in the work. It's God's gift! God deals out joy in the present, the *now*. It's useless to brood over how long we might live.

## Things Are Bad

**06.** I looked long and hard at what goes on around here, and let me tell you, things are bad. And people feel it. There are people, for instance, on whom God showers everything — money, property, reputation — all they ever wanted or dreamed of. And then God doesn't let them enjoy it. Some stranger comes along and has all the fun. It's more of what I'm calling *smoke*. A bad business.

Say a couple have scores of children and live a long, long life but never enjoy themselves — even though they end up with a big funeral! I'd say that a stillborn baby gets the better deal. It gets its start in a mist and ends up in the dark — unnamed. It sees nothing and knows nothing, but is better off by far than anyone living.

Even if someone lived a thousand years — make it two thousand! — but didn't enjoy anything, what's the point? Doesn't everyone end up in the same place?

We work to feed our appetites;
Meanwhile our souls go hungry.

So what advantage has a sage over a fool, or over some poor wretch who barely gets by? Just grab whatever you can while you can; don't assume something better might turn up by and by. All it amounts to anyway is smoke. And spitting into the wind.

Whatever happens, happens. Its destiny is fixed.
You can't argue with fate.

The more words that are spoken, the more smoke there is in the air. And who is any better off? And who knows what's best for us as we live out our meager smoke-and-shadow lives? And who can tell any of us the next chapter of our lives?

## Don't Take Anything for Granted

**07.** A good reputation is better than a fat bank account.
Your death date tells more than your birth date.

You learn more at a funeral than at a feast —
After all, that's where we'll end up. We might discover
    something from it.

Crying is better than laughing.
It blotches the face but it scours the heart.

Sages invest themselves in hurt and grieving.
Fools waste their lives in fun and games.

You'll get more from the rebuke of a sage
Than from the song and dance of fools.

The giggles of fools are like the crackling of twigs
Under the cooking pot. And like smoke.

Brutality stupefies even the wise
And destroys the strongest heart.

Endings are better than beginnings.
Sticking to it is better than standing out.

Don't be quick to fly off the handle.
Anger boomerangs. You can spot a fool by the lumps on his
    head.

Don't always be asking, "Where are the good old days?"
Wise folks don't ask questions like that.

Wisdom is better when it's paired with money,
Especially if you get both while you're still living.
Double protection: wisdom and wealth!
Plus this bonus: Wisdom energizes its owner.

Take a good look at God's work.
Who could simplify and reduce Creation's curves and angles
To a plain straight line?

On a good day, enjoy yourself;
On a bad day, examine your conscience.
God arranges for both kinds of days
So that we won't take anything for granted.

### Stay in Touch with Both Sides

I've seen it all in my brief and pointless life — here a good person cut
down in the middle of doing good, there a bad person living a long

life of sheer evil. So don't knock yourself out being good, and don't go overboard being wise. Believe me, you won't get anything out of it. But don't press your luck by being bad, either. And don't be reckless. Why die needlessly?

It's best to stay in touch with both sides of an issue. A person who fears God deals responsibly with all of reality, not just a piece of it.

Wisdom puts more strength in one wise person
Than ten strong men give to a city.

There's not one totally good person on earth,
Not one who is truly pure and sinless.

---

Is mankind inherently good or inherently evil? Our answer to this question reveals much about our worldview.

Throughout the ancient Scriptures, we're taught that all of humanity fails the "goodness" test—all of us fall short in some way or another. What do our own lives reveal? Although most of us recoil at the notion of being labeled "bad," deep down, when we truly examine our own hearts and motivations, we know we miss the mark.

---

Don't eavesdrop on the conversation of others.
What if the gossip's about you and you'd rather not hear it?
You've done that a few times, haven't you — said things
Behind someone's back you wouldn't say to his face?

## How to Interpret the Meaning of Life

I tested everything in my search for wisdom. I set out to be wise, but it was beyond me, far beyond me, and deep — oh so deep! Does anyone ever find it? I concentrated with all my might, studying and exploring and seeking wisdom — the meaning of life. I also wanted to identify evil and stupidity, foolishness and craziness.

One discovery: A woman can be a bitter pill to swallow, full of seductive scheming and grasping. The lucky escape her; the undiscerning get caught. At least this is my experience — what I, the Quester, have pieced together as I've tried to make sense of life. But the wisdom I've looked for I haven't found. I didn't find one man or woman in a thousand worth my while. Yet I did spot one ray of light in this murk: God made men and women true and upright; *we're* the ones who've made a mess of things.

**08.** There's nothing better than being wise,
Knowing how to interpret the meaning of life.
Wisdom puts light in the eyes,
And gives gentleness to words and manners.

### No One Can Control the Wind

Do what your king commands; you gave a sacred oath of obedience. Don't worryingly second-guess your orders or try to back out when the task is unpleasant. You're serving his pleasure, not yours. The king has the last word. Who dares say to him, "What are you doing?" Carrying out orders won't hurt you a bit; the wise person obeys promptly and accurately. Yes, there's a right time and way for everything, even though, unfortunately, we miss it for the most part. It's true that no one knows what's going to happen, or when. Who's around to tell us?

No one can control the wind or lock it in a box.
No one has any say-so regarding the day of death.
No one can stop a battle in its tracks.
No one who does evil can be saved by evil.

All this I observed as I tried my best to understand all that's going on in this world. As long as men and women have the power to hurt each other, this is the way it is.

## One Fate for Everybody

One time I saw wicked men given a solemn burial in holy ground. When the people returned to the city, they delivered flowery eulogies — and in the very place where wicked acts were done by those very men! More smoke. Indeed.

Because the sentence against evil deeds is so long in coming, people in general think they can get by with murder.

Even though a person sins and gets by with it hundreds of times throughout a long life, I'm still convinced that the good life is reserved for the person who fears God, who lives reverently in his presence, and that the evil person will not experience a "good" life. No matter how many days he lives, they'll all be as flat and colorless as a shadow — because he doesn't fear God.

———

Here's something that happens all the time and makes no sense at all: Good people get what's coming to the wicked, and bad people get what's coming to the good. I tell you, this makes no sense. It's smoke.

So, I'm all for just going ahead and having a good time — the best possible. The only earthly good men and women can look forward to is to eat and drink well and have a good time — compensation for the struggle for survival these few years God gives us on earth.

When I determined to load up on wisdom and examine everything taking place on earth, I realized that if you keep your eyes open day and night without even blinking, you'll still never figure out the meaning of what God is doing on this earth. Search as hard as you like, you're not going to make sense of it. No matter how smart you are, you won't get to the bottom of it.

**09.** Well, I took all this in and thought it through, inside and out. Here's what I understood: The good, the wise, and all that they do are in God's hands — but, day by day, whether it's love or hate they're dealing with, they don't know.

Anything's possible. It's one fate for everybody — righteous and wicked, good people, bad people, the nice and the nasty, worshipers and non-worshipers, committed and uncommitted. I find this outrageous — the worst thing about living on this earth — that everyone's lumped together in one fate. Is it any wonder that so many people are obsessed with evil? Is it any wonder that people go crazy right and left? Life leads to death. That's it.

**Seize Life!**

Still, anyone selected out for life has hope, for, as they say, "A living dog is better than a dead lion." The living at least know *something*, even if it's only that they're going to die. But the dead know nothing and get nothing. They're a minus that no one remembers. Their loves, their hates, yes, even their dreams, are long gone. There's not a trace of them left in the affairs of this earth.

> Seize life! Eat bread with gusto,
> Drink wine with a robust heart.
> Oh yes — God takes pleasure in *your* pleasure!
> Dress festively every morning.
> Don't skimp on colors and scarves.
> Relish life with the spouse you love
> Each and every day of your precarious life.
> Each day is God's gift. It's all you get in exchange
> For the hard work of staying alive.
> Make the most of each one!
> Whatever turns up, grab it and do it. And heartily!
> This is your last and only chance at it,
> For there's neither work to do nor thoughts to think
> In the company of the dead, where you're most certainly
>     headed.

Nearly five thousand years ago, Gilgamesh was the King of Uruk in Sumeria, a city state on the Euphrates River in modern-day Iraq. Gilgamesh was the central hero in numerous adventures and legendary tales for hundreds of years after his life. Many of these stories were recorded on ancient clay tablets dating back more than four thousand years, and these collections of cuneiform texts are now known collectively as *The Epic of Gilgamesh*.

*The Epic of Gilgamesh* is organized into two main parts. The first is a powerful story of adventure, where the heroic king defeats incredible monsters, evades terrible gods, and woos numerous fair maidens. However, the second part of the Epic reveals a much different side of the great conquering king.

Near the end of his heroic life, Gilgamesh meets a barmaid named Siduri. Initially, Siduri fears Gilgamesh because of his rugged and bloodstained presence, but soon discovers the depth of this warrior's painful past. As Gilgamesh boasts of his feats and foes, Siduri breaks through his larger-than-life façade. Gilgamesh soon crushes under the weight of life's vanity, and Siduri shoots straight for the heart of the matter in Tablet 10 (translated by Yanita Chen, 1994):

> O Mighty King, remember now that only gods stay in eternal
>     watch.
> Humans come then go, that is the way fate decreed on the
>     Tablets of Destiny.
> So someday you will depart, but till that distant day
> Sing, and dance.
>
> Eat your fill of warm cooked food and cool jugs of beer.
> Cherish the children your love gave life.
> Bathe away life's dirt in warm drawn waters.
> Pass the time in joy with your chosen wife.

On the Tablets of Destiny it is decreed
For you to enjoy short pleasures for your short days.

Similar to Quester, mighty Gilgamesh is forced to face his fragile state of humanity. Near the end of his life he realizes the simple truths of existence and embarks on a new quest for eternal meaning.

I took another walk around the neighborhood and realized that on this earth as it is —

> The race is not always to the swift,
> Nor the battle to the strong,
> Nor satisfaction to the wise,
> Nor riches to the smart,
> Nor grace to the learned.
> Sooner or later bad luck hits us all.
>
> No one can predict misfortune.
> Like fish caught in a cruel net or birds in a trap,
> So men and women are caught
> By accidents evil and sudden.

## Wisdom Is Better Than Muscle

One day as I was observing how wisdom fares on this earth, I saw something that made me sit up and take notice. There was a small town with only a few people in it. A strong king came and mounted an attack, building trenches and attack posts around it. There was a poor but wise man in that town whose wisdom saved the town, but he was promptly forgotten. (He was only a poor man, after all.)

All the same, I still say that wisdom is better than muscle, even though the wise poor man was treated with contempt and soon forgotten.

The quiet words of the wise are more effective
Than the ranting of a king of fools.

Wisdom is better than warheads,
But one hothead can ruin the good earth.

**10.** Dead flies in perfume make it stink,
And a little foolishness decomposes much wisdom.

Wise thinking leads to right living;
Stupid thinking leads to wrong living.

Fools on the road have no sense of direction.
The way they walk tells the story: "There goes the fool again!"

If a ruler loses his temper against you, don't panic;
A calm disposition quiets intemperate rage.

———

Here's a piece of bad business I've seen on this earth,
An error that can be blamed on whoever is in charge:
Immaturity is given a place of prominence,
While maturity is made to take a backseat.
I've seen unproven upstarts riding in style,
While experienced veterans are put out to pasture.

———

Caution: The trap you set might catch you.
Warning: Your accomplice in crime might double-cross you.

Safety first: Quarrying stones is dangerous.
Be alert: Felling trees is hazardous.

Remember: The duller the ax the harder the work;

Use your head: The more brains, the less muscle.

If the snake bites before it's been charmed,
What's the point in then sending for the charmer?

———

The words of a wise person are gracious.
The talk of a fool self-destructs —
He starts out talking nonsense
And ends up spouting insanity and evil.

Fools talk way too much,
Chattering stuff they know nothing about.

A decent day's work so fatigues fools
That they can't find their way back to town.

———

Unlucky the land whose king is a young pup,
And whose princes party all night.
Lucky the land whose king is mature,
Where the princes behave themselves
And don't drink themselves silly.

———

A shiftless man lives in a tumbledown shack;
A lazy woman ends up with a leaky roof.

Laughter and bread go together,
And wine gives sparkle to life —
But it's money that makes the world go around.

Don't bad-mouth your leaders, not even under your breath,
And don't abuse your betters, even in the privacy of your home.

Loose talk has a way of getting picked up and spread around.
Little birds drop the crumbs of your gossip far and wide.

# 11. Be generous: Invest in acts of charity.
Charity yields high returns.

Don't hoard your goods; spread them around.
Be a blessing to others. This could be your last night.

When the clouds are full of water, it rains.
When the wind blows down a tree, it lies where it falls.
Don't sit there watching the wind. Do your own work.
Don't stare at the clouds. Get on with your life.

Just as you'll never understand
        the mystery of life forming in a pregnant woman,
So you'll never understand
        the mystery at work in all that God does.

---

In the ancient world, the miracles of pregnancy, gestation, and birth were constant reminders of the divine. Fertility was such an incredible mystery that nearly all cultures attributed the process to God or some polytheistic hierarchy of gods.

In the last few decades, technology has provided us a glimpse into the miraculous. Through advanced *in utero* imaging techniques, we can now witness the life-making process in its full wonder. Remarkably, some of us use these technological advances to discredit the divine. Without pondering, we quickly make the leap from "observing the miraculous" to "understanding the miraculous."

So, what's the logical conclusion? The ancient days are gone. We now "understand" the world around us. Therefore, we don't need God anymore (any kind of god).

How did that happen? Why don't the latest scientific and technological discoveries drive us toward the divine? Shouldn't the latest images and insights reconnect us to the miracle and mystery of it all?

---

Go to work in the morning
        and stick to it until evening without watching the clock.

You never know from moment to moment
how your work will turn out in the end.

## Before the Years Take Their Toll

Oh, how sweet the light of day,
And how wonderful to live in the sunshine!
Even if you live a long time, don't take a single day for granted.
Take delight in each light-filled hour,
Remembering that there will also be many dark days
And that most of what comes your way is smoke.

You who are young, make the most of your youth.
Relish your youthful vigor.
Follow the impulses of your heart.
If something looks good to you, pursue it.
But know also that not just anything goes;
You have to answer to God for every last bit of it.

Live footloose and fancy-free —
You won't be young forever.
Youth lasts about as long as smoke.

**12.** Honor and enjoy your Creator while you're still young,
Before the years take their toll and your vigor wanes,
Before your vision dims and the world blurs
And the winter years keep you close to the fire.

In old age, your body no longer serves you so well.
Muscles slacken, grip weakens, joints stiffen.
The shades are pulled down on the world.
You can't come and go at will. Things grind to a halt.
The hum of the household fades away.
You are wakened now by bird-song.

Hikes to the mountains are a thing of the past.
Even a stroll down the road has its terrors.
Your hair turns apple-blossom white,
Adorning a fragile and impotent matchstick body.
Yes, you're well on your way to eternal rest,
While your friends make plans for your funeral.

Life, lovely while it lasts, is soon over.
Life as we know it, precious and beautiful, ends.
The body is put back in the same ground it came from.
The spirit returns to God, who first breathed it.

It's all smoke, nothing but smoke.
The Quester says that everything's smoke.

## The Final Word

Besides being wise himself, the Quester also taught others knowledge. He weighed, examined, and arranged many proverbs. The Quester did his best to find the right words and write the plain truth.

The words of the wise prod us to live well.
They're like nails hammered home, holding life together.
They are given by God, the one Shepherd.

But regarding anything beyond this, dear friend, go easy. There's no end to the publishing of books, and constant study wears you out so you're no good for anything else. The last and final word is this:

Fear God.
Do what he tells you.

And that's it. Eventually God will bring everything that we do out into the open and judge it according to its hidden intent, whether it's good or evil.

# JOB

Job suffered. His name is synonymous with suffering. He asked, "Why?" He asked, "Why me?" And he put his questions to God. He asked his questions persistently, passionately, and eloquently. He refused to take silence for an answer. He refused to take clichés for an answer. He refused to let God off the hook.

Job did not take his sufferings quietly or piously. He disdained going for a second opinion to outside physicians or philosophers. Job took his stance before *God,* and there he protested his suffering, protested mightily.

It is not only because Job suffered that he is important to us. It is because he suffered in the same ways that *we* suffer—in the vital areas of family, personal health, and material things. Job is also important to us because he searchingly questioned and boldly protested his suffering. Indeed, he went "to the top" with his questions.

It is not suffering as such that troubles us. It is undeserved suffering.

Almost all of us in our years of growing up have the experience of disobeying our parents and getting punished for it. When that discipline was connected with wrongdoing, it had a certain sense of justice to it: *When we do wrong, we get punished.*

One of the surprises as we get older, however, is that we come to see that there is no real correlation between the amount of wrong we commit and the amount of pain we experience. An even larger surprise is that very often there is something quite the opposite: We do right and get knocked down. We do the best we are capable of doing, and just as we are reaching out to receive our reward we are hit from the blind side and sent reeling.

*This* is the suffering that first bewilders and then outrages us. This is the kind of suffering that bewildered and outraged Job, for Job was doing everything right when suddenly everything went wrong. And it is this kind of suffering to which Job gives voice when he protests to God.

Job gives voice to his sufferings so well, so accurately and honestly, that anyone who has ever suffered—which includes every last one of us—can recognize his or her personal pain in the voice of Job. Job says boldly what some of us are too timid to say. He makes poetry out of what in many of us is only a tangle of confused whimpers. He shouts out to God what a lot of us mutter behind our sleeves. He refuses to accept the role of a defeated victim.

It is also important to note what Job does *not* do, lest we expect something from him that he does not intend. Job does not curse God as his wife suggests he should do, getting rid of the problem by getting rid of God. But neither does Job *explain* suffering. He does not instruct us in how to live so that we can avoid suffering. Suffering is a mystery, and Job comes to respect the mystery.

**01.** Job was a man who lived in Uz. He was honest inside and out, a man of his word, who was totally devoted to God and hated evil with a passion. He had seven sons and three daughters. He was also very wealthy — seven thousand head of sheep, three thousand camels, five hundred teams of oxen, five hundred donkeys, and a huge staff of servants — the most influential man in all the East!

His sons used to take turns hosting parties in their homes, always inviting their three sisters to join them in their merrymaking. When the parties were over, Job would get up early in the morning and sacrifice a burnt offering for each of his children, thinking, "Maybe one of them sinned by defying God inwardly." Job made a habit of this sacrificial atonement, just in case they'd sinned.

## The First Test: Family and Fortune

One day when the angels came to report to GOD, Satan, who was the Designated Accuser, came along with them. GOD singled out Satan and said, "What have you been up to?"

Satan answered GOD, "Going here and there, checking things out on earth."

GOD said to Satan, "Have you noticed my friend Job? There's no one quite like him — honest and true to his word, totally devoted to God and hating evil."

Satan retorted, "So do you think Job does all that out of the sheer goodness of his heart? Why, no one ever had it so good! You pamper him like a pet, make sure nothing bad ever happens to him or his family or his possessions, bless everything he does — he can't lose!

"But what do you think would happen if you reached down and took away everything that is his? He'd curse you right to your face, that's what."

GOD replied, "We'll see. Go ahead — do what you want with all that is his. Just don't hurt *him*." Then Satan left the presence of GOD.

Sometime later, while Job's children were having one of their parties at the home of the oldest son, a messenger came to Job and said, "The oxen were plowing and the donkeys grazing in the field next to us when Sabeans attacked. They stole the animals and killed the field hands. I'm the only one to get out alive and tell you what happened."

While he was still talking, another messenger arrived and said, "Bolts of lightning struck the sheep and the shepherds and fried them — burned them to a crisp. I'm the only one to get out alive and tell you what happened."

While he was still talking, another messenger arrived and said, "Chaldeans coming from three directions raided the camels and massacred the camel drivers. I'm the only one to get out alive and tell you what happened."

While he was still talking, another messenger arrived and said, "Your children were having a party at the home of the oldest brother when a tornado swept in off the desert and struck the house. It collapsed on the young people and they died. I'm the only one to get out alive and tell you what happened."

Job got to his feet, ripped his robe, shaved his head, then fell to the ground and worshiped:

Naked I came from my mother's womb,
    naked I'll return to the womb of the earth.
GOD gives, GOD takes.
    God's name be ever blessed.

Not once through all this did Job sin; not once did he blame God.

---

▶ Tearing one's clothes was an expression of severe grief in the ancient world. Since hair was often considered a symbol of personal glory, shaving one's head was the ultimate sign of humility and loss.

Yes, Job was stripped of everything, yet he accepted God's will in both the good and bad of life. God's sovereignty was the perspective of Job's life—even during his personal pain. Remarkably, as Job grieved, he worshiped God.

---

### The Second Test: Health

**02.** One day when the angels came to report to GOD, Satan also showed up. GOD singled out Satan, saying, "And what have you been up to?" Satan answered GOD, "Oh, going here and there, checking things out." Then GOD said to Satan, "Have you noticed my friend Job? There's no one quite like him, is there — honest and true to his word, totally devoted to God and hating evil? He still has a firm grip on his integrity! You tried to trick me into destroying him, but it didn't work."

Satan answered, "A human would do anything to save his life. But what do you think would happen if you reached down and took away his health? He'd curse you to your face, that's what."

GOD said, "All right. Go ahead—you can do what you like with him. But mind you, don't kill him."

Satan left GOD and struck Job with terrible sores. Job was ulcers and scabs from head to foot. They itched and oozed so badly that he took a piece of broken pottery to scrape himself, then went and sat on a trash heap, among the ashes.

His wife said, "Still holding on to your precious integrity, are you? Curse God and be done with it!"

He told her, "You're talking like an empty-headed fool. We take the good days from God—why not also the bad days?"

Not once through all this did Job sin. He said nothing against God.

## Job's Three Friends

Three of Job's friends heard of all the trouble that had fallen on him. Each traveled from his own country—Eliphaz from Teman, Bildad from Shuhah, Zophar from Naamath—and went together to Job to keep him company and comfort him. When they first caught sight of him, they couldn't believe what they saw—they hardly recognized him! They cried out in lament, ripped their robes, and dumped dirt on their heads as a sign of their grief. Then they sat with him on the ground. Seven days and nights they sat there without saying a word. They could see how rotten he felt, how deeply he was suffering.

What a gut-wrenching scene.

Job, formerly the chief citizen of a large city, now sits on a heap of ashes outside its gates. He's oozing and reeking, destitute and devastated—rejected by former friends, peers, and business associates. His immense influence and affluence totally gone.

Many believe Job's disease was a form of leprosy complicated by elephantiasis, one of the most painful and publicly humiliating afflictions in the ancient world. Job was shunned. Overnight, he went from extravagance to exile.

Job's three "friends" were likely desert chiefs and nomadic princes from other powerful tribal regions. Eliphaz was a descendant of Esau living in Teman, an ancient city of the Edomites, who later conquered the entire area. Bildad was a descendant of Abraham and Keturah living in Shuhu, an Aramaean city on the Euphrates River. Zophar was from Naamah, an unknown region in Arabia.

Each man showed up with his own reason to see Job in this state. Each man had his own set of personal, political, and providential motivations. Each man viewed Job's plight through his own religious lens.

## JOB CRIES OUT
### What's the Point of Life?

**03.** Then Job broke the silence. He spoke up and cursed his fate:

"Obliterate the day I was born.
    Blank out the night I was conceived!
Let it be a black hole in space.
    May God above forget it ever happened.
    Erase it from the books!
May the day of my birth be buried in deep darkness,
    shrouded by the fog,
    swallowed by the night.
And the night of my conception — the devil take it!
    Rip the date off the calendar,
    delete it from the almanac.
Oh, turn that night into pure nothingness —
    no sounds of pleasure from that night, ever!
May those who are good at cursing curse that day.
    Unleash the sea beast, Leviathan, on it.
May its morning stars turn to black cinders,
    waiting for a daylight that never comes,
    never once seeing the first light of dawn.
And why? Because it released me from my mother's womb
    into a life with so much trouble.

"Why didn't I die at birth,
    my first breath out of the womb my last?
Why were there arms to rock me,
    and breasts for me to drink from?
I could be resting in peace right now,
    asleep forever, feeling no pain,
In the company of kings and statesmen
    in their royal ruins,
Or with princes resplendent
    in their gold and silver tombs.
Why wasn't I stillborn and buried
    with all the babies who never saw light,
Where the wicked no longer trouble anyone
    and bone-weary people get a long-deserved rest?
Prisoners sleep undisturbed,
    never again to wake up to the bark of the guards.
The small and the great are equals in that place,
    and slaves are free from their masters.

"Why does God bother giving light to the miserable,
    why bother keeping bitter people alive,
Those who want in the worst way to die, and can't,
    who can't imagine anything better than death,
Who count the day of their death and burial
    the happiest day of their life?
What's the point of life when it doesn't make sense,
    when God blocks all the roads to meaning?

"Instead of bread I get groans for my supper,
    then leave the table and vomit my anguish.
The worst of my fears has come true,
    what I've dreaded most has happened.
My repose is shattered, my peace destroyed.
    No rest for me, ever — death has invaded life."

## ELIPHAZ SPEAKS OUT
### Now *You're* the One in Trouble

**04.** Then Eliphaz from Teman spoke up:

"Would you mind if I said something to you?
    Under the circumstances it's hard to keep quiet.
You yourself have done this plenty of times, spoken words
    that clarify, encouraged those who were about to quit.
Your words have put stumbling people on their feet,
    put fresh hope in people about to collapse.
But now *you're* the one in trouble — you're hurting!
    You've been hit hard and you're reeling from the blow.
But shouldn't your devout life give you confidence now?
    Shouldn't your exemplary life give you hope?

"Think! Has a truly innocent person ever ended up on the scrap
        heap?
    Do genuinely upright people ever lose out in the end?
It's my observation that those who plow evil
    and sow trouble reap evil and trouble.
One breath from God and they fall apart,
    one blast of his anger and there's nothing left of them.
The mighty lion, king of the beasts, roars mightily,
    but when he's toothless he's useless —
No teeth, no prey — and the cubs
    wander off to fend for themselves.

"A word came to me in secret —
    a mere whisper of a word, but I heard it clearly.
It came in a scary dream one night,
    after I had fallen into a deep, deep sleep.
Dread stared me in the face, and Terror.
    I was scared to death — I shook from head to foot.

A spirit glided right in front of me —
>the hair on my head stood on end.
I couldn't tell what it was that appeared there —
>a blur . . . and then I heard a muffled voice:

"'How can mere mortals be more righteous than God?
>How can humans be purer than their Creator?
Why, God doesn't even trust his own servants,
>doesn't even cheer his angels,
So how much less these bodies composed of mud,
>fragile as moths?
These bodies of ours are here today and gone tomorrow,
>and no one even notices — gone without a trace.
When the tent stakes are ripped up, the tent collapses —
>we die and are never the wiser for having lived.'"

## Don't Blame Fate When Things Go Wrong

**05.** "Call for help, Job, if you think anyone will answer!
>To which of the holy angels will you turn?
The hot temper of a fool eventually kills him,
>the jealous anger of a simpleton does her in.
I've seen it myself — seen fools putting down roots,
>and then, suddenly, their houses are cursed.
Their children out in the cold, abused and exploited,
>with no one to stick up for them.
Hungry people off the street plunder their harvests,
>cleaning them out completely, taking thorns and all,
>insatiable for everything they have.
Don't blame fate when things go wrong —
>trouble doesn't come from nowhere.
It's human! Mortals are born and bred for trouble,
>as certainly as sparks fly upward.

## What a Blessing When God Corrects You!

"If I were in your shoes, I'd go straight to God,
    I'd throw myself on the mercy of God.
After all, he's famous for great and unexpected acts;
    there's no end to his surprises.
He gives rain, for instance, across the wide earth,
    sends water to irrigate the fields.
He raises up the down-and-out,
    gives firm footing to those sinking in grief.
He aborts the schemes of conniving crooks,
    so that none of their plots come to term.
He catches the know-it-alls in their conspiracies —
    all that intricate intrigue swept out with the trash!
Suddenly they're disoriented, plunged into darkness;
    they can't see to put one foot in front of the other.
But the downtrodden are saved by God,
    saved from the murderous plots, saved from the iron fist.
And so the poor continue to hope,
    while injustice is bound and gagged.

"So, what a blessing when God steps in and corrects you!
    Mind you, don't despise the discipline of Almighty God!
True, he wounds, but he also dresses the wound;
    the same hand that hurts you, heals you.
From one disaster after another he delivers you;
    no matter what the calamity, the evil can't touch you —

"In famine, he'll keep you from starving,
    in war, from being gutted by the sword.
You'll be protected from vicious gossip
    and live fearless through any catastrophe.
You'll shrug off disaster and famine,
    and stroll fearlessly among wild animals.

You'll be on good terms with rocks and mountains;
    wild animals will become your good friends.
You'll know that your place on earth is safe,
    you'll look over your goods and find nothing amiss.
You'll see your children grow up,
    your family lovely and lissome as orchard grass.
You'll arrive at your grave ripe with many good years,
    like sheaves of golden grain at harvest.

"Yes, this is the way things are — my word of honor!
    Take it to heart and you won't go wrong."

## SEARCHER ON THE WAY
*Grappling with the God-Pain Paradox*

Augustine was born in AD 354, the son of a Roman official in North Africa. When he was nineteen, he read an essay by Cicero on the meaning of "truth," and it was then and there that Augustine dedicated himself to pursuing such an intriguing, yet illusive, notion.

During his philosophical journey, Augustine experienced a great deal of pain and suffering. He went through phases of severe depression and debilitating grief. He witnessed things that just couldn't be reconciled with theological doctrine. It was this irreconcilable tradeoff between truth and evil that kept Augustine jumping from philosophy to philosophy for more than a decade.

At the age of thirty-one, Augustine had a supernatural experience "as if a light of relief from all anxiety flooded into my heart." It was then that "all the shadows of doubt were dispelled" and he accepted God as part of his life.

Although Augustine would become a great man of faith, he continued to struggle with the obvious pain, suffering, and evil allowed by God. In his first book, *On Order* (AD 386), Augustine wrote:

> There is nothing that even the most gifted people
> desire more than to finally understand how, taking
> into account the amount of evil in this world, one
> can still believe that God cares about human affairs.

For the next forty years, Augustine grappled with the reality of this paradox. He focused on God's nature in Scripture and God's apparent desire for humanity. He determined that God created us for a relationship with him, and that authentic relationship is impossible with puppets. Apparently, God wanted us to have the capacity to freely choose or reject him. Of course, if we have free will, we have the capacity to choose love or hate—good or evil. After four decades of writing on the subject, Augustine concluded that "God judged it better to bring good out of evil than to suffer no evil at all."

## JOB REPLIES TO ELIPHAZ
### God Has Dumped the Works on Me

# 06.
Job answered:

"If my misery could be weighed,
    if you could pile the whole bitter load on the scales,
It would be heavier than all the sand of the sea!
    Is it any wonder that I'm screaming like a caged cat?
The arrows of God Almighty are in me,
    poison arrows — and I'm poisoned all through!
    God has dumped the whole works on me.
Donkeys bray and cows moo when they run out of pasture —
    so don't expect me to keep quiet in this.
Do you see what God has dished out for me?
    It's enough to turn anyone's stomach!
Everything in me is repulsed by it —
    it makes me sick.

### Pressed Past the Limits

"All I want is an answer to one prayer,
    a last request to be honored:
Let God step on me — squash me like a bug,
    and be done with me for good.
I'd at least have the satisfaction
    of not having blasphemed the Holy God,
    before being pressed past the limits.
Where's the strength to keep my hopes up?
    What future do I have to keep me going?
Do you think I have nerves of steel?
    Do you think I'm made of iron?
Do you think I can pull myself up by my bootstraps?
    Why, I don't even have any boots!

The book of Job is not only a witness to the dignity of suffering and God's presence in our suffering, but is also our primary biblical protest against religion that has been reduced to explanations or "answers." Many of the answers that Job's so-called friends give him are technically true. But it is the "technical" part that ruins them. They are answers without personal relationship, intellect without intimacy. The answers are slapped onto Job's ravaged life like labels on a specimen bottle. Job rages against this secularized wisdom that has lost touch with the living realities of God.

In every generation there are men and women who pretend to be able to instruct us in a way of life that guarantees we will be "healthy, wealthy, and wise." According to the propaganda of these people, anyone who lives intelligently and morally is exempt from suffering. From their point of view, it is lucky for us that they are now at hand to provide the intelligent and moral answers we need.

## My So-Called Friends

"When desperate people give up on God Almighty,
    their friends, at least, should stick with them.
But my brothers are fickle as a gulch in the desert—
    one day they're gushing with water
From melting ice and snow
    cascading out of the mountains,
But by midsummer they're dry,
    gullies baked dry in the sun.
Travelers who spot them and go out of their way for a drink
    end up in a waterless gulch and die of thirst.
Merchant caravans from Tema see them and expect water,
    tourists from Sheba hope for a cool drink.
They arrive so confident—but what a disappointment!
    They get there, and their faces fall!
And you, my so-called friends, are no better—
        there's nothing to you!
    One look at a hard scene and you shrink in fear.
It's not as though I asked you for anything—
    I didn't ask you for one red cent—

Nor did I beg you to go out on a limb for me.
    So why all this dodging and shuffling?

"Confront me with the truth and I'll shut up,
    show me where I've gone off the track.
Honest words never hurt anyone,
    but what's the point of all this pious bluster?
You pretend to tell me what's wrong with my life,
    but treat my words of anguish as so much hot air.
Are people mere things to you?
    Are friends just items of profit and loss?

"Look me in the eyes!
    Do you think I'd lie to your face?
Think it over — no double-talk!
    Think carefully — my integrity is on the line!
Can you detect anything false in what I say?
    Don't you trust me to discern good from evil?"

### There's Nothing to My Life

**07.** "Human life is a struggle, isn't it?
    It's a life sentence to hard labor.
Like field hands longing for quitting time
    and working stiffs with nothing to hope for but payday,
I'm given a life that meanders and goes nowhere —
    months of aimlessness, nights of misery!
I go to bed and think, 'How long till I can get up?'
    I toss and turn as the night drags on — and I'm fed up!
I'm covered with maggots and scabs.
    My skin gets scaly and hard, then oozes with pus.
My days come and go swifter than the click of knitting needles,
    and then the yarn runs out — an unfinished life!

"God, don't forget that I'm only a puff of air!
     These eyes have had their last look at goodness.
And your eyes have seen the last of me;
     even while you're looking, there'll be nothing left to look at.
When a cloud evaporates, it's gone for good;
     those who go to the grave never come back.
They don't return to visit their families;
     never again will friends drop in for coffee.

"And so I'm not keeping one bit of this quiet,
     I'm laying it all out on the table;
     my complaining to high heaven is bitter, but honest.
Are you going to put a muzzle on me,
     the way you quiet the sea and still the storm?
If I say, 'I'm going to bed, then I'll feel better.
     A little nap will lift my spirits,'
You come and so scare me with nightmares
     and frighten me with ghosts
That I'd rather strangle in the bedclothes
     than face this kind of life any longer.
I hate this life! Who needs any more of this?
     Let me alone! There's nothing to my life — it's nothing
          but smoke.

"What are mortals anyway, that you bother with them,
     that you even give them the time of day?
That you check up on them every morning,
     looking in on them to see how they're doing?
Let up on me, will you?
     Can't you even let me spit in peace?
Even suppose I'd sinned — how would that hurt you?
     You're responsible for every human being.
Don't you have better things to do than pick on me?
     Why make a federal case out of me?

Why don't you just forgive my sins
    and start me off with a clean slate?
The way things are going, I'll soon be dead.
    You'll look high and low, but I won't be around."

## BILDAD'S RESPONSE
### Does God Mess Up?

**08.** Bildad from Shuhah was next to speak:

"How can you keep on talking like this?
    You're talking nonsense, and noisy nonsense at that.
Does God mess up?
    Does God Almighty ever get things backward?
It's plain that your children sinned against him —
    otherwise, why would God have punished them?
Here's what you must do — and don't put it off any longer:
    Get down on your knees before God Almighty.
If you're as innocent and upright as you say,
    it's not too late — he'll come running;
    he'll set everything right again, reestablish your fortunes.
Even though you're not much right now,
    you'll end up better than ever.

### To Hang Your Life from One Thin Thread

"Put the question to our ancestors,
    study what they learned from their ancestors.
For we're newcomers at this, with a lot to learn,
    and not too long to learn it.
So why not let the ancients teach you, tell you what's what,
    instruct you in what they knew from experience?
Can mighty pine trees grow tall without soil?
    Can luscious tomatoes flourish without water?

Blossoming flowers look great before they're cut or picked,
    but without soil or water they wither more quickly than grass.
That's what happens to all who forget God —
    all their hopes come to nothing.
They hang their life from one thin thread,
    they hitch their fate to a spider web.
One jiggle and the thread breaks,
    one jab and the web collapses.
Or they're like weeds springing up in the sunshine,
    invading the garden,
Spreading everywhere, overtaking the flowers,
    getting a foothold even in the rocks.
But when the gardener rips them out by the roots,
    the garden doesn't miss them one bit.
The sooner the godless are gone, the better;
    then good plants can grow in their place.

"There's no way that God will reject a good person,
    and there is no way he'll help a bad one.
God will let you laugh again;
    you'll raise the roof with shouts of joy,
With your enemies thoroughly discredited,
    their house of cards collapsed."

## JOB CONTINUES
### How Can Mere Mortals Get Right with God?

**09.** Job continued by saying:

"So what's new? I know all this.
    The question is, 'How can mere mortals get right with God?'
If we wanted to bring our case before him,
    what chance would we have? Not one in a thousand!
God's wisdom is so deep, God's power so immense,

who could take him on and come out in one piece?
He moves mountains before they know what's happened,
     flips them on their heads on a whim.
He gives the earth a good shaking up,
     rocks it down to its very foundations.
He tells the sun, 'Don't shine,' and it doesn't;
     he pulls the blinds on the stars.
All by himself he stretches out the heavens
     and strides on the waves of the sea.
He designed the Big Dipper and Orion,
     the Pleiades and Alpha Centauri.
We'll never comprehend all the great things he does;
     his miracle-surprises can't be counted.

---

How can we fathom the immensity of it all? Our sun is about 93 million miles from the earth, and it takes about 8.5 minutes for its light to reach us. Alpha Centauri is the next closest star—about 25.2 trillion miles away! It takes 4.2 years for Alpha Centauri's light to reach us!

Let's put that in some kind of perspective. Place a marble (our earth) about nine inches from a basketball (our sun). If you imagine that each inch represents about 10,000,000 miles, your model represents the distance from the earth to the sun. Now, let's say you want to add Alpha Centauri, the next nearest star, to your model. You would need to grab another basketball and walk 40 miles away. And that's the closest one!

---

Somehow, though he moves right in front of me, I don't see him;
     quietly but surely he's active, and I miss it.
If he steals you blind, who can stop him?
     Who's going to say, 'Hey, what are you doing?'
God doesn't hold back on his anger;
     even dragon-bred monsters cringe before him.

"So how could I ever argue with him,
     construct a defense that would influence God?
Even though I'm innocent I could never prove it;

I can only throw myself on the Judge's mercy.
If I called on God and he himself answered me,
    then, and only then, would I believe that he'd heard me.
As it is, he knocks me about from pillar to post,
    beating me up, black-and-blue, for no good reason.
He won't even let me catch my breath,
    piles bitterness upon bitterness.
If it's a question of who's stronger, he wins, hands down!
    If it's a question of justice, who'll serve him the subpoena?
Even though innocent, anything I say incriminates me;
    blameless as I am, my defense just makes me sound worse.


## If God's Not Responsible, Who Is?

"Believe me, I'm blameless.
    I don't understand what's going on.
    I hate my life!
Since either way it ends up the same, I can only conclude
    that God destroys the good right along with the bad.
When calamity hits and brings sudden death,
    he folds his arms, aloof from the despair of the innocent.
He lets the wicked take over running the world,
    he installs judges who can't tell right from wrong.
    If he's not responsible, who is?

"My time is short — what's left of my life races off
    too fast for me to even glimpse the good.
My life is going fast, like a ship under full sail,
    like an eagle plummeting to its prey.
Even if I say, 'I'll put all this behind me,
    I'll look on the bright side and force a smile,'
All these troubles would still be like grit in my gut
    since it's clear you're not going to let up.
The verdict has already been handed down — 'Guilty!' —

so what's the use of protests or appeals?
Even if I scrub myself all over
　　and wash myself with the strongest soap I can find,
It wouldn't last — you'd push me into a pigpen, or worse,
　　so nobody could stand me for the stink.

"God and I are not equals; I can't bring a case against him.
　　We'll never enter a courtroom as peers.
How I wish we had an arbitrator
　　to step in and let me get on with life —
To break God's death grip on me,
　　to free me from this terror so I could breathe again.
Then I'd speak up and state my case boldly.
　　As things stand, there is no way I can do it."

## To Find Some Skeleton in My Closet

**10.** "I can't stand my life — I hate it!
　　I'm putting it all out on the table,
　　　　all the bitterness of my life — I'm holding back nothing."

Job prayed:

"Here's what I want to say:
Don't, God, bring in a verdict of guilty
　　without letting me know the charges you're bringing.
How does this fit into what you once called 'good' —
　　giving me a hard time, spurning me,
　　a life you shaped by your very own hands,
　　and then blessing the plots of the wicked?
You don't look at things the way we mortals do.
　　You're not taken in by appearances, are you?
Unlike us, you're not working against a deadline.
　　You have all eternity to work things out.

So what's this all about, anyway — this compulsion
　　　to dig up some dirt, to find some skeleton in my closet?
You know good and well I'm not guilty.
　　　You also know no one can help me.

"You made me like a handcrafted piece of pottery —
　　　and now are you going to smash me to pieces?
Don't you remember how beautifully you worked my clay?
　　　Will you reduce me now to a mud pie?
Oh, that marvel of conception as you stirred together
　　　semen and ovum —
What a miracle of skin and bone,
　　　muscle and brain!
You gave me life itself, and incredible love.
　　　You watched and guarded every breath I took.

"But you never told me about this part.
　　　I should have known that there was more to it —
That if I so much as missed a step, you'd notice and pounce,
　　　wouldn't let me get by with a thing.
If I'm truly guilty, I'm doomed.
　　　But if I'm innocent, it's no better — I'm still doomed.
My belly is full of bitterness.
　　　I'm up to my ears in a swamp of affliction.
I try to make the best of it, try to brave it out,
　　　but you're too much for me,
　　　relentless, like a lion on the prowl.
You line up fresh witnesses against me.
　　　You compound your anger
　　　and pile on the grief and pain!

"So why did you have me born?
　　　I wish no one had ever laid eyes on me!
I wish I'd never lived — a stillborn,

buried without ever having breathed.
Isn't it time to call it quits on my life?

Can't you let up, and let me smile just once
Before I die and am buried,

before I'm nailed into my coffin, sealed in the ground,
And banished for good to the land of the dead,

blind in the final dark?"

---

## The Shadow Proves the Sunshine

Sunshine won't you be my mother?
Sunshine come and help me sing
My heart is darker than these oceans
My heart is frozen underneath
Crooked soul trying to stay up straight
Dry eyes in the pouring rain
The shadow proves the sunshine
Two scared little runaways
Hold fast 'till the break of daylight
When the shadow proves the sunshine
Oh Lord, why did you forsake me
Oh Lord, don't be far away, away
Storm clouds gathering beside me
Please Lord, don't look the other way
I'm a crooked soul trying to stay up straight
Shine on me
Let my shadows prove the sunshine

— Jonathan Foreman, 2005

---

## ZOPHAR'S COUNSEL
## How Wisdom Looks from the Inside

**11.** Now it was the turn of Zophar from Naamath:

"What a flood of words! Shouldn't we put a stop to it?

Should this kind of loose talk be permitted?
Job, do you think you can carry on like this and we'll say nothing?
That we'll let you rail and mock and not step in?
You claim, 'My doctrine is sound
and my conduct impeccable.'
How I wish God would give you a piece of his mind,
tell you what's what!
I wish he'd show you how wisdom looks from the inside,
for true wisdom is mostly 'inside.'
But you can be sure of this,
you haven't gotten half of what you deserve.


"Do you think you can explain the mystery of God?
Do you think you can diagram God Almighty?
God is far higher than you can imagine,
far deeper than you can comprehend,
Stretching farther than earth's horizons,
far wider than the endless ocean.
If he happens along, throws you in jail
then hauls you into court, can you do anything about it?
He sees through vain pretensions,
spots evil a long way off —
no one pulls the wool over *his* eyes!
Hollow men, hollow women, will wise up
about the same time mules learn to talk.


### Reach Out to God

"Still, if you set your heart on God
and reach out to him,
If you scrub your hands of sin
and refuse to entertain evil in your home,
You'll be able to face the world unashamed
and keep a firm grip on life, guiltless and fearless.

You'll forget your troubles;
> they'll be like old, faded photographs.
Your world will be washed in sunshine,
> every shadow dispersed by dayspring.
Full of hope, you'll relax, confident again;
> you'll look around, sit back, and take it easy.
Expansive, without a care in the world,
> you'll be hunted out by many for your blessing.
But the wicked will see none of this.
>> They're headed down a dead-end road
>> with nothing to look forward to — nothing."

---

> The moment we find ourselves in trouble of any kind—sick in the hospital, bereaved by a friend's death, dismissed from a job or relationship, depressed or bewildered—people start showing up telling us exactly what is wrong with us and what we must do to get better. Sufferers attract fixers the way roadkill attracts vultures. At first we are impressed that they bother with us and amazed at their facility with answers. They know so much! How did they get to be such experts in living?
>
> More often than not, these people use the Word of God frequently and loosely. They are full of spiritual diagnosis and prescription. It all sounds so hopeful. But then we begin to wonder, "Why is it that for all their apparent compassion we feel worse instead of better after they've had their say?"

---

## JOB ANSWERS ZOPHAR
### Put Your Ear to the Earth

**12.** Job answered:

"I'm sure you speak for all the experts,
> and when you die there'll be no one left to tell us how to live.
But don't forget that I also have a brain —
> I don't intend to play second fiddle to you.
> It doesn't take an expert to know these things.

"I'm ridiculed by my friends:
> 'So that's the man who had conversations with God!'
Ridiculed without mercy:
> 'Look at the man who never did wrong!'
It's easy for the well-to-do to point their fingers in blame,
> for the well-fixed to pour scorn on the strugglers.
Crooks reside safely in high-security houses,
> insolent blasphemers live in luxury;
> > they've bought and paid for a god who'll protect them.

"But ask the animals what they think — let them teach you;
> let the birds tell you what's going on.
Put your ear to the earth — learn the basics.
> Listen — the fish in the ocean will tell you their stories.
Isn't it clear that they all know and agree
> that GOD is sovereign, that he holds all things in his hand —
Every living soul, yes,
> every breathing creature?
Isn't this all just common sense,
> as common as the sense of taste?
Do you think the elderly have a corner on wisdom,
> that you have to grow old before you understand life?


### From God We Learn How to Live

"True wisdom and real power belong to God;
> from him we learn how to live,
> and also what to live for.
If he tears something down, it's down for good;
> if he locks people up, they're locked up for good.
If he holds back the rain, there's a drought;
> if he lets it loose, there's a flood.
Strength and success belong to God;
> both deceived and deceiver must answer to him.

He strips experts of their vaunted credentials,
    exposes judges as witless fools.
He divests kings of their royal garments,
    then ties a rag around their waists.
He strips priests of their robes,
    and fires high officials from their jobs.
He forces trusted sages to keep silence,
    deprives elders of their good sense and wisdom.
He dumps contempt on famous people,
    disarms the strong and mighty.
He shines a spotlight into caves of darkness,
    hauls deepest darkness into the noonday sun.
He makes nations rise and then fall,
    builds up some and abandons others.
He robs world leaders of their reason,
    and sends them off into no-man's-land.
They grope in the dark without a clue,
    lurching and staggering like drunks."

## I'm Taking My Case to God

**13.** "Yes, I've seen all this with my own eyes,
    heard and understood it with my very own ears.
Everything you know, I know,
    so I'm not taking a backseat to any of you.
I'm taking my case straight to God Almighty;
    I've had it with you — I'm going directly to God.
You graffiti my life with lies.
    You're a bunch of pompous quacks!
I wish you'd shut your mouths —
    silence is your only claim to wisdom.

"Listen now while I make my case,
    consider my side of things for a change.

Or are you going to keep on lying 'to do God a service'?
> to make up stories 'to get him off the hook'?
Why do you always take his side?
> Do you think he needs a lawyer to defend himself?
How would you fare if you were in the dock?
> Your lies might convince a jury — but would they
> > convince *God*?
He'd reprimand you on the spot
> if he detected a bias in your witness.
Doesn't his splendor put you in awe?
> Aren't you afraid to speak cheap lies before him?
Your wise sayings are knickknack wisdom,
> good for nothing but gathering dust.

"So hold your tongue while I have my say,
> then I'll take whatever I have coming to me.
Why do I go out on a limb like this
> and take my life in my hands?
Because even if he killed me, I'd keep on hoping.
> I'd defend my innocence to the very end.
Just wait, this is going to work out for the best — my salvation!
> If I were guilt-stricken do you think I'd be doing this —
> > laying myself on the line before God?

▶ **Do you see all the legal language? It's as if Job's "friends" are self-appointed defense attorneys blowing it before the judge. Job finally stepped in and said, "Enough! I'll represent myself!"**

**Of course, the judge is God, and Job realized that presenting his case directly before God meant risking his life. In fact, it appears that Job expected God to kill him for what he was about to declare at trial. However, at this point in his suffering, Job wanted answers more than life itself.**

**Yes, Job was ready for death, but he also had a well-prepared case for the judge. His ultimate hope still rested in God's system of cosmic justice — whatever that looked like in the final thump of the gavel.**

You'd better pay attention to what I'm telling you,
      listen carefully with both ears.
Now that I've laid out my defense,
      I'm sure that I'll be acquitted.
Can anyone prove charges against me?
      I've said my piece. I rest my case.


## Why Does God Stay Hidden and Silent?

"Please, God, I have two requests;
      grant them so I'll know I count with you:
First, lay off the afflictions;
      the terror is too much for me.
Second, address me directly so I can answer you,
      or let me speak and then you answer me.
How many sins have been charged against me?
      Show me the list — how bad is it?
Why do you stay hidden and silent?
      Why treat me like I'm your enemy?
Why kick me around like an old tin can?
      Why beat a dead horse?
You compile a long list of mean things about me,
      even hold me accountable for the sins of my youth.
You hobble me so I can't move about.
      You watch every move I make,
      and brand me as a dangerous character.


"Like something rotten, human life fast decomposes,
      like a moth-eaten shirt or a mildewed blouse."

## SEARCHER ON THE WAY

*God and the Skeptical Barber*

---

The Internet is full of searchers. Many are cynical. Many are hurting. Many have been led astray. Websites, blogs, and e-mails are littered with barbs and bravado—many people denying God—many people defending him.

When it comes to pain, suffering, and the questioning of God, here's an e-mail story that got me thinking.

A man went to a barbershop to have his hair cut and his beard trimmed. As the barber worked, they had a good conversation. They talked about many things. When they eventually touched on the subject of God, the barber said, "I don't believe that God exists."

"Why do you say that?" asked the customer.

"Well, you just have to go out in the street to realize that God doesn't exist. Tell me. If God exists, would there be so many sick people? Would there be abandoned children? If God existed, there would be neither suffering nor pain. I can't imagine a loving God who allows all of these things."

The customer didn't respond because he didn't want to start an argument. The barber finished his job and the customer left the shop. Just after he left, the customer saw a man in the street with long, dirty hair and an untrimmed beard. He looked totally disheveled. The customer returned to the shop and said to the barber: "You know what? Barbers do not exist."

"How can you say that?" asked the surprised barber. "I am here, and I am a barber. I just cut your hair!"

**If We Die, Will We Live Again?**

**14.** "We're all adrift in the same boat:
too few days, too many troubles.
We spring up like wildflowers in the desert and then wilt,
transient as the shadow of a cloud.
Do you occupy your time with such fragile wisps?
Why even bother hauling me into court?
There's nothing much to us to start with;
how do you expect us to amount to anything?
Mortals have a limited life span.
You've already decided how long we'll live —
you set the boundary and no one can cross it.
So why not give us a break? Ease up!
Even ditchdiggers get occasional days off.
For a tree there is always hope.
Chop it down and it still has a chance —
its roots can put out fresh sprouts.
Even if its roots are old and gnarled,
its stump long dormant,
At the first whiff of water it comes to life,
buds and grows like a sapling.
But men and women? They die and stay dead.
They breathe their last, and that's it.
Like lakes and rivers that have dried up,
parched reminders of what once was,
So mortals lie down and never get up,
never wake up again — never.
Why don't you just bury me alive,
get me out of the way until your anger cools?
But don't leave me there!
Set a date when you'll see me again.
If we humans die, will we live again? That's my question.
All through these difficult days I keep hoping,

waiting for the final change — for resurrection!
Homesick with longing for the creature you made,
    you'll call — and I'll answer!
You'll watch over every step I take,
    but you won't keep track of my missteps.
My sins will be stuffed in a sack
    and thrown into the sea — sunk in deep ocean.


"Meanwhile, mountains wear down
    and boulders break up,
Stones wear smooth
    and soil erodes,
    as you relentlessly grind down our hope.
You're too much for us.
    As always, you get the last word.
We don't like it and our faces show it,
    but you send us off anyway.
If our children do well for themselves, we never know it;
    if they do badly, we're spared the hurt.
Body and soul, that's it for us —
    a lifetime of pain, a lifetime of sorrow."

## SEARCHER ON THE WAY
*From Suffering to Life in the Hoop*

Black Elk was born in 1863 as a member of the Oglala Sioux tribe. At the age of nine, he received a great vision that drove him to a life of prayer. In the vision, Black Elk was given tremendous power and a special gift—"the center of the nation's hoop to make it live."

Black Elk became an influential medicine man and experienced a number of monumental events in history, including the Battle of Little Big Horn and the Massacre at Wounded Knee. Although he was known as a powerful man, Black Elk experienced intense mental suffering throughout his early life. In *Black Elk: Holy Man of the Oglala* by Michael Steltenkamp, family members share his deep physical, psychological, and spiritual struggles, including seasons of crushing inner torment.

In 1904, severe anxiety and painful ulcers forced Black Elk into a hospital. While there, his friend, Kills Brave, shared the Great God of the Bible with him. Shortly thereafter, Black Elk committed to following this Great God and was healed of his ulcers. As it turns out, his physical and psychological issues never returned.

Black Elk followed the Great God for the last thirty years of his life. He returned to his people on the Midwestern plains of North America and reconnected to the roots of his tribal life. Although he rejected his prior ways as a medicine man, many of his people came back to him for advice, treatment, and prayer.

With new understanding, he would chant well-known tribal prayers to the Great Spirit, Sun Father, Grandfather, and Creator. Black Elk would lovingly care for his people as he shared his journey with them. History records that many Oglala Sioux ultimately followed his path to the Great God. Black Elk's childhood vision of bringing life to "the center of the nation's hoop" was realized.

## ELIPHAZ ATTACKS AGAIN
### You Trivialize Religion

**15.** Eliphaz of Teman spoke a second time:

"If you were truly wise, would you sound so much like a
    windbag, belching hot air?
Would you talk nonsense in the middle of a serious argument,
    babbling baloney?
Look at you! You trivialize religion,
    turn spiritual conversation into empty gossip.
It's your sin that taught you to talk this way.
    You chose an education in fraud.
Your own words have exposed your guilt.
    It's nothing I've said — you've incriminated yourself!
Do you think you're the first person to have to deal with
        these things?
    Have you been around as long as the hills?
Were you listening in when God planned all this?
    Do you think you're the only one who knows anything?
What do you know that we don't know?
    What insights do you have that we've missed?
Gray beards and white hair back us up —
    old folks who've been around a lot longer than you.
Are God's promises not enough for you,
    spoken so gently and tenderly?
Why do you let your emotions take over,
    lashing out and spitting fire,
Pitting your whole being against God
    by letting words like this come out of your mouth?
Do you think it's possible for any mere mortal to be sinless
        in God's sight,
    for anyone born of a human mother to get it all together?
Why, God can't even trust his holy angels.

He sees the flaws in the very heavens themselves,
So how much less we humans, smelly and foul,
>who lap up evil like water?


## Always at Odds with God

"I've a thing or two to tell you, so listen up!
>I'm letting you in on my views;
It's what wise men and women have always taught,
>holding nothing back from what *they* were taught
By their parents, back in the days
>when they had this land all to themselves:
Those who live by their own rules, not God's, can expect
>nothing but trouble,
>and the longer they live, the worse it gets.
Every little sound terrifies them.
>Just when they think they have it made, disaster strikes.
They despair of things ever getting better—
>they're on the list of people for whom things always turn out
>for the worst.
They wander here and there,
>never knowing where the next meal is coming from—
>every day is doomsday!
They live in constant terror,
>always with their backs up against the wall
Because they insist on shaking their fists at God,
>defying God Almighty to his face,
Always and ever at odds with God,
>always on the defensive.


"Even if they're the picture of health,
>trim and fit and youthful,
They'll end up living in a ghost town
>sleeping in a hovel not fit for a dog,

a ramshackle shack.
They'll never get ahead,
    never amount to a hill of beans.
And then death — don't think they'll escape that!
    They'll end up shriveled weeds,
    brought down by a puff of God's breath.
There's a lesson here: Whoever invests in lies,
    gets lies for interest,
Paid in full before the due date.
    Some investment!
They'll be like fruit frost-killed before it ripens,
    like buds sheared off before they bloom.
The godless are fruitless — a barren crew;
    a life built on bribes goes up in smoke.
They have sex with sin and give birth to evil.
    Their lives are wombs for breeding deceit."

## JOB DEFENDS HIMSELF
### If You Were in My Shoes

**16.** Then Job defended himself:

"I've had all I can take of your talk.
    What a bunch of miserable comforters!
Is there no end to your windbag speeches?
    What's your problem that you go on and on like this?
If you were in my shoes,
    I could talk just like you.
I could put together a terrific harangue
    and really let you have it.
But I'd never do that. I'd console and comfort,
    make things better, not worse!

"When I speak up, I feel no better;

if I say nothing, that doesn't help either.
I feel worn down.

God, you have wasted me totally — me and my family!

---

▶ Throughout history, the "problem of pain" has kept many people from God. The recurring philosophical question is: "How can an all-loving and all-powerful God allow pain, suffering, and evil in the world?"

According to the ancient Scriptures, all pain, suffering, and death in this world (disease, natural disasters, and all) are ultimately consequences of mankind's initial and ongoing rebellion against God. However, the Scriptures also declare that evil will be done away with when God's purpose is achieved.

In a philosophical nutshell, it's about changing our perspective. Rather than treating the existence of suffering as a theoretical stumbling block keeping us from God, maybe we should view suffering as a profound and temporary mystery driving us ever and ever closer to him.

Philosopher Alvin Plantinga writes, "An all loving, all powerful, all knowing Being could permit as much evil as He pleased without forfeiting His claim to being all loving, so long as for every evil state of affairs He permits there is an accompanying greater good."

---

You've shriveled me like a dried prune,
    showing the world that you're against me.
My gaunt face stares back at me from the mirror,
    a mute witness to your treatment of me.
Your anger tears at me,
    your teeth rip me to shreds,
    your eyes burn holes in me — God, my enemy!
People take one look at me and gasp.
    Contemptuous, they slap me around
    and gang up against me.
And God just stands there and lets them do it,
    lets wicked people do what they want with me.
I was contentedly minding my business when God beat me up.
    He grabbed me by the neck and threw me around.
He set me up as his target,
    then rounded up archers to shoot at me.

Merciless, they shot me full of arrows;
     bitter bile poured from my gut to the ground.
He burst in on me, onslaught after onslaught,
     charging me like a mad bull.

"I sewed myself a shroud and wore it like a shirt;
     I lay facedown in the dirt.
Now my face is blotched red from weeping;
     look at the dark shadows under my eyes,
Even though I've never hurt a soul
     and my prayers are sincere!

## The One Who Represents Mortals Before God

"O Earth, don't cover up the wrong done to me!
     Don't muffle my cry!
There must be Someone in heaven who knows the truth about me,
     in highest heaven, some Attorney who can clear my name —
My Champion, my Friend,
     while I'm weeping my eyes out before God.
I appeal to the One who represents mortals before God
     as a neighbor stands up for a neighbor.

"Only a few years are left
     before I set out on the road of no return."

**17.** "My spirit is broken,
     my days used up,
          my grave dug and waiting.
See how these mockers close in on me?
     How long do I have to put up with their insolence?

"O God, pledge your support for me.
     Give it to me in writing, with your signature.

You're the only one who can do it!
These people are so useless!
You know firsthand how stupid they can be.
You wouldn't let them have the last word, would you?
Those who betray their own friends
leave a legacy of abuse to their children.

"God, you've made me the talk of the town —
people spit in my face;
I can hardly see from crying so much;
I'm nothing but skin and bones.
Decent people can't believe what they're seeing;
the good-hearted wake up and insist I've given up on God.

"But principled people hold tight, keep a firm grip on life,
sure that their clean, pure hands will get stronger and stronger!

"Maybe you'd all like to start over,
to try it again, the bunch of you.
So far I haven't come across one scrap
of wisdom in anything you've said.
My life's about over. All my plans are smashed,
all my hopes are snuffed out —
My hope that night would turn into day,
my hope that dawn was about to break.
If all I have to look forward to is a home in the graveyard,
if my only hope for comfort is a well-built coffin,
If a family reunion means going six feet under,
and the only family that shows up is worms,
Do you call that hope?
Who on earth could find any hope in that?
No. If hope and I are to be buried together,
I suppose you'll all come to the double funeral!"

## BILDAD'S SECOND ATTACK
### Plunged from Light into Darkness

**18.** Bildad from Shuhah chimed in:

"How monotonous these word games are getting!
Get serious! We need to get down to business.
Why do you treat your friends like slow-witted animals?
You look down on us as if we don't know anything.
Why are you working yourself up like this?
Do you want the world redesigned to suit you?
Should reality be suspended to accommodate you?

"Here's the rule: The light of the wicked is put out.
Their flame dies down and is extinguished.
Their house goes dark—
every lamp in the place goes out.
Their strong strides weaken, falter;
they stumble into their own traps.
They get all tangled up
in their own red tape,
Their feet are grabbed and caught,
their necks in a noose.
They trip on ropes they've hidden,
and fall into pits they've dug themselves.
Terrors come at them from all sides.
They run helter-skelter.
The hungry grave is ready
to gobble them up for supper,
To lay them out for a gourmet meal,
a treat for ravenous Death.
They are snatched from their home sweet home
and marched straight to the death house.
Their lives go up in smoke;
acid rain soaks their ruins.

Their roots rot
 and their branches wither.
They'll never again be remembered —
 nameless in unmarked graves.
They are plunged from light into darkness,
 banished from the world.
And they leave empty-handed — not one single child —
 nothing to show for their life on this earth.
Westerners are aghast at their fate,
 easterners are horrified:
'Oh no! So this is what happens to perverse people.
 This is how the God-ignorant end up!' "

## How Do You Know?

I've got my doubts and I've got my questions
It's nothing new 'cause I've seen them before
I've had my share of false revelations
It always seems they're knockin' on my door

You said that I should see the light
But sometimes faith is blind

How do you know, how do you know
What I'm supposed to be doing
Why do you do, why do you go on
Thinking you know my fate
So many times I've lost my step
But never lost my way
How do you know, how do you know
When I don't know myself

You're thinking that you've got all the answers
You've got my situation figured out
But you're only seeing part of the picture
There's so much more that you don't know about
And here you come to speak your mind
But I'll say one more time

— Mac Powell, 2005

## JOB ANSWERS BILDAD
### I Call for Help and No One Bothers

# 19. Job answered:

"How long are you going to keep battering away at me,
    pounding me with these harangues?
Time after time after time you jump all over me.
    Do you have no conscience, abusing me like this?
Even if I have, somehow or other, gotten off the track,
    what business is that of yours?
Why do you insist on putting me down,
    using my troubles as a stick to beat me?
Tell it to God — he's the one behind all this,
    he's the one who dragged me into this mess.

"Look at me — I shout 'Murder!' and I'm ignored;
    I call for help and no one bothers to stop.
God threw a barricade across my path — I'm stymied;
    he turned out all the lights — I'm stuck in the dark.
He destroyed my reputation,
    robbed me of all self-respect.
He tore me apart piece by piece — I'm ruined!
    Then he yanked out hope by the roots.
He's angry with me — oh, how he's angry!
    He treats me like his worst enemy.
He has launched a major campaign against me,
    using every weapon he can think of,
    coming at me from all sides at once.

### I Know That God Lives

"God alienated my family from me;
    everyone who knows me avoids me.

My relatives and friends have all left;
>      houseguests forget I ever existed.
The servant girls treat me like a bum off the street,
>      look at me like they've never seen me before.
I call my attendant and he ignores me,
>      ignores me even though I plead with him.
My wife can't stand to be around me anymore.
>      I'm repulsive to my family.
Even street urchins despise me;
>      when I come out, they taunt and jeer.
Everyone I've ever been close to abhors me;
>      my dearest loved ones reject me.
I'm nothing but a bag of bones;
>      my life hangs by a thread.

"Oh, friends, dear friends, take pity on me.
>      God has come down hard on me!
Do you have to be hard on me, too?
>      Don't you ever tire of abusing me?

"If only my words were written in a book —
>      better yet, chiseled in stone!
Still, I know that God lives — the One who gives me back my life —
>      and eventually he'll take his stand on earth.
And I'll see him — even though I get skinned alive! —
>      see God myself, with my very own eyes.
>      Oh, how I long for that day!

---

> Five chapters back, Job asked, "If we humans die, will we live again? That's my question. All through these difficult days I keep hoping, waiting for the final change—for resurrection!"
>
> Here, five chapters further into his suffering, Job delivers his great declaration of faith: "I know that God lives—the One who gives me back my life—and eventually he'll take his stand on earth."
>
> Wow! Even though Job acknowledges that his nasty disease will ultimately bring

"If you're thinking, 'How can we get through to him,
      get him to see that his trouble is all his own fault?'
Forget it. Start worrying about *yourselves*.
      Worry about your own sins and God's coming judgment,
      for judgment is most certainly on the way.'"

## ZOPHAR ATTACKS JOB — THE SECOND ROUND
### Savoring Evil as a Delicacy

**20.** Zophar from Naamath again took his turn:

"I can't believe what I'm hearing!
      You've put my teeth on edge, my stomach in a knot.
How dare you insult my intelligence like this!
      Well, here's a piece of my mind!

"Don't you even know the basics,
      how things have been since the earliest days,
      when Adam and Eve were first placed on earth?
The good times of the wicked are short-lived;
      godless joy is only momentary.
The evil might become world famous,
      strutting at the head of the celebrity parade,
But still end up in a pile of dung.
      Acquaintances look at them with disgust and say, 'What's that?'
They fly off like a dream that can't be remembered,
      like a shadowy illusion that vanishes in the light.
Though once notorious public figures, now they're nobodies,
      unnoticed, whether they come or go.
Their children will go begging on skid row,

and they'll have to give back their ill-gotten gain.
Right in the prime of life,
>and youthful and vigorous, they'll die.


"They savor evil as a delicacy,
>roll it around on their tongues,
Prolong the flavor, a dalliance in decadence —
>real gourmets of evil!
But then they get stomach cramps,
>a bad case of food poisoning.
They gag on all that rich food;
>God makes them vomit it up.
They gorge on evil, make a diet of that poison —
>a deadly diet — and it kills them.
No quiet picnics for them beside gentle streams
>with fresh-baked bread and cheese, and tall, cool drinks.
They spit out their food half-chewed,
>unable to relax and enjoy anything they've worked for.
And why? Because they exploited the poor,
>took what never belonged to them.


"Such God-denying people are never content with what they have
>>or who they are;
>their greed drives them relentlessly.
They plunder everything
>but they can't hold on to any of it.
Just when they think they have it all, disaster strikes;
>they're served up a plate full of misery.
When they've filled their bellies with that,
>God gives them a taste of his anger,
>and they get to chew on that for a while.
As they run for their lives from one disaster,
>they run smack into another.
They're knocked around from pillar to post,

beaten to within an inch of their lives.
They're trapped in a house of horrors,
    and see their loot disappear down a black hole.
Their lives are a total loss —
    not a penny to their name, not so much as a bean.
God will strip them of their sin-soaked clothes
    and hang their dirty laundry out for all to see.
Life is a complete wipeout for them,
    nothing surviving God's wrath.
There! That's God's blueprint for the wicked —
    what they have to look forward to."

## JOB'S RESPONSE
### Why Do the Wicked Have It So Good?

**21.** Job replied:

"Now listen to me carefully, please listen,
    at least do me the favor of listening.
Put up with me while I have my say —
    then you can mock me later to your heart's content.

"It's not *you* I'm complaining to — it's *God*.
    Is it any wonder I'm getting fed up with his silence?
Take a good look at me. Aren't you appalled by what's happened?
    No! Don't say anything. I can do without your comments.
When I look back, I go into shock,
    my body is racked with spasms.
Why do the wicked have it so good,
    live to a ripe old age and get rich?
They get to see their children succeed,
    get to watch and enjoy their grandchildren.
Their homes are peaceful and free from fear;
    they never experience God's disciplining rod.

Their bulls breed with great vigor
    and their cows calve without fail.
They send their children out to play
    and watch them frolic like spring lambs.
They make music with fiddles and flutes,
    have good times singing and dancing.
They have a long life on easy street,
    and die painlessly in their sleep.
They say to God, 'Get lost!
    We've no interest in you or your ways.
Why should we have dealings with God Almighty?
    What's there in it for us?'
But they're wrong, dead wrong — they're not gods.
    It's beyond me how they can carry on like this!

"Still, how often does it happen that the wicked fail,
    or disaster strikes,
    or they get their just deserts?
How often are they blown away by bad luck?
    Not very often.
You might say, 'God is saving up the punishment for their children.'
    I say, 'Give it to them right now so they'll know what
        they've done!'
They deserve to experience the effects of their evil,
    feel the full force of God's wrath firsthand.
What do they care what happens to their families
    after they're safely tucked away in the grave?

**Fancy Funerals with All the Trimmings**

"But who are we to tell God how to run his affairs?
    He's dealing with matters that are way over our heads.
Some people die in the prime of life,
    with everything going for them —
        fat and sassy.

Others die bitter and bereft,
        never getting a taste of happiness.
They're laid out side by side in the cemetery,
        where the worms can't tell one from the other.

"I'm not deceived. I know what you're up to,
        the plans you're cooking up to bring me down.
Naively you claim that the castles of tyrants fall to pieces,
        that the achievements of the wicked collapse.
Have you ever asked world travelers how they see it?
        Have you not listened to their stories
Of evil men and women who got off scot-free,
        who never had to pay for their wickedness?
Did anyone ever confront them with their crimes?
        Did they ever have to face the music?
Not likely — they're given fancy funerals
        with all the trimmings,
Gently lowered into expensive graves,
        with everyone telling lies about how wonderful they were.

"So how do you expect me to get any comfort from your nonsense?
        Your so-called comfort is a tissue of lies."

## ELIPHAZ ATTACKS JOB — THE THIRD ROUND
### Come to Terms with God

**22.** Once again Eliphaz the Temanite took up his theme:

"Are any of us strong enough to give God a hand,
        or smart enough to give him advice?
So what if you were righteous — would God Almighty even notice?
        Even if you gave a perfect performance, do you think
                he'd applaud?
Do you think it's because he cares about your purity

that he's disciplining you, putting you on the spot?
Hardly! It's because you're a first-class moral failure,
    because there's no end to your sins.
When people came to you for help,
    you took the shirts off their backs, exploited their helplessness.
You wouldn't so much as give a drink to the thirsty,
    or food, not even a scrap, to the hungry.
And there you sat, strong and honored by everyone,
    surrounded by immense wealth!
You turned poor widows away from your door;
    heartless, you crushed orphans.
Now *you're* the one trapped in terror, paralyzed by fear.
    Suddenly the tables have turned!
How do you like living in the dark, sightless,
    up to your neck in flood waters?

"You agree, don't you, that God is in charge?
    He runs the universe — just look at the stars!
Yet you dare raise questions: 'What does God know?
    From that distance and darkness, how can he judge?
He roams the heavens wrapped in clouds,
    so how can he see us?'

"Are you going to persist in that tired old line
    that wicked men and women have always used?
Where did it get them? They died young,
    flash floods sweeping them off to their doom.
They told God, 'Get lost!
    What good is God Almighty to us?'
And yet it was God who gave them everything they had.
    It's beyond me how they can carry on like this!

"Good people see bad people crash, and call for a celebration.
    Relieved, they crow,

'At last! Our enemies — wiped out.
    Everything they had and stood for is up in smoke!'

"Give in to God, come to terms with him
    and everything will turn out just fine.
Let him tell you what to do;
    take his words to heart.
Come back to God Almighty
    and he'll rebuild your life.
Clean house of everything evil.
    Relax your grip on your money
    and abandon your gold-plated luxury.
God Almighty will be your treasure,
    more wealth than you can imagine.

"You'll take delight in God, the Mighty One,
    and look to him joyfully, boldly.
You'll pray to him and he'll listen;
    he'll help you do what you've promised.
You'll decide what you want and it will happen;
    your life will be bathed in light.
To those who feel low you'll say, 'Chin up! Be brave!'
    and God will save them.
Yes, even the guilty will escape,
    escape through God's grace in your life."

## JOB'S DEFENSE
### I'm Completely in the Dark

**23.** Job replied:

"I'm not letting up — I'm standing my ground.
    My complaint is legitimate.
God has no right to treat me like this —

it isn't fair!
If I knew where on earth to find him,
    I'd go straight to him.
I'd lay my case before him face-to-face,
    give him all my arguments firsthand.
I'd find out exactly what he's thinking,
    discover what's going on in his head.
Do you think he'd dismiss me or bully me?
    No, he'd take me seriously.
He'd see a straight-living man standing before him;
    my Judge would acquit me for good of all charges.

"I travel East looking for him — I find no one;
    then West, but not a trace;
I go North, but he's hidden his tracks;
    then South, but not even a glimpse.

---

### Where Is the Wonderful

Where is the wonderful abode,
The holy, secret, searchless shrine,
Where dwells the immaterial God,
The all-pervading and benign.
O! that He were revealed to me,
Fully and palpably displayed
In all the awful majesty

Of heaven's consummate pomp arrayed.
My Father and my Brother and my God!
Touch me with sorrow! Soften me with grief!
Until this battled wall of unbelief
Built around my warring spirit fall away!
Then take me to thyself – a full-eared-sheaf
Ripe for the harvest on an autumn day.

— Alfred Tennyson (1809-1892)

"But he knows where I am and what I've done.
>He can cross-examine me all he wants, and I'll pass the test
>>with honors.
I've followed him closely, my feet in his footprints,
>not once swerving from his way.
I've obeyed every word he's spoken,
>and not just obeyed his advice — I've *treasured* it.

"But he is singular and sovereign. Who can argue with him?
>He does what he wants, when he wants to.
He'll complete in detail what he's decided about me,
>and whatever else he determines to do.
Is it any wonder that I dread meeting him?
>Whenever I think about it, I get scared all over again.
God makes my heart sink!
>God Almighty gives me the shudders!
I'm completely in the dark,
>I can't see my hand in front of my face."

## An Illusion of Security

**24.** "But if Judgment Day isn't hidden from the Almighty,
why are we kept in the dark?
There are people out there getting by with murder —
>stealing and lying and cheating.
They rip off the poor
>and exploit the unfortunate,
Push the helpless into the ditch,
>bully the weak so that they fear for their lives.
The poor, like stray dogs and cats,
>scavenge for food in back alleys.
They sort through the garbage of the rich,
>eke out survival on handouts.
Homeless, they shiver through cold nights on the street;
>they've no place to lay their heads.

Exposed to the weather, wet and frozen,
    they huddle in makeshift shelters.
Nursing mothers have their babies snatched from them;
    the infants of the poor are kidnapped and sold.
They go about patched and threadbare;
    even the hard workers go hungry.
No matter how backbreaking their labor,
    they can never make ends meet.
People are dying right and left, groaning in torment.
    The wretched cry out for help
    and God does nothing, acts like nothing's wrong!

"Then there are those who avoid light at all costs,
    who scorn the light-filled path.
When the sun goes down, the murderer gets up —
    kills the poor and robs the defenseless.
Sexual predators can't wait for nightfall,
    thinking, 'No one can see us now.'
Burglars do their work at night,
    but keep well out of sight through the day.
    They want nothing to do with light.
Deep darkness is morning for that bunch;
    they make the terrors of darkness their companions in crime.

Free will is a blessing and a curse. God has given all of us the absolute ability to make choices in life. We have the ability to choose good or evil, right or wrong, self or others. Unfortunately, from the beginning of time, we have chosen evil quite often. Many argue that mankind is generally good. Actually, mankind is generally bad. Just look at history. Just look at small children (we don't have to teach them how to lie, steal, or strike siblings).

Why did God give us free will then? Wouldn't it have been easier and better to create mankind as inherently good? Well, as we'll see, God's purpose for humanity is to have eternal relationships with those who truly love him. Therefore, to create us as inherently good robots, without the potential for the opposite character, evil, would not allow for true love. For only love that comes from a free choice of the will is true love. Voluntary choice is the key—love isn't genuine if there's no other option.

"They are scraps of wood floating on the water—
    useless, cursed junk, good for nothing.
As surely as snow melts under the hot, summer sun,
    sinners disappear in the grave.
The womb has forgotten them, worms have relished them—
    nothing that is evil lasts.
Unscrupulous,
    they prey on those less fortunate.
However much they strut and flex their muscles,
    there's nothing to them. They're hollow.
They may have an illusion of security,
    but God has his eye on them.
They may get their brief successes,
    but then it's over, nothing to show for it.
Like yesterday's newspaper,
    they're used to wrap up the garbage.
You're free to try to prove me a liar,
    but you won't be able to do it."


## BILDAD'S THIRD ATTACK
### Even the Stars Aren't Perfect in God's Eyes

**25.** Bildad the Shuhite again attacked Job:

"God is sovereign, God is fearsome—
    everything in the cosmos fits and works in his plan.
Can anyone count his angel armies?
    Is there any place where his light doesn't shine?
How can a mere mortal presume to stand up to God?
    How can an ordinary person pretend to be guiltless?
Why, even the moon has its flaws,
    even the stars aren't perfect in God's eyes,
So how much less, plain men and women—
    slugs and maggots by comparison!"

## JOB'S DEFENSE
### God Sets a Boundary Between Light and Darkness

# 26.
Job answered:

"Well, you've certainly been a great help to a helpless man!
>    You came to the rescue just in the nick of time!
What wonderful advice you've given to a mixed-up man!
>    What amazing insights you've provided!
Where in the world did you learn all this?
>    How did you become so inspired?

"All the buried dead are in torment,
>    and all who've been drowned in the deep, deep sea.
Hell is ripped open before God,
>    graveyards dug up and exposed.
He spreads the skies over unformed space,
>    hangs the earth out in empty space.
He pours water into cumulus cloud-bags
>    and the bags don't burst.
He makes the moon wax and wane,
>    putting it through its phases.
He draws the horizon out over the ocean,
>    sets a boundary between light and darkness.
Thunder crashes and rumbles in the skies.
>    Listen! It's God raising his voice!
By his power he stills sea storms,
>    by his wisdom he tames sea monsters.
With one breath he clears the sky,
>    with one finger he crushes the sea serpent.
And this is only the beginning,
>    a mere whisper of his rule.
>    Whatever would we do if he *really* raised his voice!"

> Throughout Job, we see incredible scientific insights. At a time when other ancient thinkers described the earth as a stone tablet riding on the backs of cosmic elephants, Job described the earth as a sphere (Hebrew: *khug*) hanging on nothing in space. Job also refers to God "stretching out" the heavens, a phrase repeated by the ancients throughout Scripture.
>
> It's fascinating that modern astronomers, living about four thousand years after Job, speak of an "expanding universe." The biblical writers used the picture of a tent or canvas being spread out over an empty structure. Today's scientists describe the cosmos as a four-dimensional fabric of space and time spreading out over emptiness since its initial moment of creation (the so-called "bang").

## No Place to Hide

**27.** Having waited for Zophar, Job now resumed his defense:

"God-Alive! He's denied me justice!
    God Almighty! He's ruined my life!
But for as long as I draw breath,
    and for as long as God breathes life into me,
I refuse to say one word that isn't true.
    I refuse to confess to any charge that's false.
There is no way I'll ever agree to your accusations.
    I'll not deny my integrity even if it costs me my life.
I'm holding fast to my integrity and not loosening my grip —
    and, believe me, I'll never regret it.

"Let my enemy be exposed as wicked!
    Let my adversary be proven guilty!
What hope do people without God have when life is cut short?
    when God puts an end to life?
Do you think God will listen to their cry for help
    when disaster hits?
What interest have they ever shown in the Almighty?
    Have they ever been known to pray before?

"I've given you a clear account of God in action,
     suppressed nothing regarding God Almighty.
The evidence is right before you. You can all see it for yourselves,
     so why do you keep talking nonsense?

"I'll quote your own words back to you:

" 'This is how God treats the wicked,
     this is what evil people can expect from God Almighty:
Their children — all of them — will die violent deaths;
     they'll never have enough bread to put on the table.
They'll be wiped out by the plague,
     and none of the widows will shed a tear when they're gone.
Even if they make a lot of money
     and are resplendent in the latest fashions,
It's the good who will end up wearing the clothes
     and the decent who will divide up the money.
They build elaborate houses
     that won't survive a single winter.
They go to bed wealthy
     and wake up poor.
Terrors pour in on them like flash floods —
     a tornado snatches them away in the middle of the night,
A cyclone sweeps them up — gone!
     Not a trace of them left, not even a footprint.
Catastrophes relentlessly pursue them;
     they run this way and that, but there's no place to hide —
Pummeled by the weather,
     blown to kingdom come by the storm.' "

## Where Does Wisdom Come From?

**28.** "We all know how silver seams the rocks,
     we've seen the stuff from which gold is refined,

We're aware of how iron is dug out of the ground
    and copper is smelted from rock.
Miners penetrate the earth's darkness,
    searching the roots of the mountains for ore,
    digging away in the suffocating darkness.
Far from civilization, far from the traffic,
    they cut a shaft,
    and are lowered into it by ropes.
Earth's surface is a field for grain,
    but its depths are a forge
Firing sapphires from stones
    and chiseling gold from rocks.
Vultures are blind to its riches,
    hawks never lay eyes on it.
Wild animals are oblivious to it,
    lions don't know it's there.
Miners hammer away at the rock,
    they uproot the mountains.
They tunnel through the rock
    and find all kinds of beautiful gems.
They discover the origins of rivers,
    and bring earth's secrets to light.

"But where, oh where, will they find Wisdom?
    Where does Insight hide?
Mortals don't have a clue,
    haven't the slightest idea where to look.
Earth's depths say, 'It's not here';
    ocean deeps echo, 'Never heard of it.'
It can't be bought with the finest gold;
    no amount of silver can get it.
Even famous Ophir gold can't buy it,
    not even diamonds and sapphires.
Neither gold nor emeralds are comparable;

extravagant jewelry can't touch it.
Pearl necklaces and ruby bracelets — why bother?
  None of this is even a down payment on Wisdom!
Pile gold and African diamonds as high as you will,
  they can't hold a candle to Wisdom.

"So where does Wisdom come from?
  And where does Insight live?
It can't be found by looking, no matter
  how deep you dig, no matter how high you fly.
If you search through the graveyard and question the dead,
  they say, 'We've only heard rumors of it.'

"God alone knows the way to Wisdom,
  he knows the exact place to find it.
He knows where everything is on earth,
  he sees everything under heaven.
After he commanded the winds to blow
  and measured out the waters,
Arranged for the rain
  and set off explosions of thunder and lightning,
He focused on Wisdom,
  made sure it was all set and tested and ready.
Then he addressed the human race: 'Here it is!
  Fear-of-the-Lord — that's Wisdom,
  and Insight means shunning evil.'"

> Job gives us an entire chapter on mining techniques. What's that all about? Well, archaeology reveals that civilizations were mining and smelting ore at the time of Job. Although still very difficult and dangerous, humanity had managed the task of processing iron and copper.
>
> The point of this passage was to compare the very difficult process of mining ore with the even more difficult notion of mining the world for wisdom and understanding. Job described mankind's tremendous technological leap in great detail and foreshadowed that mankind would continue to make such leaps. However, no matter how far we advance, we'll

never achieve total Wisdom.

**The conclusion: "God alone knows the way to Wisdom."**

## When God Was Still by My Side

**29.** Job now resumed his response:

"Oh, how I long for the good old days,
    when God took such very good care of me.
He always held a lamp before me
    and I walked through the dark by its light.
Oh, how I miss those golden years
    when God's friendship graced my home,
When the Mighty One was still by my side
    and my children were all around me,
When everything was going my way,
    and nothing seemed too difficult.

"When I walked downtown
    and sat with my friends in the public square,
Young and old greeted me with respect;
    I was honored by everyone in town.
When I spoke, everyone listened;
    they hung on my every word.
People who knew me spoke well of me;
    my reputation went ahead of me.
I was known for helping people in trouble
    and standing up for those who were down on their luck.
The dying blessed me,
    and the bereaved were cheered by my visits.
All my dealings with people were good.
    I was known for being fair to everyone I met.
I was eyes to the blind

and feet to the lame,
Father to the needy,
    and champion of abused aliens.
I grabbed street thieves by the scruff of the neck
    and made them give back what they'd stolen.
I thought, 'I'll die peacefully in my own bed,
    grateful for a long and full life,
A life deep-rooted and well-watered,
    a life limber and dew-fresh,
My soul suffused with glory
    and my body robust until the day I die.'

"Men and women listened when I spoke,
    hung expectantly on my every word.
After I spoke, they'd be quiet,
    taking it all in.
They welcomed my counsel like spring rain,
    drinking it all in.
When I smiled at them, they could hardly believe it;
    their faces lit up, their troubles took wing!
I was their leader, establishing the mood
    and setting the pace by which they lived.
    Where I led, they followed."

### The Pain Never Lets Up

**30.** "But no longer. Now I'm the butt of their jokes —
    young ruffians! whippersnappers!
Why, I considered their fathers
    mere inexperienced pups.
But they are worse than dogs — good for nothing,
    stray, mangy animals,
Half-starved, scavenging the back alleys,
    howling at the moon;

Homeless guttersnipes
      chewing on old bones and licking old tin cans;
Outcasts from the community,
      cursed as dangerous delinquents.
Nobody would put up with them;
      they were driven from the neighborhood.
You could hear them out there at the edge of town,
      yelping and barking, huddled in junkyards,
A gang of beggars and no-names,
      thrown out on their ears.

"But now I'm the one they're after,
      mistreating me, taunting and mocking.
They abhor me, they abuse me.
      How dare those scoundrels — they spit in my face!
Now that God has undone me and left me in a heap,
      they hold nothing back. Anything goes.
They come at me from my blind side,
      trip me up, then jump on me while I'm down.
They throw every kind of obstacle in my path,
      determined to ruin me —
      and no one lifts a finger to help me!
They violate my broken body,
      trample through the rubble of my ruined life.
Terrors assault me —
      my dignity in shreds,
      salvation up in smoke.

"And now my life drains out,
      as suffering seizes and grips me hard.
Night gnaws at my bones;
      the pain never lets up.
I am tied hand and foot, my neck in a noose.
      I twist and turn.

Thrown facedown in the muck,

    I'm a muddy mess, inside and out.

## What Did I Do to Deserve This?

"I shout for help, God, and get nothing, no answer!

    I stand to face you in protest, and you give me a blank stare!

You've turned into my tormenter —

    you slap me around, knock me about.

You raised me up so I was riding high

    and then dropped me, and I crashed.

I know you're determined to kill me,

    to put me six feet under.

"What did I do to deserve this?

    Did I ever hit anyone who was calling for help?

Haven't I wept for those who live a hard life,

    been heartsick over the lot of the poor?

But where did it get me?

    I expected good but evil showed up.

    I looked for light but darkness fell.

My stomach's in a constant churning, never settles down.

    Each day confronts me with more suffering.

I walk under a black cloud. The sun is gone.

    I stand in the congregation and protest.

I howl with the jackals,

    I hoot with the owls.

I'm black-and-blue all over,

    burning up with fever.

My fiddle plays nothing but the blues;

    my mouth harp wails laments."

When it comes to human existence, it seems there's a hoped-for standard of fairness and justice in all of us. At one extreme, there's the full and content life—a good person who does it all and dies painlessly in her sleep at the age of ninety-nine. Now that's fairness—that's a portrait of a just and meaningful world.

At the other extreme, there's the helpless child who dies at the age of four after a long and painful battle with cancer. Now that's absolutely unfair—that's a snapshot of an unjust and incomprehensible world.

Of course, most lives fall somewhere in between these extremes—somewhere on humanity's sliding scale of fairness and justice.

As we read Job and witness real life, we're faced with perplexing questions: Who wrote the unwritten rules of human fairness? Where did our sliding scale of life justice come from in the first place?

From Job, we learn that God's standards may be operating outside our man-made definitions—fairness and justice may be eternal, spiritual concepts that don't quite mesh with our limited framework of the temporal and the physical.

---

## What Can I Expect from God?

**31.** "I made a solemn pact with myself
        never to undress a girl with my eyes.
So what can I expect from God?
        What do I deserve from God Almighty above?
Isn't calamity reserved for the wicked?
        Isn't disaster supposed to strike those who do wrong?
Isn't God looking, observing how I live?
        Doesn't he mark every step I take?

"Have I walked hand in hand with falsehood,
        or hung out in the company of deceit?
Weigh me on a set of honest scales
        so God has proof of my integrity.
If I've strayed off the straight and narrow,
        wanted things I had no right to,
        messed around with sin,
Go ahead, then —
        give my portion to someone who deserves it.

"If I've let myself be seduced by a woman
and conspired to go to bed with her,
Fine, my wife has every right to go ahead
and sleep with anyone she wants to.
For disgusting behavior like that,
I'd deserve the worst punishment you could hand out.
Adultery is a fire that burns the house down;
I wouldn't expect anything I count dear to survive it.

"Have I ever been unfair to my employees
when they brought a complaint to me?
What, then, will I do when God confronts me?
When God examines my books, what can I say?
Didn't the same God who made me, make them?
Aren't we all made of the same stuff, equals before God?

"Have I ignored the needs of the poor,
turned my back on the indigent,
Taken care of my own needs and fed my own face
while they languished?
Wasn't my home always open to them?
Weren't they always welcome at my table?

"Have I ever left a poor family shivering in the cold
when they had no warm clothes?
Didn't the poor bless me when they saw me coming,
knowing I'd brought coats from my closet?

"If I've ever used my strength and influence
to take advantage of the unfortunate,
Go ahead, break both my arms,
cut off all my fingers!

The fear of God has kept me from these things —
    how else could I ever face him?

## If Only Someone Would Give Me a Hearing!

"Did I set my heart on making big money
    or worship at the bank?
Did I boast about my wealth,
    show off because I was well-off?
Was I ever so awed by the sun's brilliance
    and moved by the moon's beauty
That I let myself become seduced by them
    and worshiped them on the sly?
If so, I would deserve the worst of punishments,
    for I would be betraying God himself.

.

"Did I ever crow over my enemy's ruin?
    Or gloat over my rival's bad luck?
No, I never said a word of detraction,
    never cursed them, even under my breath.

"Didn't those who worked for me say,
    'He fed us well. There were always second helpings'?
And no stranger ever had to spend a night in the street;
    my doors were always open to travelers.
Did I hide my sin the way Adam did,
    or conceal my guilt behind closed doors
Because I was afraid what people would say,
    fearing the gossip of the neighbors so much
That I turned myself into a recluse?
    You know good and well that I didn't.

---

▶ Job lived hundreds of years before Moses and the writing of Genesis, yet here Job
refered to Adam and his sin. Job's whole point here is that he fears God and would

"Oh, if only someone would give me a hearing!
    I've signed my name to my defense — let the
        Almighty One answer!
    I want to see my indictment in writing.
Anyone's welcome to read my defense;
    I'll write it on a poster and carry it around town.
I'm prepared to account for every move I've ever made —
    to anyone and everyone, prince or pauper.

"If the very ground that I farm accuses me,
    if even the furrows fill with tears from my abuse,
If I've ever raped the earth for my own profit
    or dispossessed its rightful owners,
Then curse it with thistles instead of wheat,
    curse it with weeds instead of barley."

        The words of Job to his three friends were finished.

## ELIHU SPEAKS
### God's Spirit Makes Wisdom Possible

**32.** Job's three friends now fell silent. They were talked out, stymied because Job wouldn't budge an inch — wouldn't admit to an ounce of guilt. Then Elihu lost his temper. (Elihu was the son of Barakel the Buzite from the clan of Ram.) He blazed out in anger against Job for pitting his righteousness against God's. He was also angry with the three friends because they had neither come up with an answer nor proved Job wrong. Elihu had waited with Job while they spoke because they were all older than he. But when he saw that the three other men had exhausted their arguments, he exploded with pent-up anger.

This is what Elihu, son of Barakel the Buzite, said:

"I'm a young man,
> and you are all old and experienced.
That's why I kept quiet
> and held back from joining the discussion.
I kept thinking, 'Experience will tell.
> The longer you live, the wiser you become.'
But I see I was wrong — it's God's Spirit in a person,
> the breath of the Almighty One, that makes wise human insight
> possible.
The experts have no corner on wisdom;
> getting old doesn't guarantee good sense.
So I've decided to speak up. Listen well!
> I'm going to tell you exactly what I think.

"I hung on your words while you spoke,
> listened carefully to your arguments.
While you searched for the right words,
> I was all ears.
And now what have you proved? Nothing.
> Nothing you say has even touched Job.
And don't excuse yourselves by saying, 'We've done our best.
> Now it's up to God to talk sense into him.'
Job has yet to contend with me.
> And rest assured, I won't be using *your* arguments!

"Do you three have nothing else to say?
> Of *course* you don't! You're total frauds!
Why should I wait any longer,
> now that you're stopped dead in your tracks?

I'm ready to speak my piece. That's right!
  It's my turn — and it's about time!
I've got a lot to say,
  and I'm bursting to say it.
The pressure has built up, like lava beneath the earth.
  I'm a volcano ready to blow.
I *have* to speak — I have no choice.
  I have to say what's on my heart,
And I'm going to say it straight —
  the truth, the whole truth, and nothing but the truth.
I was never any good at bootlicking;
  my Maker would make short work of me if I started in now!"

## 33.
"So please, Job, hear me out,
  honor me by listening to me.
What I'm about to say
  has been carefully thought out.
I have no ulterior motives in this;
  I'm speaking honestly from my heart.
The Spirit of God made me what I am,
  the breath of God Almighty gave me life!

### God Always Answers, One Way or Another

"And if you think you can prove me wrong, do it.
  Lay out your arguments. Stand up for yourself!
Look, I'm human — no better than you;
  we're both made of the same kind of mud.
So let's work this through together;
  don't let my aggressiveness overwhelm you.

"Here's what you said.
  I heard you say it with my own ears.
You said, 'I'm pure — I've done nothing wrong.

Believe me, I'm clean — my conscience is clear.
But God keeps picking on me;
  he treats me like I'm his enemy.
He's thrown me in jail;
  he keeps me under constant surveillance.'

"But let me tell you, Job, you're wrong, dead wrong!
  God is far greater than any human.
So how dare you haul him into court,
  and then complain that he won't answer your charges?
God always answers, one way or another,
  even when people don't recognize his presence.

"In a dream, for instance, a vision at night,
  when men and women are deep in sleep,
  fast asleep in their beds —
God opens their ears
  and impresses them with warnings
To turn them back from something bad they're planning,
  from some reckless choice,
And keep them from an early grave,
  from the river of no return.

"Or, God might get their attention through pain,
  by throwing them on a bed of suffering,
So they can't stand the sight of food,
  have no appetite for their favorite treats.
They lose weight, wasting away to nothing,
  reduced to a bag of bones.
They hang on the cliff-edge of death,
  knowing the next breath may be their last.

"But even then an angel could come,
  a champion — there are thousands of them! —

to take up your cause,
A messenger who would mercifully intervene,
    canceling the death sentence with the words:
        'I've come up with the ransom!'
Before you know it, you're healed,
    the very picture of health!

"Or, you may fall on your knees and pray — to God's delight!
    You'll see God's smile and celebrate,
    finding yourself set right with God.
You'll sing God's praises to everyone you meet,
    testifying, 'I messed up my life —
    and let me tell you, it wasn't worth it.
But God stepped in and saved me from certain death.
    I'm alive again! Once more I see the light!'

"This is the way God works.
    Over and over again
He pulls our souls back from certain destruction
    so we'll see the light — and *live* in the light!

---

### No Coward Soul Is Mine

No coward soul is mine,
No trembler in the world's storm-troubled sphere:
I see Heaven's glories shine,
And faith shines equal, arming me from fear.

O God within my breast,
Almighty, ever-present Deity!
Life, that in me has rest,
As I, undying life, have power in Thee!

Vain are the thousand creeds
That move men's hearts: unutterably vain;

**Worthless as withered weeds,**
**Or idlest froth amid the boundless main,**

**To waken doubt in one**
**Holding so fast by Thy infinity,**
**So surely anchored on**
**The steadfast rock of immortality.**

**Though earth and moon were gone,**
**And suns and universes ceased to be,**
**And Thou wert left alone,**
**Every existence would exist in Thee.**

**— Emily Brontë (1818-1848)**

---

"Keep listening, Job.
    Don't interrupt — I'm not finished yet.
But if you think of anything I should know, tell me.
    There's nothing I'd like better than to see your name cleared.
Meanwhile, keep listening. Don't distract me with interruptions.
    I'm going to teach you the basics of wisdom."

## ELIHU'S SECOND SPEECH
### It's Impossible for God to Do Evil

**34.** Elihu continued:

"So, my fine friends — listen to me,
    and see what you think of this.
Isn't it just common sense —
    as common as the sense of taste —
To put our heads together
    and figure out what's going on here?

"We've all heard Job say, 'I'm in the right,

but God won't give me a fair trial.
When I defend myself, I'm called a liar to my face.
I've done nothing wrong, and I get punished anyway.'
Have you ever heard anything to beat this?
Does nothing faze this man Job?
Do you think he's spent too much time in bad company,
hanging out with the wrong crowd,
So that now he's parroting their line:
'It doesn't pay to try to please God'?

"You're veterans in dealing with these matters;
certainly we're of one mind on this.
It's impossible for God to do anything evil;
no way can the Mighty One do wrong.
He makes us pay for exactly what we've done — no more, no less.
Our chickens always come home to roost.
It's impossible for God to do anything wicked,
for the Mighty One to subvert justice.
He's the one who runs the earth!
He cradles the whole world in his hand!
If he decided to hold his breath,
every man, woman, and child would die for lack of air.

### God Is Working Behind the Scenes

"So, Job, use your head;
this is all pretty obvious.
Can someone who hates order, keep order?
Do you dare condemn the righteous, mighty God?
Doesn't God always tell it like it is,
exposing corrupt rulers as scoundrels and criminals?
Does he play favorites with the rich and famous and slight the poor?
Isn't he equally responsible to everybody?
Don't people who deserve it die without notice?

Don't wicked rulers tumble to their doom?
When the so-called great ones are wiped out,
    we know God is working behind the scenes.

"He has his eyes on every man and woman.
    He doesn't miss a trick.
There is no night dark enough, no shadow deep enough,
    to hide those who do evil.
God doesn't need to gather any more evidence;
    their sin is an open-and-shut case.
He deposes the so-called high and mighty without asking questions,
    and replaces them at once with others.
Nobody gets by with anything; overnight,
    judgment is signed, sealed, and delivered.
He punishes the wicked for their wickedness
    out in the open where everyone can see it,
Because they quit following him,
    no longer even thought about him or his ways.
Their apostasy was announced by the cry of the poor;
    the cry of the afflicted got God's attention.

**Because You Refuse to Live on God's Terms**

"If God is silent, what's that to you?
    If he turns his face away, what can you do about it?
But whether silent or hidden, he's there, ruling,
    so that those who hate God won't take over
    and ruin people's lives.

"So why don't you simply confess to God?
    Say, 'I sinned, but I'll sin no more.
Teach me to see what I still don't see.
    Whatever evil I've done, I'll do it no more.'
Just because you refuse to live on God's terms,
    do you think he should start living on yours?

You choose. I can't do it for you.
    Tell me what you decide.

"All right-thinking people say —
    and the wise who have listened to me concur —
'Job is an ignoramus.
    He talks utter nonsense.'
Job, you need to be pushed to the wall and called to account
    for wickedly talking back to God the way you have.
You've compounded your original sin
    by rebelling against God's discipline,
Defiantly shaking your fist at God,
    piling up indictments against the Almighty One."

## ELIHU'S THIRD SPEECH
### When God Makes Creation a Classroom

**35.** Elihu lit into Job again:

"Does this kind of thing make any sense?
    First you say, 'I'm perfectly innocent before God.'
And then you say, 'It doesn't make a bit of difference
    whether I've sinned or not.'

"Well, I'm going to show you
    that you don't know what you're talking about,
    neither you nor your friends.
Look up at the sky. Take a long hard look.
    See those clouds towering above you?
If you sin, what difference could that make to God?
    No matter how much you sin, will it matter to him?
Even if you're good, what would God get out of that?
    Do you think he's dependent on your accomplishments?
The only ones who care whether you're good or bad

are your family and friends and neighbors.
  God's not dependent on your behavior.

"When times get bad, people cry out for help.
  They cry for relief from being kicked around,
But never give God a thought when things go well,
  when God puts spontaneous songs in their hearts,
When God sets out the entire creation as a science classroom,
  using birds and beasts to teach wisdom.
People are arrogantly indifferent to God—
  until, of course, they're in trouble,
  and then God is indifferent to them.
There's nothing behind such prayers except panic;
  the Almighty pays them no mind.
So why would he notice you
  just because you say you're tired of waiting to be heard,
Or waiting for him to get good and angry
  and do something about the world's problems?

"Job, you talk sheer nonsense—
  nonstop nonsense!"

## Those Who Learn from Their Suffering

**36.** Here Elihu took a deep breath, but kept going:

"Stay with me a little longer. I'll convince you.
  There's still more to be said on God's side.
I learned all this firsthand from the Source;
  everything I know about justice I owe to my Maker himself.
Trust me, I'm giving you undiluted truth;
  believe me, I know these things inside and out.

"It's true that God is all-powerful,

but he doesn't bully innocent people.
For the wicked, though, it's a different story —
    he doesn't give them the time of day,
    but champions the rights of their victims.
He never takes his eyes off the righteous;
    he honors them lavishly, promotes them endlessly.
When things go badly,
    when affliction and suffering descend,
God tells them where they've gone wrong,
    shows them how their pride has caused their trouble.
He forces them to heed his warning,
    tells them they must repent of their bad life.
If they obey and serve him,
    they'll have a good, long life on easy street.
But if they disobey, they'll be cut down in their prime
    and never know the first thing about life.
Angry people without God pile grievance upon grievance,
    always blaming others for their troubles.
Living it up in sexual excesses,
    virility wasted, they die young.
But those who learn from their suffering,
    God delivers from their suffering.

## SEARCHER ON THE WAY
*God's Great Sunrise*

Elizabeth Barrett was born in England in 1806. She was homeschooled by her father and learned several languages, including Greek and Latin, before she was a teenager. Her first poem was published in 1819, when she was only thirteen years old.

At age fifteen, Elizabeth seriously injured her back in a nasty fall and began spending a great deal of time at home. After the death of her brother, she became a total recluse, retreating to her room to write poetry and letters. Elizabeth immersed herself in the mystery of pain, while clinging to the hope of love.

At age thirty-eight, Elizabeth received her first letter from Robert Browning, who had been reading her deep and powerful poems. In 1846, at age forty, Elizabeth became a first-hand witness to the miracle of love—she left her room and secretly married Robert. Shortly thereafter, they moved to Italy, where Elizabeth's health improved dramatically. The couple would become famous, living and writing in Italy until Elizabeth died in Robert's arms at the age of fifty-five.

> So oft the doing of God's will
> Our foolish heart undoeth!
> And yet what idle dream breaks ill,
> Which morning-light subdueth?
> And who would murmur and misdoubt,
> When God's great sunrise find him out?

In her letters, Elizabeth Barrett Browning wrote that "God is the perfect poet," who "keeps his holy mysteries just on the outside of man's dream." Indeed, Elizabeth lived the total mystery of God's plan, from pain and loneliness to the miraculous realization of her hopes and dreams.

> God hath transfixed us,—we, so moved before,
> Attain to a calm. Ay, shouldering weights of pain,

We anchor in deep waters, safe from the shore,
And hear submissive o'er the stormy main
God's chartered judgments walk for evermore.


## Obsessed with Putting the Blame on God

"Oh, Job, don't you see how God's wooing you
    from the jaws of danger?
How he's drawing you into wide-open places —
    inviting you to feast at a table laden with blessings?
And here you are laden with the guilt of the wicked,
    obsessed with putting the blame on *God*!
Don't let your great riches mislead you;
    don't think you can bribe your way out of this.
Did you plan to buy your way out of this?
    Not on your life!
And don't think that night,
    when people sleep off their troubles,
    will bring you any relief.
Above all, don't make things worse with more evil —
    that's what's behind your suffering as it is!

"Do you have any idea how powerful God is?
    Have you ever heard of a teacher like him?
Has anyone ever had to tell him what to do,
    or correct him, saying, 'You did that all wrong!'?
Remember, then, to praise his workmanship,
    which is so often celebrated in song.
Everybody sees it;
    nobody is too far away to see it.

## No One Can Escape from God

"Take a long, hard look. See how great he is — infinite,
    greater than anything you could ever imagine or figure out!

"He pulls water up out of the sea,
    distills it, and fills up his rain-cloud cisterns.
Then the skies open up
    and pour out soaking showers on everyone.
Does anyone have the slightest idea how this happens?
    How he arranges the clouds, how he speaks in thunder?
Just look at that lightning, his sky-filling light show
    illumining the dark depths of the sea!
These are the symbols of his sovereignty,
    his generosity, his loving care.
He hurls arrows of light,
    taking sure and accurate aim.
The High God roars in the thunder,
    angry against evil."

**37.** "Whenever this happens, my heart stops —
    I'm stunned, I can't catch my breath.
Listen to it! Listen to his thunder,
    the rolling, rumbling thunder of his voice.
He lets loose his lightnings from horizon to horizon,
    lighting up the earth from pole to pole.
In their wake, the thunder echoes his voice,
    powerful and majestic.
He lets out all the stops, he holds nothing back.
    No one can mistake that voice —
His word thundering so wondrously,
    his mighty acts staggering our understanding.
He orders the snow, 'Blanket the earth!'
    and the rain, 'Soak the whole countryside!'

No one can escape the weather — it's *there*.
And no one can escape from God.
Wild animals take shelter,
crawling into their dens,
When blizzards roar out of the north
and freezing rain crusts the land.
It's God's breath that forms the ice,
it's God's breath that turns lakes and rivers solid.
And yes, it's God who fills clouds with rainwater
and hurls lightning from them every which way.
He puts them through their paces — first this way, then that —
commands them to do what he says all over the world.
Whether for discipline or grace or extravagant love,
he makes sure they make their mark.

## A Terrible Beauty Streams from God

"Job, are you listening? Have you noticed all this?
Stop in your tracks! Take in God's miracle-wonders!
Do you have any idea how God does it all,
how he makes bright lightning from dark storms,
How he piles up the cumulus clouds —
all these miracle-wonders of a perfect Mind?
Why, you don't even know how to keep cool
on a sweltering hot day,
So how could you even dream
of making a dent in that hot-tin-roof sky?

"If you're so smart, give us a lesson in how to address God.
We're in the dark and can't figure it out.
Do you think I'm dumb enough to challenge God?
Wouldn't that just be asking for trouble?
No one in his right mind stares straight at the sun
on a clear and cloudless day.

As gold comes from the northern mountains,
    so a terrible beauty streams from God.

"Mighty God! Far beyond our reach!
    Unsurpassable in power and justice!
    It's unthinkable that he'd treat anyone unfairly.
So bow to him in deep reverence, one and all!
    If you're wise, you'll most certainly worship him."

---

> On behalf of all of us who have been misled by the platitudes of the nice people who show up to tell us everything is going to be all right if we simply think such-and-such and do such-and-such, Job issued an anguished rejoinder. He rejected the kind of advice and teaching that has God all figured out, that provides glib explanations for every circumstance. Job's honest defiance continues to be the best defense against the clichés of positive thinkers and the prattle of religious small talk.
>
> The honest, innocent Job was placed in a setting of immense suffering and then surrounded by the conventional religious wisdom of the day in the form of speeches by Eliphaz, Bildad, Zophar, and Elihu. The contrast is unforgettable. The counselors methodically and pedantically recited their bookish precepts to Job. At first Job raged in pain and roared out his protests, but then he became silent in awestruck faith before God, who spoke out of a storm—a "whirlwind" of Deity. Real faith cannot be reduced to spiritual bromides and merchandised in success stories. It is refined in the fires and the storms of pain.

---

## GOD CONFRONTS JOB
### Have You Gotten to the Bottom of Things?

**38.** And now, finally, GOD answered Job from the eye of a violent storm. He said:

"Why do you confuse the issue?
    Why do you talk without knowing what you're talking about?
Pull yourself together, Job!
    Up on your feet! Stand tall!
I have some questions for you,

and I want some straight answers.
Where were you when I created the earth?
  Tell me, since you know so much!
Who decided on its size? Certainly you'll know that!
  Who came up with the blueprints and measurements?
How was its foundation poured,
  and who set the cornerstone,
While the morning stars sang in chorus
  and all the angels shouted praise?
And who took charge of the ocean
  when it gushed forth like a baby from the womb?
That was me! I wrapped it in soft clouds,
  and tucked it in safely at night.
Then I made a playpen for it,
  a strong playpen so it couldn't run loose,
And said, 'Stay here, this is your place.
  Your wild tantrums are confined to this place.'

"And have you ever ordered Morning, 'Get up!'
  told Dawn, 'Get to work!'
So you could seize Earth like a blanket
  and shake out the wicked like cockroaches?
As the sun brings everything to light,
  brings out all the colors and shapes,
The cover of darkness is snatched from the wicked —
  they're caught in the very act!

"Have you ever gotten to the true bottom of things,
  explored the labyrinthine caves of deep ocean?
Do you know the first thing about death?
  Do you have one clue regarding death's dark mysteries?
And do you have any idea how large this earth is?
  Speak up if you have even the beginning of an answer.

"Do you know where Light comes from
        and where Darkness lives
So you can take them by the hand
        and lead them home when they get lost?
Why, of *course* you know that.
        You've known them all your life,
        grown up in the same neighborhood with them!

"Have you ever traveled to where snow is made,
        seen the vault where hail is stockpiled,
The arsenals of hail and snow that I keep in readiness
        for times of trouble and battle and war?
Can you find your way to where lightning is launched,
        or to the place from which the wind blows?
Who do you suppose carves canyons
        for the downpours of rain, and charts
        the route of thunderstorms
That bring water to unvisited fields,
        deserts no one ever lays eyes on,
Drenching the useless wastelands
        so they're carpeted with wildflowers and grass?
And who do you think is the father of rain and dew,
        the mother of ice and frost?
You don't for a minute imagine
        these marvels of weather just happen, do you?

"Can you catch the eye of the beautiful Pleiades sisters,
        or distract Orion from his hunt?
Can you get Venus to look your way,
        or get the Great Bear and her cubs to come out and play?
Do you know the first thing about the sky's constellations
        and how they affect things on Earth?

Why do we see three aligned stars in the night sky and say that's the belt of a hunter named Orion? I don't see it. Do you? How about the cluster known as *Ursa Major* (the "Big Dipper")? Does anyone truly see a "picture" of a Great Bear and her cubs? Of course not.

Actually, when the ancients named the heavenly bodies, it wasn't based on pictures they saw in the night sky. Rather, the bodies of light were viewed as awesome "signs" from God, and those signs each came with an underlying story. The story was then summarized in the name and picture associated with that sign, so that the entire narrative of the zodiac could be passed along more easily.

The Hebrew name for the zodiac is the *Mazzeroth*. Although a zodiac chart today is in a slightly different order, it's interesting how the story of the *Mazzeroth* begins with *Virgo* (the Virgin) and ends with *Leo* (the Lion of the Tribe of Judah).

"Can you get the attention of the clouds,
    and commission a shower of rain?
Can you take charge of the lightning bolts
    and have them report to you for orders?

## SEARCHER ON THE WAY
*Carp and the Theory of Everything*

As a young child, Michio Kaku spent hours watching carp at the Japanese Tea Garden in San Francisco. He imagined the pond as an entire two-dimensional universe, where the carp could only swim forward and backward, left and right. The concept of "up," beyond the lily pads, was totally alien to the fish.

Michio wondered, *What if I could reach down and grab a carp and lift him up into my universe?* What a wondrous story the carp would tell the others! He would babble on about new laws of physics and unbelievable creatures that move without fins and breathe without gills. However, without such a visit to the third dimension, how could a "thinking" carp know anything about the unseen world above?

One day it rained, and Michio saw the drops form ripples on the surface of the pond. Then he understood. The carp could see the rippling shadows. The third dimension was invisible to them, but vibrations in this dimension were clearly visible. The ripples might even be felt by the carp, who would invent scientific concepts such as "light" and "gravity" to help describe the unseen "force." Of course, the other carp in the pond would laugh at the notion, since carp know there's no "force" at all, just the rippling of the water.

Today, Michio Kaku believes we are the carp swimming in our tiny pond, blissfully unaware of invisible universes hovering just above us in hyperspace. As described on his self-named website, twenty-first century physicists can now "see" and "feel" the "ripples," and Michio is leading the charge toward a scientific formula that explains it all—the "Theory of Everything" as Einstein called it. He is the leading scientist in "superstring" theory, a ten-dimensional model of unseen "strings" vibrating at the quantum level that provides a unification of all forces in the cosmos.

## What Do You Have to Say for Yourself?

"Who do you think gave weather-wisdom to the ibis,
    and storm-savvy to the rooster?
Does anyone know enough to number all the clouds
    or tip over the rain barrels of heaven
When the earth is cracked and dry,
    the ground baked hard as a brick?

"Can you teach the lioness to stalk her prey
    and satisfy the appetite of her cubs
As they crouch in their den,
    waiting hungrily in their cave?
And who sets out food for the ravens
    when their young cry to God,
        fluttering about because they have no food?"

**39.** "Do you know the month when mountain goats give birth?
    Have you ever watched a doe bear her fawn?
Do you know how many months she is pregnant?
    Do you know the season of her delivery,
        when she crouches down and drops her offspring?

Her young ones flourish and are soon on their own;
    they leave and don't come back.

"Who do you think set the wild donkey free,
    opened the corral gates and let him go?
I gave him the whole wilderness to roam in,
    the rolling plains and wide-open places.
He laughs at his city cousins, who are harnessed and harried.
    He's oblivious to the cries of teamsters.
He grazes freely through the hills,
    nibbling anything that's green.

"Will the wild buffalo condescend to serve you,
    volunteer to spend the night in your barn?
Can you imagine hitching your plow to a buffalo
    and getting him to till your fields?
He's hugely strong, yes, but could you trust him,
    would you dare turn the job over to him?
You wouldn't for a minute depend on him, would you,
    to do what you said when you said it?

"The ostrich flaps her wings futilely —
    all those beautiful feathers, but useless!
She lays her eggs on the hard ground,
    leaves them there in the dirt, exposed to the weather,
Not caring that they might get stepped on and cracked
    or trampled by some wild animal.
She's negligent with her young, as if they weren't even hers.
    She cares nothing about anything.
She wasn't created very smart, that's for sure,
    wasn't given her share of good sense.
But when she runs, oh, how she runs,
    laughing, leaving horse and rider in the dust.

"Are you the one who gave the horse his prowess
    and adorned him with a shimmering mane?
Did you create him to prance proudly
    and strike terror with his royal snorts?
He paws the ground fiercely, eager and spirited,
    then charges into the fray.
He laughs at danger, fearless,
    doesn't shy away from the sword.
The banging and clanging
    of quiver and lance don't faze him.
He quivers with excitement, and at the trumpet blast
    races off at a gallop.

At the sound of the trumpet he neighs mightily,
    smelling the excitement of battle from a long way off,
    catching the rolling thunder of the war cries.

"Was it through your know-how that the hawk learned to fly,
    soaring effortlessly on thermal updrafts?
Did you command the eagle's flight,
    and teach her to build her nest in the heights,
Perfectly at home on the high cliff face,
    invulnerable on pinnacle and crag?
From her perch she searches for prey,
    spies it at a great distance.
Her young gorge themselves on carrion;
    wherever there's a roadkill, you'll see her circling."

# 40.

GOD then confronted Job directly:

"Now what do you have to say for yourself?
    Are you going to haul me, the Mighty One, into court and
        press charges?"

## JOB ANSWERS GOD
### I'm Ready to Shut Up and Listen

Job answered:

"I'm speechless, in awe — words fail me.
    I should never have opened my mouth!
I've talked too much, way too much.
    I'm ready to shut up and listen."

## GOD'S SECOND SET OF QUESTIONS
### I Want Straight Answers

GOD addressed Job next from the eye of the storm, and this is what
he said:

"I have some more questions for you,
and I want straight answers.

"Do you presume to tell me what I'm doing wrong?
Are you calling me a sinner so you can be a saint?
Do you have an arm like my arm?
Can you shout in thunder the way I can?
Go ahead, show your stuff.
Let's see what you're made of, what you can do.
Unleash your outrage.
Target the arrogant and lay them flat.
Target the arrogant and bring them to their knees.
Stop the wicked in their tracks — make mincemeat of them!
Dig a mass grave and dump them in it —
faceless corpses in an unmarked grave.
I'll gladly step aside and hand things over to you —
you can surely save yourself with no help from me!

"Look at the land beast, Behemoth. I created him as well as you.
Grazing on grass, docile as a cow —
Just look at the strength of his back,
the powerful muscles of his belly.
His tail sways like a cedar in the wind;
his huge legs are like beech trees.
His skeleton is made of steel,
every bone in his body hard as steel.
Most magnificent of all my creatures,
but I still lead him around like a lamb!

The grass-covered hills serve him meals,
    while field mice frolic in his shadow.
He takes afternoon naps under shade trees,
    cools himself in the reedy swamps,
Lazily cool in the leafy shadows
    as the breeze moves through the willows.
And when the river rages he doesn't budge,
    stolid and unperturbed even when the Jordan goes wild.
But you'd never want him for a pet—
    you'd never be able to housebreak him!"

## I Run This Universe

**41.** "Or can you pull in the sea beast, Leviathan, with a fly rod
    and stuff him in your creel?
Can you lasso him with a rope,
    or snag him with an anchor?
Will he beg you over and over for mercy,
    or flatter you with flowery speech?
Will he apply for a job with you
    to run errands and serve you the rest of your life?
Will you play with him as if he were a pet goldfish?
    Will you make him the mascot of the neighborhood children?
Will you put him on display in the market
    and have shoppers haggle over the price?
Could you shoot him full of arrows like a pin cushion,
    or drive harpoons into his huge head?
If you so much as lay a hand on him,
    you won't live to tell the story.
What hope would you have with such a creature?
    Why, one look at him would do you in!
If you can't hold your own against his glowering visage,
    how, then, do you expect to stand up to *me*?
Who could confront me and get by with it?

I'm *in charge* of all this — I run this universe!

"But I've more to say about Leviathan, the sea beast,
    his enormous bulk, his beautiful shape.
Who would even dream of piercing that tough skin
    or putting those jaws into bit and bridle?
And who would dare knock at the door of his mouth
    filled with row upon row of fierce teeth?
His pride is invincible;
    nothing can make a dent in that pride.
Nothing can get through that proud skin —
    impervious to weapons and weather,
The thickest and toughest of hides,
    impenetrable!

"He snorts and the world lights up with fire,
    he blinks and the dawn breaks.
Comets pour out of his mouth,
    fireworks arc and branch.
Smoke erupts from his nostrils
    like steam from a boiling pot.
He blows and fires blaze;
    flames of fire stream from his mouth.
All muscle he is — sheer and seamless muscle.
    To meet him is to dance with death.
Sinewy and lithe,
    there's not a soft spot in his entire body —
As tough inside as out,
    rock-hard, invulnerable.
Even angels run for cover when he surfaces,
    cowering before his tail-thrashing turbulence.
Javelins bounce harmlessly off his hide,
    harpoons ricochet wildly.
Iron bars are so much straw to him,

bronze weapons beneath notice.
Arrows don't even make him blink;
   bullets make no more impression than raindrops.
A battle ax is nothing but a splinter of kindling;
   he treats a brandished harpoon as a joke.
His belly is armor-plated, inexorable —
   unstoppable as a barge.
He roils deep ocean the way you'd boil water,
   he whips the sea like you'd whip an egg into batter.
With a luminous trail stretching out behind him,
   you might think Ocean had grown a gray beard!
There's nothing on this earth quite like him,
   not an ounce of fear in *that* creature!
He surveys all the high and mighty —
   king of the ocean, king of the deep!"

---

Many people don't realize that paleontology (the study of past geological ages based primarily on the study of fossils) is a relatively new science. In fact, the concept of "dinosaurs" only surfaced in its present form less than 180 years ago. Prior to that, anyone who found a large fossilized bone assumed it came from an elephant, dragon, or giant. It wasn't until 1841 that English scientist Richard Owens suggested that the group of "newly discovered" animals be called "dinosaurs" (meaning "terrible lizards"). Therefore, we shouldn't expect to see dinosaurs in the Bible, but we should expect to see descriptions of "dragons" and other large creatures. In fact, we do!

A search for the word *tannin* in the original Hebrew produces thirty-four separate matches across ten different books of the Jewish Scriptures. *Tannin* directly translates as "sea or land monsters," and is often translated as "dragon." Even more dramatic than general references to sea and land monsters, Job gives us fantastic details about the great land creature, Behemoth, and the great water creature, Leviathan.

## JOB WORSHIPS GOD
### I Babbled On About Things Far Beyond Me

**42.** Job answered GOD:

"I'm convinced: You can do anything and everything.
    Nothing and no one can upset your plans.
You asked, 'Who is this muddying the water,
    ignorantly confusing the issue, second-guessing my purposes?'
I admit it. I was the one. I babbled on about things far beyond me,
    made small talk about wonders way over my head.
You told me, 'Listen, and let me do the talking.
    Let me ask the questions. *You* give the answers.'
I admit I once lived by rumors of you;
    now I have it all firsthand—from my own eyes and ears!
I'm sorry—forgive me. I'll never do that again, I promise!
    I'll never again live on crusts of hearsay, crumbs of rumor."

---

> In the course of facing, questioning, and respecting suffering, Job found himself in an even larger mystery—the mystery of God. Perhaps the greatest mystery in suffering is how it can bring a person into the presence of God in a state of worship, full of wonder, love, and praise. Suffering does not inevitably do that, but it does it far more often than we would expect. It certainly did that for Job. Even in his answer to his wife, he spoke the language of an uncharted irony, a dark and difficult kind of truth: "We take the good days from God—why not also the bad days?"

---

## GOD RESTORES JOB
### I Will Accept His Prayer

After GOD had finished addressing Job, he turned to Eliphaz the Temanite and said, "I've had it with you and your two friends. I'm fed up! You haven't been honest either with me or about me—not the way my friend Job has. So here's what you must do. Take seven bulls and seven rams, and go to my friend Job. Sacrifice a burnt offering on your own behalf. My friend Job will pray for you, and I will accept his prayer. He will ask me not to treat you as you deserve for talking nonsense about me, and for not being honest with me, as he has."

They did it. Eliphaz the Temanite, Bildad the Shuhite, and Zophar the Naamathite did what GOD commanded. And GOD accepted Job's prayer.

After Job had interceded for his friends, GOD restored his fortune — and then doubled it! All his brothers and sisters and friends came to his house and celebrated. They told him how sorry they were, and consoled him for all the trouble GOD had brought him. Each of them brought generous housewarming gifts.

GOD blessed Job's later life even more than his earlier life. He ended up with fourteen thousand sheep, six thousand camels, one thousand teams of oxen, and one thousand donkeys. He also had seven sons and three daughters. He named the first daughter Dove, the second, Cinnamon, and the third, Darkeyes. There was not a woman in that country as beautiful as Job's daughters. Their father treated them as equals with their brothers, providing the same inheritance.

Job lived on another 140 years, living to see his children and grandchildren — four generations of them! Then he died — an old man, a full life.

---

▶ In our compassion, we don't like to see people suffer. And so our instincts are aimed at preventing and alleviating suffering. No doubt, that is a good impulse. But if we really want to reach out to others who are suffering, we should be careful not to be like Job's friends. We shouldn't "help" with the presumption that we can fix things, get rid of the pain, or make it "better." We may look at our suffering friends and imagine how they could have better marriages, better-behaved children, better mental and emotional health. But when we rush in to fix suffering, we need to keep in mind several things.

First, no matter how insightful we may be, we don't *really* understand the full nature of our friends' problems. Second, our friends may not *want* our advice. Third, the ironic fact of the matter is that, more often than not, people do not suffer *less* when they are committed to following God, but *more*. When these people go through suffering, their lives are often transformed, deepened, marked with beauty and holiness, in remarkable ways that could never have been anticipated before the suffering.

So, instead of continuing to focus on preventing suffering—which we simply won't be very successful at anyway—perhaps we should begin *entering* the suffering, participating insofar as we are able—entering the mystery and looking around for God. In other words, we need to quit feeling sorry for people who suffer and instead look up to them, learn from them, and—if they will let us—join them in protest and prayer. Pity can be nearsighted and condescending; shared suffering can be dignifying and life-changing. As we look at Job's suffering and praying and worshiping, we see that he has already blazed a trail of courage and integrity for us to follow.

But sometimes it's hard to know just how to follow Job's lead when we feel so alone in our suffering, unsure of what God wants us to do. What we must realize during those times of darkness is that the God who appeared to Job in the whirlwind is calling out to all of us. Although God may not appear to us in a vision, he makes himself known to us in all the many ways that he describes to Job—from the macro to the micro, from the wonders of the galaxies to the little things we take for granted. He is the Creator of the unfathomable universe all around us—and he is also the Creator of the universe inside of us. And so we gain hope, not from the darkness of our suffering, not from pat answers in books, but from the God who sees our suffering and shares our pain.

Reading Job prayerfully and meditatively leads us to face the questions that arise when our lives don't turn out the way we expect them to. First we hear all the stock answers. Then we ask the questions again, with variations—and hear the answers again, with variations. Over and over and over. Every time we let Job give voice to our own questions, our suffering gains in dignity and we are brought a step closer to the threshold of the voice and mystery of God. Every time we persist with Job in rejecting the quick-fix counsel of people who see us and hear us but do not understand us, we deepen our availability and openness to the revelation that comes only out of the tempest. The mystery of God eclipses the darkness and the struggle. We realize that suffering calls *our* lives into question, not God's. The tables are turned: God-Alive is present to us. God is speaking to us. And so Job's experience is confirmed and repeated once again in our suffering and our vulnerable humanity.

Job lived the full spectrum of existence. In the end, he wrapped the good times and the bad times, the joy and the pain, the miraculous and the mysterious, into one tight bundle and buried it in the backyard. Job lived the extremes of human-ness, and through it all became sure of only one thing: God.

When religion has said its last word,
there is little that we need other than God Himself.

— A. W. Tozer

# HABAKKUK

## INTRODUCTION TO HABAKKUK

Living by faith is a bewildering venture. We rarely know what's coming next, and not many things turn out the way we anticipate. It is natural to assume that since I am God's chosen and beloved, I will get favorable treatment from the God who favors me so extravagantly. It is not unreasonable to expect that from the time that I become his follower, I will be exempt from dead ends, muddy detours, and cruel treatment from the travelers I meet daily who are walking the other direction. That God-followers don't get preferential treatment in life always comes as a surprise. But it's also a surprise to find that there are a few men and women *within* the Bible who show up alongside us at such moments.

The prophet Habakkuk is one of them, and a most welcome companion he is. Most prophets, most of the time, speak God's Word *to us.* They are preachers calling us to listen to God's words of judgment and salvation, confrontation and comfort. They face us with God as he is, not as we imagine him to be. Most prophets are in-your-face assertive, not given to tact, not diplomatic, as they insist that we pay attention to God. But Habakkuk speaks our word *to God.* He gives voice to our bewilderment, articulates our puzzled attempts to make sense of things, faces God with our disappointment with God. He insists that God pay attention to us, and he insists with a prophet's characteristic no-nonsense bluntness.

The circumstance that aroused Habakkuk took place in the seventh century BC. The prophet realized that God was going to use the godless military machine of Babylon to bring God's judgment on God's own people—using a godless nation to punish a godly nation! It didn't make sense, and Habakkuk was quick and bold to say so. He dared to voice his feelings that God didn't know his own God business. Not a day has passed since then that one of us hasn't picked up and repeated Habakkuk's bafflement: "God, you don't seem to make sense!"

But this prophet companion who stands at our side does something even more important: He waits and he listens. It is in his waiting and listening—which then turns into his praying—that he found himself inhabiting the large world of God's sovereignty. Only there did he eventually realize that the believing-in-God life, the steady trusting-in-God life, is the full life, the only real life. Habakkuk started out exactly where we start out with our puzzled complaints and God-accusations, but he didn't stay there. He ended up in a world, along with us, where every detail in our lives of love for God is worked into something good.

## Justice Is a Joke

**01.** The problem as God gave Habakkuk to see it:

GOD, how long do I have to cry out for help
  before you listen?
How many times do I have to yell, "Help! Murder! Police!"
  before you come to the rescue?
Why do you force me to look at evil,
  stare trouble in the face day after day?
Anarchy and violence break out,
  quarrels and fights all over the place.
Law and order fall to pieces.
  Justice is a joke.
The wicked have the righteous hamstrung
  and stand justice on its head.

## God Says, "Look!"

"Look around at the godless nations.
    Look long and hard. Brace yourself for a shock.
Something's about to take place
    and you're going to find it hard to believe.
I'm about to raise up Babylonians to punish you,
    Babylonians, fierce and ferocious —
World-conquering Babylon,
    grabbing up nations right and left,
A dreadful and terrible people,
    making up its own rules as it goes.
Their horses run like the wind,
    attack like bloodthirsty wolves.
A stampede of galloping horses
    thunders out of nowhere.
They descend like vultures
    circling in on carrion.
They're out to kill. Death is on their minds.
    They collect victims like squirrels gathering nuts.
They mock kings,
    poke fun at generals,
Spit on forts,
    and leave them in the dust.
They'll all be blown away by the wind.
    Brazen in sin, they call strength their god."

## Why Is God Silent Now?

GOD, you're from eternity, aren't you?
    Holy God, we aren't going to die, are we?
GOD, you chose *Babylonians* for your judgment work?
    Rock-Solid God, you gave *them* the job of discipline?
But you can't be serious!

*You* can't condone evil!
So why don't you do something about this?
     Why are you silent *now*?
This outrage! Evil men swallow up the righteous
     and you stand around and *watch*!

———

> **Where is God when we really need him?**
>
> At times, even the most faithful believers get absolutely perplexed with their condition. In the late sixth century BC, Habakkuk, a faithful man of God, watched as his people committed injustice and atrocity. In the holy city of Jerusalem, God was nowhere to be found—just death, destruction, and despair all around.
>
> When God finally answered Habakkuk, the message was far from what Habakkuk expected. Instead of a message of awakening and reconciliation for the Jewish people, God announced that his people would suffer at the hands of an even more unjust and atrocious people—the Babylonian Empire.
>
> Initially, Habakkuk was shocked! Where's the cosmic justice in this?
>
> However, Habakkuk didn't use this as a reason to turn away from God, instead he dug in deeper and prayerfully sought God in the depths of his dismay. Unlike many "religious" people today, Habakkuk was honest with himself and honest with God. God-followers are often taught to "put on a happy face" in all situations. Questions, doubts, and fears are unacceptable signs of faithlessness. Habakkuk teaches us that authenticity is the beginning of true relationship.

You're treating men and women
     as so many fish in the ocean,
Swimming without direction,
     swimming but not getting anywhere.
Then this evil Babylonian arrives and goes fishing.
     He pulls in a good catch.
He catches his limit and fills his creel—
     a good day of fishing! He's happy!
He praises his rod and reel,
     piles his fishing gear on an altar and worships it!

It's made his day,
  and he's going to eat well tonight!

_____

Are you going to let this go on and on?
  Will you let this Babylonian fisherman
Fish like a weekend angler,
  killing people as if they're nothing but fish?

---

Rolling into the sixth century BC, the Babylonian Empire was recognized as the most powerful civilization on Earth. Babylon itself was considered the most awesome city in the ancient world, covering more than six square miles along the Euphrates River in present-day Iraq.

Babylon was known for its fantastic palaces, gates, and walls—walls so thick that a four-horse chariot could make a turn on top of them. While the peaceful and beautiful hanging gardens of Babylon were recorded as one of the seven wonders of the ancient world, the armies of Babylon were the anecdote for peace—an absolutely fierce and ruthless hoard conquering all peoples in its path.

The Assyrian Empire fell to the Babylonian armies at Nineveh in 612 BC. The fall of the Egyptian Empire to the Babylonians was close behind, with the final battle at Carchemish in 605 BC. Although Jerusalem escaped for a time, the prophecies of its defeat at the hands of the Babylonian Empire were fulfilled in 597 BC, and the surviving people of Judah were taken in chains to Babylon. In 587 BC, Jerusalem was totally destroyed.

---

**02.** What's God going to say to my questions? I'm braced for the worst.
  I'll climb to the lookout tower and scan the horizon.
I'll wait to see what God says,
  how he'll answer my complaint.

### Full of Self, but Soul-Empty

And then GOD answered: "Write this.
  Write what you see.
Write it out in big block letters

so that it can be read on the run.
This vision-message is a witness
      pointing to what's coming.
It aches for the coming — it can hardly wait!
      And it doesn't lie.
If it seems slow in coming, wait.
      It's on its way. It will come right on time.

———

"Look at that man, bloated by self-importance —
      full of himself but soul-empty.
But the person in right standing before God
      through loyal and steady believing
      is fully alive, *really* alive.

"Note well: Money deceives.
      The arrogant rich don't last.
They are more hungry for wealth
      than the grave is for cadavers.
Like death, they always want more,
      but the 'more' they get is dead bodies.
They are cemeteries filled with dead nations,
      graveyards filled with corpses.
Don't give people like this a second thought.
      Soon the whole world will be taunting them:

"'Who do you think you are —
      getting rich by stealing and extortion?
How long do you think
      you can get away with this?'
Indeed, how long before your victims wake up,
      stand up and make *you* the victim?
You've plundered nation after nation.
      Now you'll get a taste of your own medicine.

All the survivors are out to plunder you,
    a payback for all your murders and massacres.

"Who do you think you are —
    recklessly grabbing and looting,
Living it up, acting like king of the mountain,
    acting above it all, above trials and troubles?
You've engineered the ruin of your own house.
    In ruining others you've ruined yourself.
You've undermined your foundations,
    rotted out your own soul.
The bricks of your house will speak up and accuse you.
    The woodwork will step forward with evidence.

"Who do you think you are —
    building a town by murder, a city with crime?
Don't you know that GOD-of-the-Angel-Armies
    makes sure nothing comes of that but ashes,
Makes sure the harder you work
    at that kind of thing, the less you are?
Meanwhile the earth fills up
    with awareness of GOD's glory
    as the waters cover the sea.

"Who do you think you are —
    inviting your neighbors to your drunken parties,
Giving them too much to drink,
    roping them into your sexual orgies?
You thought you were having the time of your life.
    Wrong! It's a time of disgrace.
All the time you were drinking,
    you were drinking from the cup of God's wrath.
You'll wake up holding your throbbing head, hung over —
    hung over from Lebanon violence,

Hung over from animal massacres,
   hung over from murder and mayhem,
From multiple violations
   of place and people.

"What's the use of a carved god
   so skillfully carved by its sculptor?
What good is a fancy cast god
   when all it tells is lies?
What sense does it make to be a pious god-maker
   who makes gods that can't even talk?
Who do you think you are —
   saying to a stick of wood, 'Wake up,'
Or to a dumb stone, 'Get up'?
   Can they teach you anything about anything?
There's nothing to them but surface.
   There's nothing on the inside.

"But oh! God is in his holy Temple!
   Quiet everyone — a holy silence. Listen!"

### God Racing on the Crest of the Waves

**03.** A prayer of the prophet Habakkuk, with orchestra:

God, I've heard what our ancestors say about you,
   and I'm stopped in my tracks, down on my knees.
Do among us what you did among them.
   Work among us as you worked among them.
And as you bring judgment, as you surely must,
   remember mercy.

———

## SEARCHER ON THE WAY

*A Lesson in Humility*

Nebuchadnezzar was the mighty king of the Babylonian Empire between 604 and 562 BC. Numerous cuneiform tablets and ancient texts speak of his wondrous achievements and prideful character. "Look at this, Babylon the great! And I built it all by myself, a royal palace adequate to display my honor and glory!" Nebuchadnezzar trusted in his immense wealth and powerful warriors—he had no room for God in his kingdom.

However, late in his reign, Nebuchadnezzar had a wake-up call. Overnight, he went from mighty king to wandering madman as he was stricken with a psycho-mania, which caused him to act like an animal. He grew long hair and nails, roaming about the countryside grazing on grass.

Seven years into his malady, Nebuchadnezzar returned to his senses; immediately, he knew his lifelong mistake. A once godless ruler was now a God-fearing man. In fact, his own story was recorded in the ancient texts of the prophet Daniel, who was living as a captive in Babylon:

> I, Nebuchadnezzar, looked to heaven. I was
> given my mind back and I blessed the High God,
> thanking and glorifying God, who lives forever. . . .
>
> At the same time that I was given back my mind,
> I was also given back my majesty and splendor,
> making my kingdom shine. All the leaders and
> important people came looking for me. I was
> reestablished as king in my kingdom and became
> greater than ever. And that's why I'm singing—I,
> Nebuchadnezzar—singing and praising the King of
> Heaven:
>
> "Everything he does is right,
>    and he does it the right way.

> He knows how to turn a proud person
>> into a humble man or woman."

Nebuchadnezzar was a mighty king, ruling a vast kingdom. By the world's standards, he was the most powerful man of his day. However, through a season of humbling, Nebuchadnezzar came to recognize that God is a far mightier king, ruling a kingdom that is everlasting.

God's on his way again,
     retracing the old salvation route,
Coming up from the south through Teman,
     the Holy One from Mount Paran.
Skies are blazing with his splendor,
     his praises sounding through the earth,
His cloud-brightness like dawn, exploding, spreading,
     forked-lightning shooting from his hand —
     what power hidden in that fist!
Plague marches before him,
     pestilence at his heels!
He stops. He shakes Earth.
     He looks around. Nations tremble.
The age-old mountains fall to pieces;
     ancient hills collapse like a spent balloon.
The paths God takes are older
     than the oldest mountains and hills.
I saw everyone worried, in a panic:
·    Old wilderness adversaries,
Cushan and Midian, were terrified,
     hoping he wouldn't notice them.

———

GOD, is it River you're mad at?
     Angry at old River?

Were you raging at Sea when you rode
    horse and chariot through to salvation?
You unfurled your bow
    and let loose a volley of arrows.
    You split Earth with rivers.
Mountains saw what was coming.
    They twisted in pain.
Flood Waters poured in.
    Ocean roared and reared huge waves.
Sun and Moon stopped in their tracks.
    Your flashing arrows stopped them,
    your lightning-strike spears impaled them.
Angry, you stomped through Earth.
    Furious, you crushed the godless nations.
You were out to save your people,
    to save your specially chosen people.
You beat the stuffing
    out of King Wicked,
Stripped him naked
    from head to toe,
Set his severed head on his own spear
    and blew away his army.
Scattered they were to the four winds —
    and ended up food for the sharks!
You galloped through the Sea on your horses,
    racing on the crest of the waves.
When I heard it, my stomach did flips.
    I stammered and stuttered.
My bones turned to water.
    I staggered and stumbled.
I sit back and wait for Doomsday
    to descend on our attackers.

———

Though the cherry trees don't blossom
    and the strawberries don't ripen,
Though the apples are worm-eaten
    and the wheat fields stunted,
Though the sheep pens are sheepless
    and the cattle barns empty,
I'm singing joyful praise to GOD.
    I'm turning cartwheels of joy to my Savior God.
Counting on GOD's Rule to prevail,
    I take heart and gain strength.
I run like a deer.
    I feel like I'm king of the mountain!

(For congregational use, with a full orchestra.)

---

## Naked Before God!

Whether we admit it or not, we're totally naked before God—our minds and motives are fully exposed. Therefore, as Habakkuk, we should embrace our spiritual nudity. It is utterly worthless to go through religious motions and mantras without humbly and honestly seeking God.

In Hans Christian Andersen's "The Emperor's New Clothes," the problem wasn't that the emperor was naked—he was. The problem was that he wouldn't admit it.

> He thought it better to continue the procession under the
> illusion that anyone who couldn't see his clothes was either
> stupid or incompetent. And he stood stiffly on his carriage,
> while behind him a page held his imaginary mantle.

So, how many of us are placing religion before authenticity? How much humility and honesty is giving way to pomp and ceremony? Sometimes it just takes a child, without job or agenda, to declare, "The emperor is naked."

And thus starts spiritual revival for many of us.

---

# JONAH

Everybody knows about Jonah. People who have never read the Bible know enough about Jonah to laugh at a joke about him and the "whale." Jonah has entered our folklore. There is a playful aspect to his story, a kind of slapstick clumsiness about Jonah as he bumbles his way along, trying, but always unsuccessfully, to avoid God.

But the playfulness is not frivolous. This is deadly serious. While we are smiling or laughing at Jonah, we drop the guard with which we are trying to keep God at a comfortable distance, and suddenly we find ourselves caught in the purposes and commands of God. All of us. No exceptions.

Stories are the most prominent biblical way of helping us see ourselves in "the God story," which always gets around to the story of God making and saving us. Stories, in contrast to abstract statements of truth, tease us into becoming participants in what is being said. We find ourselves involved in the action. We may start out as spectators or critics, but if the story is good (and the biblical stories are very good!), we find ourselves no longer just listening to but inhabiting the story.

One reason that the Jonah story is so enduringly important for nurturing the life of faith in us is that Jonah is not a hero too high and mighty for us to identify with—he doesn't do anything great. Instead of being held up as an ideal to admire, we find Jonah as a companion in our ineptness. Here is someone on our level. Even when Jonah does it right (like preaching, finally, in Nineveh) he does it wrong (by getting angry at God). But the whole time, God is working within and around Jonah's very ineptness and accomplishing his purposes in him. Most of us need a biblical friend or two like Jonah.

## Running Away from God

**01.** One day long ago, GOD's Word came to Jonah, Amittai's son: "Up on your feet and on your way to the big city of Nineveh! Preach to them. They're in a bad way and I can't ignore it any longer."

But Jonah got up and went the other direction to Tarshish, running away from GOD. He went down to the port of Joppa and found a ship headed for Tarshish. He paid the fare and went on board, joining those going to Tarshish — as far away from GOD as he could get.

---

▶ Nineveh was the gem of ancient Assyria. This great capital city was strategically located on the eastern bank of the Tigris River, across from Mosul in modern-day Iraq. Nineveh had a central position on the main trading route between the Mediterranean and the Indian Ocean. Thus, the expansive city was one of the most important hubs for all commercial convoys crossing the Tigris. The city's wealth was immense, and the Assyrian-controlled region was regarded as one of the great city-state civilizations.

For Jonah, Tarshish was at the opposite end of the world. Although we don't know its exact location, other ancient accounts described Tarshish as a three-year roundtrip from Israel. The Phoenicians were exporting very exotic cargoes from Tarshish, and scholars are now looking as far away as central Africa and east Asia for this exotic seaport. Regardless, Jonah was heading as far away from Ninevah as possible, to what seemed like the end of the earth in Jonah's day.

---

But GOD sent a huge storm at sea, the waves towering.

The ship was about to break into pieces. The sailors were terrified. They called out in desperation to their gods. They threw everything they were carrying overboard to lighten the ship. Meanwhile, Jonah had gone down into the hold of the ship to take a nap. He was sound asleep. The captain came to him and said, "What's this? Sleeping! Get up! Pray to your god! Maybe your god will see we're in trouble and rescue us."

Then the sailors said to one another, "Let's get to the bottom of this. Let's draw straws to identify the culprit on this ship who's responsible for this disaster."

So they drew straws. Jonah got the short straw.

Then they grilled him: "Confess. Why this disaster? What is your work? Where do you come from? What country? What family?"

He told them, "I'm a Hebrew. I worship GOD, the God of heaven who made sea and land."

At that, the men were frightened, really frightened, and said, "What on earth have you done!" As Jonah talked, the sailors realized that he was running away from GOD.

They said to him, "What are we going to do with you — to get rid of this storm?" By this time the sea was wild, totally out of control.

Jonah said, "Throw me overboard, into the sea. Then the storm will stop. It's all my fault. I'm the cause of the storm. Get rid of me and you'll get rid of the storm."

But no. The men tried rowing back to shore. They made no headway. The storm only got worse and worse, wild and raging.

Then they prayed to GOD, "O GOD! Don't let us drown because of this man's life, and don't blame us for his death. You are GOD. Do what you think is best."

They took Jonah and threw him overboard. Immediately the sea was quieted down.

The sailors were impressed, no longer terrified by the sea, but in awe of GOD. They worshiped GOD, offered a sacrifice, and made vows.

Then GOD assigned a huge fish to swallow Jonah. Jonah was in the fish's belly three days and nights.

## At the Bottom of the Sea

**02.** Then Jonah prayed to his God from the belly of the fish. He prayed:

"In trouble, deep trouble, I prayed to GOD.
　　　He answered me.
From the belly of the grave I cried, 'Help!'
　　　You heard my cry.
You threw me into ocean's depths,
　　　into a watery grave,
With ocean waves, ocean breakers
　　　crashing over me.
I said, 'I've been thrown away,
　　　thrown out, out of your sight.
I'll never again lay eyes
　　　on your Holy Temple.'
Ocean gripped me by the throat.
　　　The ancient Abyss grabbed me and held tight.
My head was all tangled in seaweed
　　　at the bottom of the sea where the mountains take root.
I was as far down as a body can go,
　　　and the gates were slamming shut behind me forever—
Yet you pulled me up from that grave alive,
　　　O GOD, my God!
When my life was slipping away,
　　　I remembered GOD,
And my prayer got through to you,
　　　made it all the way to your Holy Temple.
Those who worship hollow gods, god-frauds,
　　　walk away from their only true love.
But I'm worshiping you, GOD,
　　　calling out in thanksgiving!
And I'll do what I promised I'd do!

Salvation belongs to GOD!"

Then GOD spoke to the fish, and it vomited up Jonah on the seashore.

## Maybe God Will Change His Mind

**03.** Next, GOD spoke to Jonah a second time: "Up on your feet and on your way to the big city of Nineveh! Preach to them. They're in a bad way and I can't ignore it any longer."

This time Jonah started off straight for Nineveh, obeying GOD's orders to the letter.

Nineveh was a big city, very big — it took three days to walk across it.

> ▶ Today, Nineveh's primary ruins are located in mounds within an 1800-acre region surrounded by a brick fortification spanning over seven miles. When Jonah referred to the "very big" city that "took three days to walk across it," he was probably referring to what scholars call "Greater Nineveh," a sixty-mile area around Nineveh that included Kuyunjik, Khorsabad, and Nimrud.

Jonah entered the city, went one day's walk and preached, "In forty days Nineveh will be smashed."

The people of Nineveh listened, and trusted God. They proclaimed a citywide fast and dressed in burlap to show their repentance. Everyone did it — rich and poor, famous and obscure, leaders and followers.

When the message reached the king of Nineveh, he got up off his throne, threw down his royal robes, dressed in burlap, and sat down in the dirt. Then he issued a public proclamation throughout Nineveh, authorized by him and his leaders: "Not one drop of water, not one bite of food for man, woman, or animal, including your herds and flocks! Dress them all, both people and animals, in burlap, and send up a cry for help to God. Everyone must turn around, turn back from an evil life and the violent ways that stain their hands. Who knows? Maybe God will turn around and change his mind about us, quit being angry with us and let us live!"

God saw what they had done, that they had turned away from their evil lives. He *did* change his mind about them. What he said he would do to them he didn't do.

---

Jonah delivered his message to the Ninevites between 800 and 750 BC. Within a generation of their repentance, the Assyrians returned to their evil ways. In fact, the ancient records reveal that the Assyrian Empire became even worse than before—absolutely brutal in their conquests and pillaging. Their well-known atrocities included hanging the bodies of their victims on poles and putting the skins of their victims on the walls of their tents.

It was Sennacherib who launched a wave of Assyrian conquest and made Nineveh a truly magnificent city by around 700 BC. In addition to modern streets and market squares, Sennacherib built his huge palace, comprised of at least eighty sculpture-lined rooms.

The Assyrian Empire finally fell to the Medes and Babylonians in 612 BC. At that time, Nineveh was totally destroyed. Until the mid-1800s AD, little was known about the Assyrian Empire and its incredible capital city.

---

## SEARCHER ON THE WAY
*A Journey into Ancient Truth*

Sir Austen Henry Layard was born in Paris in 1817. He belonged to a family of doctors, bankers, and diplomats, and was educated in the top schools of England, France, Italy, and Switzerland. He loved the study of languages and fine arts and served as a lawyer-apprentice for six years. Upon entering his twenties, Layard was totally groomed for aristocratic success.

In 1839, Layard determined to follow in his father's footsteps and return to Ceylon (present-day Sri Lanka) to serve in the British civil service. Layard's family had served as diplomats in Ceylon for generations. However, rather than travel by standard aristocratic means, Layard decided to walk from England to Ceylon by way of Asia. He was twenty-two.

Once he embarked on his trek, Layard's life journey took a totally different track. He never made it to Ceylon. Instead, he spent years wandering about Persia and Turkey, fascinated by the local cultures and ancient Assyrian ruins. Ultimately, he was responsible for rediscovering the ancient ruins of Nineveh in 1847, including the lost palace of Sennacherib. He also stumbled into the famous library of Ashurbanipal, which contained 22,000 clay texts, including important finds such as *The Epic of Gilgamesh*.

Remarkably, since the fiery fall of Nineveh in 612 BC, many of the huge walls and relief sculptures of Sennacherib's throne room were still preserved under the desert sands. And right there, inscribed in cuneiform on the massive doorway, was Sennacherib's own account of his siege of Jerusalem.

Layard's discovery was stunning! The mid-nineteenth century was a time of religious skepticism and biblical revisionism in Europe. Now, the world had new and compelling evidence for a biblical event. Layard's journeys and exploits continued throughout his life, including more biblical discoveries from the ancient Assyrian ruins. In 1866, Layard became a trustee of the British Museum, where he published a number of books and articles about his phenomenal adventures into the past.

## "I Knew This Was Going to Happen!"

**04.** Jonah was furious. He lost his temper. He yelled at GOD, "GOD! I knew it—when I was back home, I knew this was going to happen! That's why I ran off to Tarshish! I knew you were sheer grace and mercy, not easily angered, rich in love, and ready at the drop of a hat to turn your plans of punishment into a program of forgiveness!

"So, GOD, if you won't kill them, kill *me*! I'm better off dead!"

GOD said, "What do you have to be angry about?"

But Jonah just left. He went out of the city to the east and sat down in a sulk. He put together a makeshift shelter of leafy branches and sat there in the shade to see what would happen to the city.

GOD arranged for a broad-leafed tree to spring up. It grew over Jonah to cool him off and get him out of his angry sulk. Jonah was pleased and enjoyed the shade. Life was looking up.

But then God sent a worm. By dawn of the next day, the worm had bored into the shade tree and it withered away. The sun came up and God sent a hot, blistering wind from the east. The sun beat down on Jonah's head and he started to faint. He prayed to die: "I'm better off dead!"

Then God said to Jonah, "What right do you have to get angry about this shade tree?"

Jonah said, "Plenty of right. It's made me angry enough to die!"

GOD said, "What's this? How is it that you can change your feelings from pleasure to anger overnight about a mere shade tree that you did nothing to get? You neither planted nor watered it. It grew up one night and died the next night. So, why can't I likewise change what I feel about Nineveh from anger to pleasure, this big city of more than 120,000 childlike people who don't yet know right from wrong, to say nothing of all the innocent animals?"

It's funny how many of us reject the message of Jonah because of the inherent "fish story." We can't get past the notion that a man survived in the belly of a great fish for three days and nights.

Thus, we miss the point of Jonah's message. Was it to prove his "fish story" to the Ninevites? Was it to record his miraculous "fish journey" for generations to come?

Well, nearly 800 years after Jonah, Jesus summed it all up for us. In the eleventh chapter of Luke, Jesus declared,

> "The mood of this age is all wrong. Everybody's looking for proof, but you're looking for the wrong kind. All you're looking for is something to titillate your curiosity, satisfy your lust for miracles. But the only proof you're going to get is the Jonah-proof given to the Ninevites, which looks like no proof at all What Jonah was to Ninevah, the Son of Man is to this age.
>
> "On Judgment Day the Ninevites will stand up and give evidence that will condemn this generation, because when Jonah preached to them they changed their lives. A far greater preacher than Jonah is here, and you squabble about 'proofs.'"

# PSALMS OF DAVID

## INTRODUCTION TO THE PSALMS OF DAVID

The book of Psalms is the largest collection of compositions in the Bible, containing 150 separate texts. Most of the Psalms read like poetic prayers set to some unknown music. In fact, the word "Psalms" comes from the Greek Septuagint, referring to songs set to the accompaniment of stringed instruments such as the harp, lyre, and lute.

Although poetic, the Psalms are often gritty—even rough. Some read like journal entries of a confused teenager, while others read like battlefield letters of a homesick soldier. All at once, a psalm may lift us to the mountaintops, and then drop us to the valley floor below. The Psalms are honest, portraying both the joyous heights and the despairing lows of existence.

Of the 150 Psalms, about half are attributed to King David, "the sweet singer of Israel." Many of us relate to David and his Psalms, because he's real and his writings "tell it like it is." He has victories, and he has defeats. He's full of faith one day, and he falls into doubt the next. As in David's life, it's when we're humbled and crumbled before God that we seek him with all our heart.

Since the Psalms of David paint a picture of his *Great Pursuit,* we've limited the next section to specific Psalms identified with David. We've chosen a selection of David's Psalms that gets to the heart of his rollercoaster journey.

Most of David's Psalms cycle through persecution, suffering, sorrow, and despair. They're often ragged and raw, exposing the heart of a

God-fearing man who's battered and confused. The power of the Psalms is found in their spiritual context. No matter what the temporal trial, David is touched by God's eternal goodness and faithfulness. Somehow, in the depths of despair, David is able to see and communicate God's indescribable love. It is here that his faith is bolstered and his perplexity is traded for praise.

# 02.

Why the big noise, nations?
Why the mean plots, peoples?
Earth-leaders push for position,
Demagogues and delegates meet for summit talks,
The God-deniers, the Messiah-defiers:
"Let's get free of God!
Cast loose from Messiah!"
Heaven-throned God breaks out laughing.
At first he's amused at their presumption;
Then he gets good and angry.
Furiously, he shuts them up:
"Don't you know there's a King in Zion? A coronation banquet
Is spread for him on the holy summit."

Let me tell you what GOD said next.
He said, "You're my son,
And today is your birthday.
What do you want? Name it:
Nations as a present? continents as a prize?
You can command them all to dance for you,
Or throw them out with tomorrow's trash."

So, rebel-kings, use your heads;
Upstart-judges, learn your lesson:
Worship GOD in adoring embrace,
Celebrate in trembling awe. Kiss Messiah!
Your very lives are in danger, you know;

His anger is about to explode,
But if you make a run for God — you won't regret it!

---

Of the 150 Psalms, David's name is actually attached to 73 of them. In addition, there are a couple of anonymous texts that are attributed to David because of their later authentication.

For instance, about thousand years after David, Peter and John were jailed for speaking about Jesus as the promised Messiah. Upon their release, they went to their friends and celebrated their escape from possible death and quoted from Psalm 2 in chapter 4 of the book of Acts:

Strong God, you made heaven and earth and sea and everything in them. By the Holy Spirit you spoke through the mouth of your servant and our father, David:

Why the big noise, nations?
Why the mean plots, peoples?
Earth's leaders push for position,
Potentates meet for summit talks,
The God-deniers, the Messiah-defiers!

For in fact they did meet—Herod and Pontius Pilate with nations and peoples, even Israel itself!—met in this very city to plot against your holy Son Jesus, the One you made Messiah, to carry out the plans you long ago set in motion.

---

## A David Psalm, When He Escaped for His Life from Absalom, His Son

**03.** GOD! Look! Enemies past counting!
Enemies sprouting like mushrooms,
Mobs of them all around me, roaring their mockery:
"Hah! No help for *him* from God!"

But you, GOD, shield me on all sides;

You ground my feet, you lift my head high;
With all my might I shout up to GOD,
His answers thunder from the holy mountain.

I stretch myself out. I sleep.
Then I'm up again — rested, tall and steady,
Fearless before the enemy mobs
Coming at me from all sides.

Up, GOD! My God, help me!
Slap their faces,
First this cheek, then the other,
Your fist hard in their teeth!

Real help comes from GOD.
Your blessing clothes your people!

**A David Psalm**

# 04.

When I call, give me answers. God, take my side!
Once, in a tight place, you gave me room;
Now I'm in trouble again: grace me! hear me!

You rabble — how long do I put up with your scorn?
How long will you lust after lies?
How long will you live crazed by illusion?

Look at this: look
Who got picked by GOD!
He listens the split second I call to him.

Complain if you must, but don't lash out.
Keep your mouth shut, and let your heart do the talking.
Build your case before God and wait for his verdict.

Why is everyone hungry for *more*? "More, more," they say.
"More, more."
I have God's more-than-enough,
More joy in one ordinary day

Than they get in all their shopping sprees.
At day's end I'm ready for sound sleep,
For you, GOD, have put my life back together.

---

A number of scholars maintain that the historical David never existed. In fact, many archaeologists and cultural anthropologists refer to the "well-established David Myth"—a literary invention drawn from heroic tradition to establish the Jewish monarchy.

Well, in 1993, the validity of the ancient biblical record regarding King David received a huge lift! Archaeologists discovered a stone inscription at the ancient city of Dan, which refers to the "House of David." The "House of David Inscription" (Tel Dan Inscription) is the first ancient reference to King David outside the Jewish Scriptures.

Specifically, the stone is a victory pillar of a king in Damascus dated a couple hundred years after David's reign, which mentions a "king of Israel of the House of David." More inscription pieces were discovered at the site between 1993 and 1994, which allowed archaeologists to reconstruct the entire declaration: "I killed Jehoram son of Ahab king of Israel and I killed Ahaziahu son of Jehoram king of the House of David." Remarkably, these are Jewish leaders linked to the lineage of David as recorded in the biblical texts.

---

## A David Psalm

**05.** Listen, GOD! Please, pay attention!
　　Can you make sense of these ramblings,
　　　　my groans and cries?
　　　　King-God, I need your help.
Every morning
　　you'll hear me at it again.
Every morning
　　I lay out the pieces of my life
　　on your altar
　　and watch for fire to descend.

You don't socialize with Wicked,
    or invite Evil over as your houseguest.
Hot-Air-Boaster collapses in front of you;
you shake your head over Mischief-Maker.
GOD destroys Lie-Speaker;
    Blood-Thirsty and Truth-Bender disgust you.

And here I am, your invited guest—
    it's incredible!
I enter your house; here I am,
    prostrate in your inner sanctum,
Waiting for directions
    to get me safely through enemy lines.

Every word they speak is a land mine;
    their lungs breathe out poison gas.
Their throats are gaping graves,
    their tongues slick as mudslides.
Pile on the guilt, God!
    Let their so-called wisdom wreck them.
Kick them out! They've had their chance.

But you'll welcome us with open arms
    when we run for cover to you.
Let the party last all night!
    Stand guard over our celebration.
You are famous, GOD, for welcoming God-seekers,
    for decking us out in delight.

---

▶ Wait. I thought God teaches us to "love our enemies." This sounds like David is actually
   praying for God to torture and annihilate his enemies. Isn't this the type of language
that religious fanatics can use to justify violence against people who don't agree with their
belief systems?

    Yes, this is tough stuff—the first of many "imprecatory psalms" where David prays for
God's judgment against godless enemies. However, as we'll see, the prayers are focused not

on the personal enemies of David, but rather, the wickedness of certain civilizations. In their purest form, "imprecations" should contain no sense of personal vindication—they should focus solely on the defeat and judgment of God's enemies, by and through God's will.

## A David Psalm

**06.** Please, GOD, no more yelling,
no more trips to the woodshed.
Treat me nice for a change;
I'm so starved for affection.

Can't you see I'm black-and-blue,
beat up badly in bones and soul?
GOD, how long will it take
for you to let up?

Break in, GOD, and break up this fight;
if you love me at all, get me out of here.
I'm no good to you dead, am I?
I can't sing in your choir if I'm buried in some tomb!

I'm tired of all this — so tired. My bed
has been floating forty days and nights
On the flood of my tears.
My mattress is soaked, soggy with tears.
The sockets of my eyes are black holes;
nearly blind, I squint and grope.

Get out of here, you Devil's crew:
at last GOD has heard my sobs.
My requests have all been granted,
my prayers are answered.

Cowards, my enemies disappear.
Disgraced, they turn tail and run.

---

**Again, this doesn't sound like the loving God I heard about in church as a kid. What's going on here?**

Throughout the ancient Scriptures, God is presented as a loving Father who, like any good father, must discipline his children from time to time. Also, the Scriptures tell us, that like any good father, God doesn't necessarily enjoy the responsibility of disciplining his children. Doing the right thing for long-term character development sometimes hurts father and child in the short-term.

Picture this. At the age of two, Dad takes me to this awful guy in a sterile room who pokes me in the backside with a huge needle after saying, "This won't hurt a bit." I scream in pain and immediately look to my father. No matter what Dad says, I'm hurt and confused. Then, when I'm six years old, Dad takes me to this same doctor for my final inoculation. This time, however, I'm a few years wiser and Dad is able to explain that the momentary pain is to protect me from a far greater pain in the future. Since my dad delivers this truth from a position of love and trust, I accept the temporary pain as a necessary part of life.

---

## A David Psalm

**07.** GOD! God! I am running to you for dear life;
　　the chase is wild.
If they catch me, I'm finished:
　　ripped to shreds by foes fierce as lions,
　　dragged into the forest and left
　　unlooked for, unremembered.

GOD, if I've done what they say—
　　betrayed my friends,
　　ripped off my enemies—
If my hands are really that dirty,
　　let them get me, walk all over me,
　　leave me flat on my face in the dirt.

Stand up, GOD; pit your holy fury
    against my furious enemies.
Wake up, God. My accusers have packed
    the courtroom; it's judgment time.
Take your place on the bench, reach for your gavel,
    throw out the false charges against me.
I'm ready, confident in your verdict:
    "Innocent."

Close the book on Evil, GOD,
    but publish your mandate for us.
You get us ready for life:
    you probe for our soft spots,
    you knock off our rough edges.
And I'm feeling so fit, so safe:
    made right, kept right.
God in solemn honor does things right,
    but his nerves are sandpapered raw.

Nobody gets by with anything.
    God is already in action —
Sword honed on his whetstone,
    bow strung, arrow on the string,
Lethal weapons in hand,
    each arrow a flaming missile.

Look at that guy!
    He had sex with sin,
    he's pregnant with evil.
Oh, look! He's having
    the baby — a Lie-Baby!

See that man shoveling day after day,
    digging, then concealing, his man-trap

down that lonely stretch of road?
Go back and look again — you'll see him in it headfirst,
    legs waving in the breeze.
That's what happens:
    mischief backfires;
    violence boomerangs.

I'm thanking God, who makes things right.
I'm singing the fame of heaven-high GOD.

## SEARCHER ON THE WAY
*From Slave-Shepherd to Saint*

Patrick was born in Roman-controlled Britain in about AD 390. When he was a youth, Irish barbarians attacked his village and took him captive to Ireland, where he was sold as a slave to a feudal king.

In Thomas Cahill's book *How the Irish Saved Civilization*, Patrick is described as a slave-shepherd. "The work of such slave-shepherds was bitterly isolated, months at a time spent alone in the hills."

As Patrick faced his first months of loneliness, hunger, illness, and despair, he began seeking God. He later wrote in his book *Confessions*, "I would pray constantly during the daylight hours" and "the love of God . . . surrounded me more and more."

After six scary years, Patrick had a life-changing dream. The message: "Your hungers are rewarded. You are going home. Look—your ship is ready." Almost immediately, Patrick snubbed his fear of punishment, left his flock, and walked two hundred miles to the Irish coast. There, he found a ship and traveled back to Britain, where he joined a monastery and became a priest.

Years later, Patrick couldn't deny his love for the Irish people and his calling to return to them. Ireland was now dominated by full-scale barbarism, where murder, rape, slavery, and even human sacrifice were commonplace. Nonetheless, Patrick wrote, "I am ready to be murdered, betrayed, enslaved—whatever may come my way." He had to return for the Irish people.

Thomas Cahill concludes, "Only this former slave had the right instincts to impart to the Irish a New Story, one that made sense of all their old stories and brought them a peace they had never known before."

So, what's the real meaning of Saint Patrick's Day? Because of Patrick, a barbarian land "lay down the swords of battle, flung away the knives of sacrifice, and cast away the chains of slavery."

**A David Psalm**

**08.** GOD, brilliant Lord,
yours is a household name.

Nursing infants gurgle choruses about you;
toddlers shout the songs
That drown out enemy talk,
and silence atheist babble.

I look up at your macro-skies, dark and enormous,
your handmade sky-jewelry,
Moon and stars mounted in their settings.
Then I look at my micro-self and wonder,
Why do you bother with us?
Why take a second look our way?

---

On the clearest night, with a full sky in view, 1,029 bodies of light can be counted with the naked eye. It was that way 3,000 years ago when David wrote, and it's the same today.

About 300 years ago, Galileo invented the first telescope. At that point in history, 3,310 celestial lights were visible. Wow! Galileo's technology more than tripled our awareness of the awesome spectacle in the cosmos.

Today, the Hubble Space Telescope and various land-based telescopes and radio telescopes have "seen" approximately 100 billion stars in our own Milky Way Galaxy alone! If you think that's huge, astronomers now estimate that there may be 100 billion galaxies in our universe! That's 100,000,000,000 x 100,000,000,000 stars!

There are two ways to live your life.
One is as though nothing is a miracle.
The other is as though everything is a miracle.

— Albert Einstein

---

Yet we've so narrowly missed being gods,
    bright with Eden's dawn light.
You put us in charge of your handcrafted world,
    repeated to us your Genesis-charge,
Made us lords of sheep and cattle,
    even animals out in the wild,
Birds flying and fish swimming,
    whales singing in the ocean deeps.

GOD, brilliant Lord,
    your name echoes around the world.

---

> *YHVH* is the Hebrew word that translates as "LORD." Found more often in the Jewish Scriptures than any other name for God (approximately 7,000 times), the title is also referred to as the *Tetragrammaton*, meaning "The Four Letters." *YHVH* comes from the Hebrew verb "to be" and is the special name that God revealed to Moses at the burning bush.

> God said to Moses, "I-AM-WHO-I-AM. Tell the People of Israel, 'I-AM sent me to you.' . . . This has always been my name, and this is how I always will be known."

> Therefore, *YHVH* declares God's absolute being—the source of everything, without beginning and without end. Although some pronounce *YHVH* as "Jehovah" or "Yaweh," scholars really don't know the proper pronunciation. The Jews stopped pronouncing this name by the third century, out of fear of breaking the commandment, "You shall not take the name of YHVH your God in vain."

---

## A David Psalm

**09.** I'm thanking you, GOD, from a full heart,
    I'm writing the book on your wonders.
I'm whistling, laughing, and jumping for joy;
    I'm singing your song, High God.

The day my enemies turned tail and ran,
>they stumbled on you and fell on their faces.
You took over and set everything right;
>when I needed you, you were there, taking charge.

You blow the whistle on godless nations;
>you throw dirty players out of the game,
>wipe their names right off the roster.
Enemies disappear from the sidelines,
>their reputation trashed,
>their names erased from the halls of fame.

GOD holds the high center,
>he sees and sets the world's mess right.
He decides what is right for us earthlings,
>gives people their just deserts.

GOD's a safe-house for the battered,
>a sanctuary during bad times.
The moment you arrive, you relax;
>you're never sorry you knocked.

Sing your songs to Zion-dwelling GOD,
>tell his stories to everyone you meet:
How he tracks down killers
>yet keeps his eye on us,
>registers every whimper and moan.

Be kind to me, GOD;
>I've been kicked around long enough.
Once you've pulled me back
>from the gates of death,
I'll write the book on Hallelujahs;
>on the corner of Main and First

I'll hold a street meeting;
I'll be the song leader; we'll fill the air
    with salvation songs.

They're trapped, those godless countries,
    in the very snares they set,
Their feet all tangled
    in the net they spread.
They have no excuse;
    the way God works is well-known.
The cunning machinery made by the wicked
    has maimed their own hands.

The wicked bought a one-way
    ticket to hell.
No longer will the poor be nameless—
    no more humiliation for the humble.
Up, GOD! Aren't you fed up with their empty strutting?
    Expose these grand pretensions!
Shake them up, GOD!
    Show them how silly they look.

**A David Psalm**

**11.** I've already run for dear life
    straight to the arms of GOD.
So why would I run away now
    when you say,

"Run to the mountains; the evil
    bows are bent, the wicked arrows
Aimed to shoot under cover of darkness
    at every heart open to God.
The bottom's dropped out of the country;

good people don't have a chance"?

But God hasn't moved to the mountains;
    his holy address hasn't changed.
He's in charge, as always, his eyes
    taking everything in, his eyelids
Unblinking, examining Adam's unruly brood
    inside and out, not missing a thing.
He tests the good and the bad alike;
    if anyone cheats, God's outraged.
Fail the test and you're out,
    out in a hail of firestones,
Drinking from a canteen
    filled with hot desert wind.

God's business is putting things right;
    he loves getting the lines straight,
Setting us straight. Once we're standing tall,
    we can look him straight in the eye.

### A David Psalm

**12.** Quick, God, I need your helping hand!
    The last decent person just went down,
All the friends I depended on gone.
Everyone talks in lie language;
Lies slide off their oily lips.
They doubletalk with forked tongues.

Slice their lips off their faces! Pull
The braggart tongues from their mouths!
I'm tired of hearing, "We can talk anyone into anything!
Our lips manage the world."

Into the hovels of the poor,
Into the dark streets where the homeless groan, God speaks:
"I've had enough; I'm on my way
To heal the ache in the heart of the wretched."

God's words are pure words,
Pure silver words refined seven times
In the fires of his word-kiln,
Pure on earth as well as in heaven.
GOD, keep us safe from their lies,
From the wicked who stalk us with lies,
From the wicked who collect honors
For their wonderful lies.

### A David Psalm

**13.** Long enough, GOD —
you've ignored me long enough.
I've looked at the back of your head
　　long enough. Long enough
I've carried this ton of trouble,
　　lived with a stomach full of pain.
Long enough my arrogant enemies
　　have looked down their noses at me.

Take a good look at me, GOD, my God;
　　I want to look life in the eye,
So no enemy can get the best of me
　　or laugh when I fall on my face.

I've thrown myself headlong into your arms —
　　I'm celebrating your rescue.
I'm singing at the top of my lungs,
　　I'm so full of answered prayers.

➤ **Why did God create such a massive, fine-tuned universe?**

Astronomer and former atheist Sir Fred Hoyle states, "commonsense interpretation of the facts is that a super-intelligence has monkeyed with physics, as well as chemistry and biology, and that there are no blind forces in nature."

Evolutionist and atheist Professor Richard Dawkins continues, "We have seen that living things are too improbable and too beautifully 'designed' to have come into existence by chance."

Molecular geneticist Dr. Michael Denton concludes, "All the evidence available in the biological sciences supports the core proposition . . . that the cosmos is a specially designed whole with life and mankind as its fundamental goal and purpose."

Simply stated, the miracle of God's universe declares the majesty of his handiwork and allows for the existence of life on earth.

## A David Psalm

**14.** Bilious and bloated, they gas,
"God is gone."
Their words are poison gas,
fouling the air; they poison
Rivers and skies;
thistles are their cash crop.

GOD sticks his head out of heaven.
He looks around.
He's looking for someone not stupid —
one man, even, God-expectant,
just one God-ready woman.

He comes up empty. A string
of zeros. Useless, unshepherded
Sheep, taking turns pretending
to be Shepherd.
The ninety and nine
follow their fellow.

Don't they know anything,
    all these impostors?
Don't they know
    they can't get away with this —
Treating people like a fast-food meal
    over which they're too busy to pray?

Night is coming for them, and nightmares,
    for God takes the side of victims.
Do you think you can mess
    with the dreams of the poor?
You can't, for God
    makes their dreams come true.

Is there anyone around to save Israel?
    Yes. God is around; GOD turns life around.
Turned-around Jacob skips rope,
    turned-around Israel sings laughter.


**A David Psalm**

**15.** GOD, who gets invited
    to dinner at your place?
How do we get on your guest list?

"Walk straight,
    act right,
        tell the truth.

"Don't hurt your friend,
    don't blame your neighbor;
        despise the despicable.

"Keep your word even when it costs you,
    make an honest living,
        never take a bribe.

"You'll never get
blacklisted
if you live like this."

---

In the nineteenth century, German Philosopher Friedrich Nietzsche declared, "God is dead!" Since that time, twentieth-century science and technology have been used to nail the coffin shut on God's existence. The general modern consensus nearing the end of the millennium was:

> Smart people with telescopes and microscopes "broke the code" once and for all. The "facts" of science trump anything religious or philosophical. Case closed.

During the past few decades, we've peered to the edge of the massive cosmos and discovered phenomenal complexity; we've delved into the intricate world of the microscopic cell and exposed literal machines; we've deciphered the digital code of the human genome that reveals a mass database of information; we've developed principles of quantum physics that establish extra-dimensionality; and we've attached complex messages to photons of light and invisibly beamed them across the world in milliseconds.

Remarkably, in the last couple of years, we've heard top scientists return to words such as "miracle," "design inherent in nature," "information from outside of pure naturalism," and "metaphysical implications." So, it seems twentieth-century science and technology somehow removed the need for God, but twenty-first-century science and technology are revealing things that can't be explained through merely assumed physical processes.

---

## A David Song

**16.** Keep me safe, O God,
    I've run for dear life to you.
I say to GOD, "Be my Lord!"
    Without you, nothing makes sense.

And these God-chosen lives all around —
    what splendid friends they make!

Don't just go shopping for a god.
    Gods are not for sale.
I swear I'll never treat god-names
    like brand-names.

My choice is you, GOD, first and only.
    And now I find I'm *your* choice!
You set me up with a house and yard.
    And then you made me your heir!

The wise counsel GOD gives when I'm awake
    is confirmed by my sleeping heart.
Day and night I'll stick with GOD;
    I've got a good thing going and I'm not letting go.

I'm happy from the inside out,
    and from the outside in, I'm firmly formed.
You canceled my ticket to hell —
    that's not my destination!

Now you've got my feet on the life path,
    all radiant from the shining of your face.
Ever since you took my hand,
    I'm on the right way.

---

The livid lightnings flashed in the clouds;
The leaden thunders crashed.
A worshipper raised his arm.
"Hearken! Hearken! The voice of God!"

"Not so," said a man.

> "The voice of God whispers in the heart
> So softly
> That the soul pauses,
> Making no noise,
> And strives for these melodies,
> Distant, sighing, like faintest breath,
> And all the being is still to hear."

> — Stephen Crane, 1895

## A David Prayer

**17.** Listen while I build my case, GOD,
    the most honest prayer you'll ever hear.
Show the world I'm innocent —
    in your heart you know I am.

Go ahead, examine me from inside out,
    surprise me in the middle of the night —
You'll find I'm just what I say I am.
    My words don't run loose.

I'm not trying to get my way
    in the world's way.
I'm trying to get *your* way,
    your Word's way.
I'm staying on your trail;
    I'm putting one foot
In front of the other.
    I'm not giving up.

I call to you, God, because I'm sure of an answer.
    So — answer! bend your ear! listen sharp!
Paint grace-graffiti on the fences;

take in your frightened children who
Are running from the neighborhood bullies
      straight to you.

Keep your eye on me;
      hide me under your cool wing feathers
From the wicked who are out to get me,
      from mortal enemies closing in.

Their hearts are hard as nails,
      their mouths blast hot air.
They are after me, nipping my heels,
      determined to bring me down,
Lions ready to rip me apart,
      young lions poised to pounce.
Up, GOD: beard them! break them!
      By your sword, free me from their clutches;
Barehanded, GOD, break these mortals,
      these flat-earth people who can't think beyond today.

I'd like to see their bellies
      swollen with famine food,
The weeds they've sown
      harvested and baked into famine bread,
With second helpings for their children
      and crusts for their babies to chew on.

And me? I plan on looking
      you full in the face. When I get up,
I'll see your full stature
      and live heaven on earth.

## SEARCHER ON THE WAY
*Humbled and Crumbled Before God*

Many remember David as the shepherd boy who defeated a giant named Goliath. Others recall David as the wise Jewish ruler who brought the tribes of Israel together as a united nation. The ancient texts also present David as a powerful warrior, cunning diplomat, and talented musician. However, with all these tremendous accolades, the foundation of David's fame and faith can be traced to a period of severe trial and doubting in his life.

Early in his journey, David was chosen to succeed Saul as the king of Judah. Although Saul was initially impressed by David's skills as a soldier, politician, and musician, Saul became wary of his successor, so he put out a contract on David's life. David was forced to live on the run, often spending weeks hiding in the network of caves surrounding the Dead Sea.

It is here that David really began his pursuit of God. Alone in the dark or on the run through enemy territory, David opened up and honestly shared his thoughts, struggles, and fears. David was frustrated with God's plan for his life, and he wrote about it in his prayer journals. Although Saul stopped at nothing to kill David, David never followed through on his opportunities to kill Saul. David's years alone with God forged his exemplary character and unflinching faith. Through loneliness and struggle, David learned to be fully dependant on God.

When Saul finally died in an unrelated battle, David returned to Judah and claimed his position as king over Judah in 1009 BC. Seven years later, the northern tribes of Israel accepted him as king, and he became ruler of a united Jewish nation until his death in 969 BC. David wasn't a perfect leader or a perfect man, but his years alone with God, humbled and crumbled in the dark, developed the soul of a legendary king and forged a legacy that endures to this day.

**A David Song, Which He Sang to God After Being
Saved from All His Enemies and from Saul**

**18.** I love you, GOD —
     you make me strong.
GOD is bedrock under my feet,
     the castle in which I live,
     my rescuing knight.
My God — the high crag
     where I run for dear life,
     hiding behind the boulders,
     safe in the granite hideout.

I sing to GOD, the Praise-Lofty,
     and find myself safe and saved.

The hangman's noose was tight at my throat;
     devil waters rushed over me.
Hell's ropes cinched me tight;
     death traps barred every exit.

A hostile world! I call to GOD,
     I cry to God to help me.
From his palace he hears my call;
     my cry brings me right into his presence —
     a private audience!

Earth wobbles and lurches;
     huge mountains shake like leaves,
Quake like aspen leaves
     because of his rage.
His nostrils flare, bellowing smoke;
     his mouth spits fire.
Tongues of fire dart in and out;

he lowers the sky.
He steps down;
    under his feet an abyss opens up.
He's riding a winged creature,
    swift on wind-wings.
Now he's wrapped himself
    in a trenchcoat of black-cloud darkness.
But his cloud-brightness bursts through,
    spraying hailstones and fireballs.
Then GOD thundered out of heaven;
    the High God gave a great shout,
    spraying hailstones and fireballs.
God shoots his arrows — pandemonium!
    He hurls his lightnings — a rout!
The secret sources of ocean are exposed,
    the hidden depths of earth lie uncovered
The moment you roar in protest,
    let loose your hurricane anger.

But me he caught — reached all the way
    from sky to sea; he pulled me out
Of that ocean of hate, that enemy chaos,
    the void in which I was drowning.
They hit me when I was down,
    but GOD stuck by me.
He stood me up on a wide-open field;
    I stood there saved — surprised to be loved!

GOD made my life complete
    when I placed all the pieces before him.
When I got my act together,
    he gave me a fresh start.
Now I'm alert to GOD's ways;
    I don't take God for granted.

Every day I review the ways he works;
    I try not to miss a trick.
I feel put back together,
    and I'm watching my step.
GOD rewrote the text of my life
    when I opened the book of my heart to his eyes.

The good people taste your goodness,
The whole people taste your health,
The true people taste your truth,
The bad ones can't figure you out.
You take the side of the down-and-out,
But the stuck-up you take down a peg.

Suddenly, GOD, you floodlight my life;
    I'm blazing with glory, God's glory!
I smash the bands of marauders,
    I vault the highest fences.

What a God! His road
    stretches straight and smooth.
Every GOD-direction is road-tested.
    Everyone who runs toward him
Makes it.

Is there any god like GOD?
    Are we not at bedrock?
Is not this the God who armed me,
    then aimed me in the right direction?
Now I run like a deer;
    I'm king of the mountain.
He shows me how to fight;
    I can bend a bronze bow!
You protect me with salvation-armor;

you hold me up with a firm hand,
 caress me with your gentle ways.
You cleared the ground under me
 so my footing was firm.
When I chased my enemies I caught them;
 I didn't let go till they were dead men.
I nailed them; they were down for good;
 then I walked all over them.
You armed me well for this fight,
 you smashed the upstarts.
You made my enemies turn tail,
 and I wiped out the haters.
They cried "uncle"
 but Uncle didn't come;
They yelled for GOD
 and got no for an answer.
I ground them to dust; they gusted in the wind.
 I threw them out, like garbage in the gutter.

You rescued me from a squabbling people;
 you made me a leader of nations.
People I'd never heard of served me;
 the moment they got wind of me they listened.
The foreign devils gave up; they came
 on their bellies, crawling from their hideouts.

Live, GOD! Blessings from my Rock,
 my free and freeing God, towering!
This God set things right for me
 and shut up the people who talked back.
He rescued me from enemy anger,
 he pulled me from the grip of upstarts,
He saved me from the bullies.

That's why I'm thanking you, GOD,
    all over the world.
That's why I'm singing songs
    that rhyme your name.
God's king takes the trophy;
    God's chosen is beloved.
I mean David and all his children—
    always.

## A David Psalm

**19.** God's glory is on tour in the skies,
    God-craft on exhibit across the horizon.
Madame Day holds classes every morning,
    Professor Night lectures each evening.

Throughout his years as a shepherd, David would look to the heavens at night and stare in utter amazement. To him, God was real and powerful. He was constantly reminded of his glory! A feeling of utter awe was generated by about 1,000 specks of light in the visible night sky.

It seems that over the last hundred years or so, many of us have become numb to God's creation. We can go many nights without even looking up. We walk from our offices and schools to our cars—we close the garage door behind us as we walk from our cars to the television. Yes, it seems we've become passive creatures with no time for simple awe.

Through the Hubble telescope and other technological eyes, maybe it's time to wake up and be amazed again! Like the psalmist, maybe it's time to look up and ponder the glorious heavens!

I share Einstein's affirmation that anyone who is not lost on the rapturous awe at the power and glory of the mind behind the universe "is as good as a burnt out candle."

—Madeleine L'Engle

Their words aren't heard,
　　their voices aren't recorded,
But their silence fills the earth:
　　unspoken truth is spoken everywhere.

God makes a huge dome
　　for the sun — a superdome!
The morning sun's a new husband
　　leaping from his honeymoon bed,
The daybreaking sun an athlete
　　racing to the tape.

That's how God's Word vaults across the skies
　　from sunrise to sunset,
Melting ice, scorching deserts,
　　warming hearts to faith.

The revelation of GOD is whole
　　and pulls our lives together.
The signposts of GOD are clear
　　and point out the right road.
The life-maps of GOD are right,
　　showing the way to joy.
The directions of GOD are plain
　　and easy on the eyes.
GOD's reputation is twenty-four-carat gold,
　　with a lifetime guarantee.
The decisions of GOD are accurate
　　down to the nth degree.

God's Word is better than a diamond,
　　better than a diamond set between emeralds.
You'll like it better than strawberries in spring,
　　better than red, ripe strawberries.

There's more: God's Word warns us of danger
     and directs us to hidden treasure.
Otherwise how will we find our way?
     Or know when we play the fool?
Clean the slate, God, so we can start the day fresh!
     Keep me from stupid sins,
     from thinking I can take over your work;
Then I can start this day sun-washed,
     scrubbed clean of the grime of sin.
These are the words in my mouth;
     these are what I chew on and pray.
Accept them when I place them
     on the morning altar,
O God, my Altar-Rock,
     God, Priest-of-My-Altar.

## SEARCHER ON THE WAY

*Pursuing the Evidence . . . Wherever It Leads*

Antony Flew, a British philosopher, Oxford professor, and leading champion of atheism for more than fifty years, honestly followed the evidence and renounced his naturalistic faith in 2004. In a published interview with another philosopher, Flew said, "My whole life has been guided by the principle of Plato's Socrates: Follow the evidence, wherever it leads."

After chewing on his scientific worldview for more than five decades, Flew concluded, "A super-intelligence is the only good explanation for the origin of life and the complexity of nature."

Previously, in his central work *The Presumption of Atheism* (1976), Flew argued that the "onus of proof [of God] must lie upon the theist." However, at the age of eighty-one, Flew shocked the world when he renounced his atheism because "the argument for Intelligent Design is enormously stronger than it was when I first met it." In the same 2004 interview, Flew shared, "It seems to me that the case for an Aristotelian God who has the characteristics of power and also intelligence, is now much stronger than it ever was before."

The story of Antony Flew reminds us that physics and metaphysics are not mutually exclusive. True science asks us to follow the observational evidence, no matter what the destination. Does life really occur in a naturalistic vacuum? Or does its design, order, and complexity necessitate something more?

Antony Flew is an honest thinker who ultimately acknowledged the existence of God. Like many of us, recognition is a huge step. However, when it comes to the *Great Pursuit,* can we rest in mere recognition? What about Dr. Flew's observations of Intelligent Design—the immensity, intensity, and intricacy of it all—don't they compel us to move forward?

**A David Psalm**

**20.** GOD answer you on the day you crash,
The name God-of-Jacob put you out of harm's reach,
Send reinforcements from Holy Hill,
Dispatch from Zion fresh supplies,
Exclaim over your offerings,
Celebrate your sacrifices,
Give you what your heart desires,
Accomplish your plans.

When you win, we plan to raise the roof
    and lead the parade with our banners.
May all your wishes come true!

That clinches it — help's coming,
    an answer's on the way,
        everything's going to work out.

See those people polishing their chariots,
    and those others grooming their horses?
        But we're making garlands for GOD our God.
The chariots will rust,
    those horses pull up lame —
        and we'll be on our feet, standing tall.

Make the king a winner, GOD;
    the day we call, give us your answer.

**A David Psalm**

**21.** Your strength, GOD, is the king's strength.
    Helped, he's hollering Hosannas.
You gave him exactly what he wanted;
    you didn't hold back.

You filled his arms with gifts;
  you gave him a right royal welcome.
He wanted a good life; you gave it to him,
  and then made it a *long* life as a bonus.
You lifted him high and bright as a cumulus cloud,
  then dressed him in rainbow colors.
You pile blessings on him;
  you make him glad when you smile.
Is it any wonder the king loves GOD?
  that he's sticking with the Best?

With a fistful of enemies in one hand
  and a fistful of haters in the other,
You radiate with such brilliance
  that they cringe as before a furnace.
Now the furnace swallows them whole,
  the fire eats them alive!
You purge the earth of their progeny,
  you wipe the slate clean.
All their evil schemes, the plots they cook up,
  have fizzled — every one.
You sent them packing;
  they couldn't face you.

Show your strength, GOD, so no one can miss it.
  We are out singing the good news!

## A David Psalm

**22.** God, God . . . my God!
  Why did you dump me
  miles from nowhere?
Doubled up with pain, I call to God
  all the day long. No answer. Nothing.

I keep at it all night, tossing and turning.

And you! Are you indifferent, above it all,
     leaning back on the cushions of Israel's praise?
We know you were there for our parents:
          they cried for your help and you gave it;
          they trusted and lived a good life.

And here I am, a nothing — an earthworm,
     something to step on, to squash.
Everyone pokes fun at me;
          they make faces at me, they shake their heads:
"Let's see how GOD handles this one;
          since God likes him so much, let *him* help him!"

And to think you were midwife at my birth,
     setting me at my mother's breasts!
When I left the womb you cradled me;
          since the moment of birth you've been my God.
Then you moved far away
          and trouble moved in next door.
I need a neighbor.

Herds of bulls come at me,
          the raging bulls stampede,
Horns lowered, nostrils flaring,
          like a herd of buffalo on the move.

I'm a bucket kicked over and spilled,
          every joint in my body has been pulled apart.
My heart is a blob
          of melted wax in my gut.
I'm dry as a bone,
          my tongue black and swollen.

They have laid me out for burial
    in the dirt.

Now packs of wild dogs come at me;
    thugs gang up on me.
They pin me down hand and foot,
    and lock me in a cage—a bag
Of bones in a cage, stared at
    by every passerby.
They take my wallet and the shirt off my back,
    and then throw dice for my clothes.

You, GOD—don't put off my rescue!
    Hurry and help me!
Don't let them cut my throat;
    don't let those mongrels devour me.
If you don't show up soon,
    I'm done for—gored by the bulls,
    meat for the lions.

Here's the story I'll tell my friends when they come to worship,
    and punctuate it with Hallelujahs:
Shout Hallelujah, you God-worshipers;
    give glory, you sons of Jacob;
    adore him, you daughters of Israel.
He has never let you down,
    never looked the other way
    when you were being kicked around.
He has never wandered off to do his own thing;
    he has been right there, listening.

Here in this great gathering for worship
    I have discovered this praise-life.

And I'll do what I promised right here
    in front of the God-worshipers.
Down-and-outers sit at GOD's table
    and eat their fill.
Everyone on the hunt for God
    is here, praising him.
"Live it up, from head to toe.
    Don't ever quit!"

From the four corners of the earth
    people are coming to their senses,
    are running back to GOD.
Long-lost families
    are falling on their faces before him.
GOD has taken charge;
    from now on he has the last word.

All the power-mongers are before him
    — worshiping!
All the poor and powerless, too
    — worshiping!
Along with those who never got it together
    — worshiping!

Our children and their children
    will get in on this
As the word is passed along
    from parent to child.
Babies not yet conceived
    will hear the good news —
    that God does what he says.

### A David Psalm

**23.** GOD, my shepherd!
    I don't need a thing.
You have bedded me down in lush meadows,
    you find me quiet pools to drink from.
True to your word,
    you let me catch my breath
    and send me in the right direction.

Even when the way goes through
    Death Valley,
I'm not afraid
    when you walk at my side.
Your trusty shepherd's crook
    makes me feel secure.

You serve me a six-course dinner
    right in front of my enemies.
You revive my drooping head;
    my cup brims with blessing.

Your beauty and love chase after me
    every day of my life.
I'm back home in the house of GOD
    for the rest of my life.

As he reflects on his life, David compares God to a shepherd. Throughout David's journey, God has been there to provide guidance, protection, nourishment, and spiritual rest. The title and role were very familiar to David, since he was an actual shepherd during his youth and the symbolic shepherd of a nation as its king.

The Jewish prophets that came after David compared the predicted Messiah to a shepherd. Later, Jesus of Nazareth claimed this title for himself. In John chapter 10, Jesus expanded on his prophetic legacy:

"I am the Good Shepherd. I know my own sheep and my own sheep know me. . . . I put the sheep before myself, sacrificing myself if necessary. You need to know that I have other sheep in addition to those in this pen. I need to gather and bring them, too. They'll also recognize my voice. Then it will be one flock, one Shepherd."

## A David Psalm

**24.** GOD claims Earth and everything in it,
GOD claims World and all who live on it.
He built it on Ocean foundations,
    laid it out on River girders.

Who can climb Mount GOD?
    Who can scale the holy north-face?
Only the clean-handed,
    only the pure-hearted;
Men who won't cheat,
    women who won't seduce.

GOD is at their side;
    with GOD's help they make it.
This, Jacob, is what happens
    to God-seekers, God-questers.

Wake up, you sleepyhead city!
Wake up, you sleepyhead people!
    King-Glory is ready to enter.

Who is this King-Glory?
    GOD, armed
    and battle-ready.

Wake up, you sleepyhead city!
Wake up, you sleepyhead people!
    King-Glory is ready to enter.

Who is this King-Glory?
    GOD-of-the-Angel-Armies:
    he is King-Glory.

## A David Psalm

**25.** My head is high, GOD, held high;
I'm looking to you, GOD;
No hangdog skulking for me.

I've thrown in my lot with you;
You won't embarrass me, will you?
Or let my enemies get the best of me?

Don't embarrass any of us
Who went out on a limb for you.
It's the traitors who should be humiliated.

Show me how you work, GOD;
School me in your ways.

Take me by the hand;
Lead me down the path of truth.
You are my Savior, aren't you?

Mark the milestones of your mercy and love, GOD;
Rebuild the ancient landmarks!

Forget that I sowed wild oats;
Mark me with your sign of love.

Plan only the best for me, GOD!

GOD is fair and just;
He corrects the misdirected,
Sends them in the right direction.

He gives the rejects his hand,
And leads them step-by-step.

From now on every road you travel
Will take you to GOD.
Follow the Covenant signs;
Read the charted directions.

Keep up your reputation, GOD;
Forgive my bad life;
It's been a very bad life.

My question: What are God-worshipers like?
Your answer: Arrows aimed at God's bull's-eye.

They settle down in a promising place;
Their kids inherit a prosperous farm.

God-friendship is for God-worshipers;
They are the ones he confides in.

If I keep my eyes on GOD,
I won't trip over my own feet.

Look at me and help me!
I'm all alone and in big trouble.

My heart and kidneys are fighting each other;

Call a truce to this civil war.

Take a hard look at my life of hard labor,
Then lift this ton of sin.

Do you see how many people
Have it in for me?
How viciously they hate me?

Keep watch over me and keep me out of trouble;
Don't let me down when I run to you.

Use all your skill to put me together;
I wait to see your finished product.

GOD, give your people a break
From this run of bad luck.


**A David Psalm**

**26.** Clear my name, GOD;
I've kept an honest shop.
I've thrown in my lot with you, GOD, and
I'm not budging.

Examine me, GOD, from head to foot,
order your battery of tests.
Make sure I'm fit
inside and out

So I never lose
sight of your love,
But keep in step with you,
never missing a beat.

I don't hang out with tricksters,
 I don't pal around with thugs;
I hate that pack of gangsters,
 I don't deal with double-dealers.

I scrub my hands with purest soap,
 then join hands with the others in the great circle,
 dancing around your altar, GOD,
Singing God-songs at the top of my lungs,
 telling God-stories.

GOD, I love living with you;
 your house glows with your glory.
When it's time for spring cleaning,
 don't sweep me out with the quacks and crooks,
Men with bags of dirty tricks,
 women with purses stuffed with bribe-money.

You know I've been aboveboard with you;
 now be aboveboard with me.
I'm on the level with you, GOD;
 I bless you every chance I get.

---

> According to scientist and philosopher Blaise Pascal (1623-1662) humankind is both
> noble and wretched. Noble because we are created in God's image; wretched because
> we are fallen and alienated from him.
>
> What kind of freak is man? What a novelty he is, how absurd he is, how chaotic and
> what a mass of contradictions, and yet what a prodigy! He is judge of all things, yet a feeble
> worm. He is repository of truth, and yet sinks into such doubt and error. He is the glory and
> the scum of the universe!

---

## A David Psalm

**27.** Light, space, zest —
that's GOD!
So, with him on my side I'm fearless,
afraid of no one and nothing.

When vandal hordes ride down
ready to eat me alive,
Those bullies and toughs
fall flat on their faces.

When besieged,
I'm calm as a baby.
When all hell breaks loose,
I'm collected and cool.

I'm asking GOD for one thing,
only one thing:
To live with him in his house
my whole life long.
I'll contemplate his beauty;
I'll study at his feet.

That's the only quiet, secure place
in a noisy world,
The perfect getaway,
far from the buzz of traffic.

God holds me head and shoulders
above all who try to pull me down.
I'm headed for his place to offer anthems
that will raise the roof!
Already I'm singing God-songs;
I'm making music to GOD.

Listen, GOD, I'm calling at the top of my lungs:
    "Be good to me! Answer me!"
When my heart whispered, "Seek God,"
    my whole being replied,
"I'm seeking him!"
    Don't hide from me now!

You've always been right there for me;
    don't turn your back on me now.
Don't throw me out, don't abandon me;
    you've always kept the door open.
My father and mother walked out and left me,
    but GOD took me in.

Point me down your highway, GOD;
    direct me along a well-lighted street;
    show my enemies whose side you're on.
Don't throw me to the dogs,
    those liars who are out to get me,
    filling the air with their threats.

I'm sure now I'll see God's goodness
    in the exuberant earth.
Stay with GOD!
    Take heart. Don't quit.
I'll say it again:
    Stay with GOD.


**A David Psalm**

**28.** Don't turn a deaf ear
    when I call you, GOD.
If all I get from you is
    deafening silence,

I'd be better off
    in the Black Hole.

I'm letting you know what I need,
    calling out for help
And lifting my arms
    toward your inner sanctum.

Don't shove me into
    the same jail cell with those crooks,
With those who are
    full-time employees of evil.
They talk a good line of "peace,"
    then moonlight for the Devil.

Pay them back for what they've done,
    for how bad they've been.
Pay them back for their long hours
    in the Devil's workshop;
Then cap it with a huge bonus.

Because they have no idea how God works
    or what he is up to,
God will smash them to smithereens
    and walk away from the ruins.

    Blessed be GOD —
    he heard me praying.
He proved he's on my side;
    I've thrown my lot in with him.

Now I'm jumping for joy,
    and shouting and singing my thanks to him.

GOD is all strength for his people,
     ample refuge for his chosen leader;
Save your people
     and bless your heritage.
Care for them;
     carry them like a good shepherd.


**A David Psalm**

**29.** Bravo, GOD, bravo!
     Gods and all angels shout, "Encore!"
In awe before the glory,
     in awe before God's visible power.
Stand at attention!
     Dress your best to honor him!

GOD thunders across the waters,
Brilliant, his voice and his face, streaming brightness —
GOD, across the flood waters.

GOD's thunder tympanic,
GOD's thunder symphonic.

GOD's thunder smashes cedars,
GOD topples the northern cedars.

The mountain ranges skip like spring colts,
The high ridges jump like wild kid goats.

GOD's thunder spits fire.
GOD thunders, the wilderness quakes;
He makes the desert of Kadesh shake.

GOD's thunder sets the oak trees dancing
A wild dance, whirling; the pelting rain strips their branches.
We fall to our knees — we call out, "Glory!"

Above the floodwaters is GOD's throne
    from which his power flows,
    from which he rules the world.

GOD makes his people strong.
GOD gives his people peace.

**A David Psalm**

**30.** I give you all the credit, GOD —
    you got me out of that mess,
you didn't let my foes gloat.

GOD, my God, I yelled for help
    and you put me together.
GOD, you pulled me out of the grave,
    gave me another chance at life
    when I was down-and-out.

All you saints! Sing your hearts out to GOD!
    Thank him to his face!
He gets angry once in a while, but across
    a lifetime there is only love.
The nights of crying your eyes out
    give way to days of laughter.

When things were going great
    I crowed, "I've got it made.
I'm GOD's favorite.

He made me king of the mountain."
Then you looked the other way
and I fell to pieces.

I called out to you, GOD;
I laid my case before you:
"Can you sell me for a profit when I'm dead?
auction me off at a cemetery yard sale?
When I'm 'dust to dust' my songs
and stories of you won't sell.
So listen! and be kind!
Help me out of this!"

You did it: you changed wild lament
into whirling dance;
You ripped off my black mourning band
and decked me with wildflowers.
I'm about to burst with song;
I can't keep quiet about you.
GOD, my God,
I can't thank you enough.

---

▶ Have you noticed one of the major themes running through David's writings? He paints a picture of utter trial and turmoil in his life, yet maintains an internal compass that always points to "true north." Whereas most of us look for happiness based on external circumstances in our lives, David has discovered a deeper joy grounded in his inner self. Most of us strive for happiness that's external and temporary. David teaches us to drive toward a place of deeper well-being, where we develop trust and hope in God that extends beyond our external realities.

Yes, deep stuff! David has learned that happiness and joy are different things. Happiness is that fleeting state of emotion that's dependant on *doing*. Today's marketers know this! However, joy is a long-term process of the mind that's dependant on *being*. For David, it's the seasons of trial and suffering—chaos and confusion—that ultimately develop deeper and more profound joy. The key is to know God as your internal compass.

---

## A David Psalm

**31.** I run to you, GOD; I run for dear life.
   Don't let me down!
      Take me seriously this time!
Get down on my level and listen,
      and please — no procrastination!
Your granite cave a hiding place,
      your high cliff aerie a place of safety.

You're my cave to hide in,
      my cliff to climb.
Be my safe leader,
      be my true mountain guide.
Free me from hidden traps;
      I want to hide in you.
I've put my life in your hands.
      You won't drop me,
      you'll never let me down.

I hate all this silly religion,
      but you, GOD, I trust.
I'm leaping and singing in the circle of your love;
      you saw my pain,
      you disarmed my tormentors,
You didn't leave me in their clutches
      but gave me room to breathe.
Be kind to me, GOD —
      I'm in deep, deep trouble again.
I've cried my eyes out;
      I feel hollow inside.
My life leaks away, groan by groan;
      my years fade out in sighs.
My troubles have worn me out,

turned my bones to powder.
To my enemies I'm a monster;
    I'm ridiculed by the neighbors.
My friends are horrified;
    they cross the street to avoid me.
They want to blot me from memory,
        forget me like a corpse in a grave,
        discard me like a broken dish in the trash.
The street-talk gossip has me
    "criminally insane"!
Behind locked doors they plot
    how to ruin me for good.


Desperate, I throw myself on you:
    *you* are my God!
Hour by hour I place my days in your hand,
    safe from the hands out to get me.
Warm me, your servant, with a smile;
    save me because you love me.
Don't embarrass me by not showing up;
    I've given you plenty of notice.
Embarrass the wicked, stand them up,
        leave them stupidly shaking their heads
        as they drift down to hell.
Gag those loudmouthed liars
        who heckle me, your follower,
        with jeers and catcalls.


What a stack of blessing you have piled up
    for those who worship you,
Ready and waiting for all who run to you
    to escape an unkind world.
You hide them safely away
    from the opposition.

As you slam the door on those oily, mocking faces,
　　you silence the poisonous gossip.
Blessed GOD!
　　His love is the wonder of the world.
Trapped by a siege, I panicked.
　　"Out of sight, out of mind," I said.
But you heard me say it,
　　you heard and listened.

Love GOD, all you saints;
　　GOD takes care of all who stay close to him,
But he pays back in full
　　those arrogant enough to go it alone.

Be brave. Be strong. Don't give up.
　　Expect GOD to get here soon.

## A David Psalm

**32.** Count yourself lucky, how happy you must be —
　　you get a fresh start,
　　　　your slate's wiped clean.

Count yourself lucky —
　　GOD holds nothing against you
　　and you're holding nothing back from him.

When I kept it all inside,
　　my bones turned to powder,
　　my words became daylong groans.

The pressure never let up;
　　all the juices of my life dried up.

Then I let it all out;

I said, "I'll make a clean breast of my failures to GOD."

Suddenly the pressure was gone —
    my guilt dissolved,
    my sin disappeared.

These things add up. Every one of us needs to pray;
    when all hell breaks loose and the dam bursts
    we'll be on high ground, untouched.

GOD's my island hideaway,
    keeps danger far from the shore,
    throws garlands of hosannas around my neck.

Let me give you some good advice;
    I'm looking you in the eye
    and giving it to you straight:

"Don't be ornery like a horse or mule
    that needs bit and bridle
    to stay on track."

---

▶ This is a great picture of human nature. Although we know the way we should go on
a certain issue, we often pick the exact opposite path. Deep down, we know what God
wants from us, but we choose something totally different. Yes, humanity is like a stubborn
ass. If we would just follow the God-given instructions in the first place, maybe we wouldn't
need so much poking, prodding, and kicking. If we each walked our selected paths, maybe
the mouth bits could be removed altogether.

---

God-defiers are always in trouble;
    GOD-affirmers find themselves loved
    every time they turn around.

Celebrate GOD.
>    Sing together — everyone!
>    All you honest hearts, raise the roof!

## 33.
Good people, cheer GOD!
>    Right-living people sound best when praising.
Use guitars to reinforce your Hallelujahs!
>    Play his praise on a grand piano!
Invent your own new song to him;
>    give him a trumpet fanfare.

For GOD's Word is solid to the core;
>    everything he makes is sound inside and out.
He loves it when everything fits,
>    when his world is in plumb-line true.
Earth is drenched
>    in GOD's affectionate satisfaction.

The skies were made by GOD's command;
>    he breathed the word and the stars popped out.
He scooped Sea into his jug,
>    put Ocean in his keg.

Earth-creatures, bow before GOD;
>    world-dwellers — down on your knees!
Here's why: he spoke and there it was,
>    in place the moment he said so.

---

▶ David said that God spoke the universe into existence. In the beginning was nothing.
Then God spoke, and there was everything. What a simple statement from an ancient
and "unenlightened" man.

The Big Bang Theory and its related Inflation Universe Theories are today's dominant
scientific conjectures about the origin of the cosmos. Simply, the universe was created
from the random, cosmic explosion (or expansion) of a subatomic ball that hurled space,
time, matter, and energy in all directions. Everything—the whole universe—came from an

initial speck of infinite density called a "singularity." This speck existed outside of space and time, and appeared from nowhere, for no reason, only to explode (start expanding) all of a sudden. This newly created space, time, matter, and energy became remarkably designed and fully functional stars, galaxies, and planets, including our Earth.

Hmmm . . . In the beginning was nothing. Then God spoke, and there was everything. Three thousand years after David, it sounds like science has almost figured it out.

(Although the author of this psalm is unknown, we've included it as a liturgy in the style of David that focuses on God as creator.)

---

GOD takes the wind out of Babel pretense,
    he shoots down the world's power-schemes.
GOD's plan for the world stands up,
    all his designs are made to last.
Blessed is the country with GOD for God;
    blessed are the people he's put in his will.

From high in the skies GOD looks around,
    he sees all Adam's brood.
From where he sits
    he overlooks all us earth-dwellers.
He has shaped each person in turn;
    now he watches everything we do.

No king succeeds with a big army alone,
    no warrior wins by brute strength.
Horsepower is not the answer;
    no one gets by on muscle alone.

Watch this: God's eye is on those who respect him,
    the ones who are looking for his love.
He's ready to come to their rescue in bad times;
    in lean times he keeps body and soul together.

We're depending on GOD;

he's everything we need.
What's more, our hearts brim with joy
     since we've taken for our own his holy name.
Love us, GOD, with all you've got —
     that's what we're depending on.

## A David Psalm, When He Outwitted Abimelech and Got Away

**34.** I bless GOD every chance I get;
my lungs expand with his praise.

I live and breathe GOD;
if things aren't going well, hear this and be happy:

Join me in spreading the news;
together let's get the word out.

GOD met me more than halfway,
he freed me from my anxious fears.

Look at him; give him your warmest smile.
Never hide your feelings from him.

When I was desperate, I called out,
and GOD got me out of a tight spot.

GOD's angel sets up a circle
of protection around us while we pray.

Open your mouth and taste, open your eyes and see —
     how good GOD is.
Blessed are you who run to him.

Worship GOD if you want the best;

worship opens doors to all his goodness.

Young lions on the prowl get hungry,
but GOD-seekers are full of God.

Come, children, listen closely;
I'll give you a lesson in GOD worship.

Who out there has a lust for life?
Can't wait each day to come upon beauty?

Guard your tongue from profanity,
and no more lying through your teeth.

Turn your back on sin; do something good.
Embrace peace — don't let it get away!

GOD keeps an eye on his friends,
his ears pick up every moan and groan.

GOD won't put up with rebels;
he'll cull them from the pack.

Is anyone crying for help? GOD is listening,
ready to rescue you.

If your heart is broken, you'll find GOD right there;
if you're kicked in the gut, he'll help you catch your breath.

Disciples so often get into trouble;
still, GOD is there every time.

He's your bodyguard, shielding every bone;
not even a finger gets broken.

The wicked commit slow suicide;
they waste their lives hating the good.

GOD pays for each slave's freedom;
no one who runs to him loses out.

**A David Psalm**

# 35.
Harass these hecklers, GOD,
   punch these bullies in the nose.
Grab a weapon, anything at hand;
   stand up for me!
Get ready to throw the spear, aim the javelin,
   at the people who are out to get me.
Reassure me; let me hear you say,
   "I'll save you."

When those thugs try to knife me in the back,
   make them look foolish.
Frustrate all those
   who are plotting my downfall.
Make them like cinders in a high wind,
   with GOD's angel working the bellows.
Make their road lightless and mud-slick,
   with GOD's angel on their tails.
Out of sheer cussedness they set a trap to catch me;
   for no good reason they dug a ditch to stop me.
Surprise them with your ambush —
   catch them in the very trap they set,
   the disaster they planned for me.

But let me run loose and free,
   celebrating GOD's great work,
Every bone in my body laughing, singing, "GOD,

there's no one like you.
You put the down-and-out on their feet
and protect the unprotected from bullies!"

Hostile accusers appear out of nowhere,
they stand up and badger me.
They pay me back misery for mercy,
leaving my soul empty.

When they were sick, I dressed in black;
instead of eating, I prayed.
My prayers were like lead in my gut,
like I'd lost my best friend, my brother.
I paced, distraught as a motherless child,
hunched and heavyhearted.

But when I was down
they threw a party!
All the nameless riffraff of the town came
chanting insults about me.
Like barbarians desecrating a shrine,
they destroyed my reputation.

GOD, how long are you going
to stand there doing nothing?
Save me from their brutalities;
everything I've got is being thrown to the lions.
I will give you full credit
when everyone gathers for worship;
When the people turn out in force
I will say my Hallelujahs.

Don't let these liars, my enemies,
have a party at my expense,

Those who hate me for no reason,
  winking and rolling their eyes.
No good is going to come
  from that crowd;
They spend all their time cooking up gossip
  against those who mind their own business.
They open their mouths
  in ugly grins,
Mocking, "Ha-ha, ha-ha, thought you'd get away with it?
  We've caught you hands down!"

Don't you see what they're doing, GOD?
  You're not going to let them
Get by with it, are you? Not going to walk off
  without *doing* something, are you?

Please get up — wake up! Tend to my case.
  My God, my Lord — my life is on the line.
Do what you think is right, GOD, my God,
  but don't make me pay for their good time.
Don't let them say to themselves,
  "Ha-ha, we got what we wanted."
Don't let them say,
  "We've chewed him up and spit him out."
Let those who are being hilarious
  at my expense
Be made to look ridiculous.
  Make them wear donkey's ears;
Pin them with the donkey's tail,
  who made themselves so high and mighty!

But those who want
  the best for me,
Let them have the last word — a glad shout! —

and say, over and over and over,
"GOD is great — everything works
    together for good for his servant."
I'll tell the world how great and good you are,
    I'll shout Hallelujah all day, every day.


**A David Psalm**

**36.** The God-rebel tunes in to sedition —
        all ears, eager to sin.
He has no regard for God,
    he stands insolent before him.
He has smooth-talked himself
    into believing
That his evil
    will never be noticed.
Words gutter from his mouth,
    dishwater dirty.
Can't remember when he
    did anything decent.
Every time he goes to bed,
    he fathers another evil plot.
When he's loose on the streets,
    nobody's safe.
He plays with fire
    and doesn't care who gets burned.


God's love is meteoric,
    his loyalty astronomic,
His purpose titanic,
    his verdicts oceanic.
Yet in his largeness
    nothing gets lost;
Not a man, not a mouse,

slips through the cracks.

How exquisite your love, O God!
How eager we are to run under your wings,
To eat our fill at the banquet you spread
as you fill our tankards with Eden spring water.
You're a fountain of cascading light,
and you open our eyes to light.

Keep on loving your friends;
do your work in welcoming hearts.
Don't let the bullies kick me around,
the moral midgets slap me down.
Send the upstarts sprawling
flat on their faces in the mud.

---

Do we all share a moral baseline? Do we all possess an inherent standard that declares murder, rape, theft, and cheating as universal wrongs? Why? Where does that come from?

When we see images of genocidal atrocities in Rwanda and Sudan, do our stomachs turn? When we read details about the twisted minds of serial killers and sexual predators, do we shirk in disgust?

Although it seems that humanity shares an ethical plumb line on the "big things," it also seems that some people are totally numb. The inner conscience is broken; the inherent checks and balances are gone; and true evil has surfaced. If there's no fear of God and his ultimate justice, the truly wicked are free to boldly pursue evil without restraint.

---

## A David Psalm

**37.** Don't bother your head with braggarts
or wish you could succeed like the wicked.
In no time they'll shrivel like grass clippings
and wilt like cut flowers in the sun.

Get insurance with GOD and do a good deed,
    settle down and stick to your last.
Keep company with GOD,
     get in on the best.

Open up before GOD, keep nothing back;
     he'll do whatever needs to be done:
He'll validate your life in the clear light of day
     and stamp you with approval at high noon.

Quiet down before GOD,
     be prayerful before him.
Don't bother with those who climb the ladder,
     who elbow their way to the top.

Bridle your anger, trash your wrath,
     cool your pipes — it only makes things worse.
Before long the crooks will be bankrupt;
     GOD-investors will soon own the store.

Before you know it, the wicked will have had it;
     you'll stare at his once famous place and — nothing!
Down-to-earth people will move in and take over,
     relishing a huge bonanza.

Bad guys have it in for the good guys,
     obsessed with doing them in.
But GOD isn't losing any sleep; to him
     they're a joke with no punch line.

Bullies brandish their swords,
     pull back on their bows with a flourish.
They're out to beat up on the harmless,
     or mug that nice man out walking his dog.

A banana peel lands them flat on their faces —
    slapstick figures in a moral circus.

Less is more and more is less.
    One righteous will outclass fifty wicked,
For the wicked are moral weaklings
    but the righteous are GOD-strong.

GOD keeps track of the decent folk;
    what they do won't soon be forgotten.
In hard times, they'll hold their heads high;
    when the shelves are bare, they'll be full.

God-despisers have had it;
    GOD's enemies are finished —
Stripped bare like vineyards at harvest time,
    vanished like smoke in thin air.

Wicked borrows and never returns;
    Righteous gives and gives.
Generous gets it all in the end;
    Stingy is cut off at the pass.

Stalwart walks in step with GOD;
    his path blazed by GOD, he's happy.
If he stumbles, he's not down for long;
    GOD has a grip on his hand.

I once was young, now I'm a graybeard —
    not once have I seen an abandoned believer,
    or his kids out roaming the streets.
Every day he's out giving and lending,
    his children making him proud.

Turn your back on evil,
    work for the good and don't quit.
GOD loves this kind of thing,
    never turns away from his friends.

Live this way and you've got it made,
    but bad eggs will be tossed out.
The good get planted on good land
    and put down healthy roots.

Righteous chews on wisdom like a dog on a bone,
    rolls virtue around on his tongue.
His heart pumps God's Word like blood through his veins;
    his feet are as sure as a cat's.

Wicked sets a watch for Righteous,
    he's out for the kill.
GOD, alert, is also on watch —
    Wicked won't hurt a hair of his head.

Wait passionately for GOD,
    don't leave the path.
He'll give you your place in the sun
    while you watch the wicked lose it.

I saw Wicked bloated like a toad,
    croaking pretentious nonsense.
The next time I looked there was nothing —
    a punctured bladder, vapid and limp.

Keep your eye on the healthy soul,
    scrutinize the straight life;
There's a future

in strenuous wholeness.
But the willful will soon be discarded;
   insolent souls are on a dead-end street.

The spacious, free life is from GOD,
   it's also protected and safe.
GOD-strengthened, we're delivered from evil —
   when we run to him, he saves us.

## A David Psalm

**38.** Take a deep breath, GOD; calm down —
   don't be so hasty with your punishing rod.
Your sharp-pointed arrows of rebuke draw blood;
   my backside smarts from your caning.

I've lost twenty pounds in two months
   because of your accusation.
My bones are brittle as dry sticks
   because of my sin.
I'm swamped by my bad behavior,
   collapsed under gunnysacks of guilt.

The cuts in my flesh stink and grow maggots
   because I've lived so badly.
And now I'm flat on my face
   feeling sorry for myself morning to night.
All my insides are on fire,
   my body is a wreck.
I'm on my last legs; I've had it —
   my life is a vomit of groans.

Lord, my longings are sitting in plain sight,
   my groans an old story to you.

My heart's about to break;
    I'm a burned-out case.
Cataracts blind me to God and good;
    old friends avoid me like the plague.
My cousins never visit,
    my neighbors stab me in the back.
My competitors blacken my name,
    devoutly they pray for my ruin.
But I'm deaf and mute to it all,
    ears shut, mouth shut.
I don't hear a word they say,
    don't speak a word in response.
What I do, GOD, is wait for you,
    wait for my Lord, my God — you *will* answer!
I wait and pray so they won't laugh me off,
    won't smugly strut off when I stumble.

I'm on the edge of losing it —
    the pain in my gut keeps burning.
I'm ready to tell my story of failure,
    I'm no longer smug in my sin.
My enemies are alive and in action,
    a lynch mob after my neck.
I give out good and get back evil
    from God-haters who can't stand a God-lover.

Don't dump me, GOD;
    my God, don't stand me up.
Hurry and help me;
    I want some wide-open space in my life!

## A David Psalm

**39.** I'm determined to watch steps and tongue
so they won't land me in trouble.
I decided to hold my tongue
as long as Wicked is in the room.
"Mum's the word," I said, and kept quiet.
But the longer I kept silence
The worse it got —
my insides got hotter and hotter.
My thoughts boiled over;
I spilled my guts.

"Tell me, what's going on, GOD?
How long do I have to live?
Give me the bad news!
You've kept me on pretty short rations;
my life is string too short to be saved.
Oh! we're all puffs of air.
Oh! we're all shadows in a campfire.
Oh! we're just spit in the wind.
We make our pile, and then we leave it.

"What am I doing in the meantime, Lord?
*Hoping,* that's what I'm doing — hoping
You'll save me from a rebel life,
save me from the contempt of dunces.
I'll say no more, I'll shut my mouth,
since you, Lord, are behind all this.
But I can't take it much longer.
When you put us through the fire
to purge us from our sin,
our dearest idols go up in smoke.
Are we also nothing but smoke?

"Ah, GOD, listen to my prayer, my
    cry — open your ears.
Don't be callous;
    just look at these tears of mine.
I'm a stranger here. I don't know my way —
    a migrant like my whole family.
Give me a break, cut me some slack
    before it's too late and I'm out of here."


## A David Psalm

**40.** I waited and waited and waited for GOD.
    At last he looked; finally he listened.
He lifted me out of the ditch,
    pulled me from deep mud.
He stood me up on a solid rock
    to make sure I wouldn't slip.
He taught me how to sing the latest God-song,
    a praise-song to our God.
More and more people are seeing this:
    they enter the mystery,
    abandoning themselves to GOD.

Blessed are you who give yourselves over to GOD,
    turn your backs on the world's "sure thing,"
    ignore what the world worships;
The world's a huge stockpile
    of GOD-wonders and God-thoughts.
Nothing and no one
    comes close to you!
I start talking about you, telling what I know,
    and quickly run out of words.
Neither numbers nor words
    account for you.

Doing something for you, bringing something to you —
    that's not what you're after.
Being religious, acting pious —
    that's not what you're asking for.
You've opened my ears
    so I can listen.

So I answered, "I'm coming.
    I read in your letter what you wrote about me,
And I'm coming to the party
    you're throwing for me."
That's when God's Word entered my life,
    became part of my very being.

I've preached you to the whole congregation,
    I've kept back nothing, GOD — you know that.
I didn't keep the news of your ways
    a secret, didn't keep it to myself.
I told it all, how dependable you are, how thorough.
    I didn't hold back pieces of love and truth
For myself alone. I told it all,
    let the congregation know the whole story.

Now GOD, don't hold out on me,
    don't hold back your passion.
Your love and truth
    are all that keeps me together.
When troubles ganged up on me,
    a mob of sins past counting,
I was so swamped by guilt
    I couldn't see my way clear.
More guilt in my heart than hair on my head,
    so heavy the guilt that my heart gave out.

Soften up, GOD, and intervene;
    hurry and get me some help,
So those who are trying to kidnap my soul
    will be embarrassed and lose face,
So anyone who gets a kick out of making me miserable
    will be heckled and disgraced,
So those who pray for my ruin
    will be booed and jeered without mercy.

But all who are hunting for you —
    oh, let them sing and be happy.
Let those who know what you're all about
    tell the world you're great and not quitting.
And me? I'm a mess. I'm nothing and have nothing:
    make something of me.
You can do it; you've got what it takes —
    but God, don't put it off.

---

Powerful insights! God's not looking for rules and rituals . . . pomp or piety. According to David, God wants all of us!

Here, the "opened ear" refers to the piercing of a large hole in the earlobe of a bond servant who chooses to remain in the service of his master, even after achieving legal freedom. Through this ancient practice, the servant was declaring his lifelong dedication to his master—voluntary slavehood. The large hole in the ear symbolized the servant's open willingness to hear and obey his master's voice.

---

**A David Psalm**

**41.** Dignify those who are down on their luck;
    you'll feel good — *that's* what GOD does.
GOD looks after us all,
    makes us robust with life —
Lucky to be in the land,
    we're free from enemy worries.

Whenever we're sick and in bed,
GOD becomes our nurse,
nurses us back to health.

I said, "GOD, be gracious!
Put me together again —
my sins have torn me to pieces."
My enemies are wishing the worst for me;
they make bets on what day I will die.
If someone comes to see me,
he mouths empty platitudes,
All the while gathering gossip about me
to entertain the street-corner crowd.
These "friends" who hate me
whisper slanders all over town.
They form committees
to plan misery for me.

The rumor goes out, "He's got some dirty,
deadly disease. The doctors
have given up on him."
Even my best friend, the one I always told everything
— he ate meals at my house all the time! —
has bitten my hand.

GOD, give grace, get me up on my feet.
I'll show them a thing or two.

Meanwhile, I'm sure you're on my side —
no victory shouts yet from the enemy camp!
You know me inside and out, you hold me together,
you never fail to stand me tall in your presence
so I can look you in the eye.

Blessed is GOD, Israel's God,
  always, always, always.
  Yes. Yes. Yes.

## A David Psalm, After He Was Confronted by Nathan About the Affair with Bathsheba

**51.** Generous in love — God, give grace!
    Huge in mercy — wipe out my bad record.
Scrub away my guilt,
  soak out my sins in your laundry.
I know how bad I've been;
  my sins are staring me down.

You're the One I've violated, and you've seen
  it all, seen the full extent of my evil.
You have all the facts before you;
  whatever you decide about me is fair.
I've been out of step with you for a long time,
  in the wrong since before I was born.
What you're after is truth from the inside out.
  Enter me, then; conceive a new, true life.

Soak me in your laundry and I'll come out clean,
  scrub me and I'll have a snow-white life.
Tune me in to foot-tapping songs,
  set these once-broken bones to dancing.
Don't look too close for blemishes,
  give me a clean bill of health.
God, make a fresh start in me,
  shape a Genesis week from the chaos of my life.
Don't throw me out with the trash,
  or fail to breathe holiness in me.
Bring me back from gray exile,

put a fresh wind in my sails!
Give me a job teaching rebels your ways
    so the lost can find their way home.
Commute my death sentence, God, my salvation God,
    and I'll sing anthems to your life-giving ways.
Unbutton my lips, dear God;
    I'll let loose with your praise.

Going through the motions doesn't please you,
    a flawless performance is nothing to you.
I learned God-worship
    when my pride was shattered.
Heart-shattered lives ready for love
    don't for a moment escape God's notice.

Make Zion the place you delight in,
    repair Jerusalem's broken-down walls.
Then you'll get real worship from us,
    acts of worship small and large,
Including all the bulls
    they can heave onto your altar!

---

David was a special king, but he was also broken like the rest of us. At one point during his reign, he saw a beautiful woman bathing and decided to search her out. It was Bathsheba, a woman married to Uriah, a soldier in David's army. Regardless, while Uriah was away in battle, David had an adulterous affair with Bathsheba, and she became pregnant.

In an effort to cover his tracks, David dug a much deeper hole by having Uriah killed "by accident" on the battlefield. As sins were piling up, God used a prophet named Nathan to deliver the following message:

> And here's what GOD, the God of Israel, has to say to you: I made you king over Israel. I freed you from the fist of Saul. I gave you your master's daughter and other wives to have and to hold. I gave you both Israel and Judah. And if that hadn't been enough, I'd have gladly thrown in much

more. So why have you treated the word of God with brazen contempt, doing this great evil?

Then David confessed to Nathan, "I've sinned against God."

This psalm is David's confession to God himself.

---

## A David Psalm, When Doeg the Edomite Reported to Saul, "David's at Ahimelech's House"

**52.** Why do you brag of evil, "Big Man"?
　　God's mercy carries the day.
You scheme catastrophe;
　　your tongue cuts razor-sharp,
　　artisan in lies.
You love evil more than good,
　　you call black white.
You love malicious gossip,
　　you foul-mouth.

God will tear you limb from limb,
　　sweep you up and throw you out,
Pull you up by the roots
　　from the land of life.

Good people will watch and
　　worship. They'll laugh in relief:
"Big Man bet on the wrong horse,
　　trusted in big money,
　　made his living from catastrophe."

And I'm an olive tree,
　　growing green in God's house.
I trusted in the generous mercy
　　of God then and now.

I thank you always
    that you went into action.
And I'll stay right here,
    your good name my hope,
    in company with your faithful friends.


**A David Psalm**

**53.** Bilious and bloated, they gas,
    "God is gone."
It's poison gas —
    they foul themselves, they poison
Rivers and skies;
    thistles are their cash crop.
God sticks his head out of heaven.
    He looks around.
He's looking for someone not stupid —
    one man, even, God-expectant,
    just one God-ready woman.


He comes up empty. A string
    of zeros. Useless, unshepherded
Sheep, taking turns pretending
    to be Shepherd.
The ninety and nine
    follow the one.


Don't they know anything,
    all these impostors?
Don't they know
    they can't get away with this,
Treating people like a fast-food meal
    over which they're too busy to pray?

Night is coming for them, and nightmare —
    a nightmare they'll never wake up from.
God will make hash of these squatters,
    send them packing for good.

Is there anyone around to save Israel?
    God turns life around.
Turned-around Jacob skips rope,
    turned-around Israel sings laughter.

## A David Psalm, When the Ziphites Reported to Saul, "David Is Hiding Out with Us"

**54.** God, for your sake, help me!
    Use your influence to clear me.
Listen, God — I'm desperate.
    Don't be too busy to hear me.

Outlaws are out to get me,
    hit men are trying to kill me.
Nothing will stop them;
    God means nothing to them.

Oh, look! God's right here helping!
    GOD's on my side,
Evil is looping back on my enemies.
    Don't let up! Finish them off!

I'm ready now to worship, so ready.
    I thank you, GOD — you're so good.
You got me out of every scrape,
    and I saw my enemies get it.

## A David Psalm

**55.** Open your ears, God, to my prayer;
don't pretend you don't hear me knocking.
Come close and whisper your answer.
    I really need you.
I shudder at the mean voice,
    quail before the evil eye,
As they pile on the guilt,
    stockpile angry slander.

My insides are turned inside out;
    specters of death have me down.
I shake with fear,
    I shudder from head to foot.
"Who will give me wings," I ask —
    "wings like a dove?"
Get me out of here on dove wings;
    I want some peace and quiet.
I want a walk in the country,
    I want a cabin in the woods.
I'm desperate for a change
    from rage and stormy weather.

Come down hard, Lord — slit their tongues.
    I'm appalled how they've split the city
Into rival gangs
    prowling the alleys
Day and night spoiling for a fight,
    trash piled in the streets,
Even shopkeepers gouging and cheating
    in broad daylight.

This isn't the neighborhood bully

mocking me — I could take that.
This isn't a foreign devil spitting
    invective — I could tune that out.
It's *you*! We grew up together!
    *You!* My best friend!
Those long hours of leisure as we walked
    arm in arm, God a third party to our conversation.

Haul my betrayers off alive to hell — let them
    experience the horror, let them
    feel every desolate detail of a damned life.

I call to God;
    GOD will help me.
At dusk, dawn, and noon I sigh
    deep sighs — he hears, he rescues.
My life is well and whole, secure
    in the middle of danger
Even while thousands
    are lined up against me.
God hears it all, and from his judge's bench
    puts them in their place.
But, set in their ways, they won't change;
    they pay him no mind.

And this, my best friend, betrayed his best friends;
    his life betrayed his word.
All my life I've been charmed by his speech,
    never dreaming he'd turn on me.
His words, which were music to my ears,
    turned to daggers in my heart.

Pile your troubles on GOD's shoulders —
    he'll carry your load, he'll help you out.

He'll never let good people
    topple into ruin.
But you, God, will throw the others
    into a muddy bog,
Cut the lifespan of assassins
    and traitors in half.

And I trust in you.

## A David Psalm, When He Was Captured by the Philistines in Gath

**56.** Take my side, God — I'm getting kicked around,
    stomped on every day.
Not a day goes by
    but somebody beats me up;
They make it their duty
    to beat me up.
When I get really afraid
    I come to you in trust.
I'm proud to praise God;
    fearless now, I trust in God.
    What can mere mortals do?

They don't let up —
    they smear my reputation
    and huddle to plot my collapse.
They gang up,
    sneak together through the alleys
To take me by surprise,
    wait their chance to get me.

Pay them back in evil!
    Get angry, God!

Down with these people!

You've kept track of my every toss and turn
through the sleepless nights,
Each tear entered in your ledger,
each ache written in your book.

If my enemies run away,
turn tail when I yell at them,
Then I'll know
that God is on my side.

I'm proud to praise God,
proud to praise GOD.
Fearless now, I trust in God;
what can mere mortals do to me?

God, you did everything you promised,
and I'm thanking you with all my heart.
You pulled me from the brink of death,
my feet from the cliff-edge of doom.
Now I stroll at leisure with God
in the sunlit fields of life.

## A David Psalm, When He Hid in a Cave from Saul

**57.** Be good to me, God — and now!
I've run to you for dear life.
I'm hiding out under your wings
until the hurricane blows over.
I call out to High God,
the God who holds me together.
He sends orders from heaven and saves me,
he humiliates those who kick me around.

God delivers generous love,
he makes good on his word.

I find myself in a pride of lions
who are wild for a taste of human flesh;
Their teeth are lances and arrows,
their tongues are sharp daggers.

Soar high in the skies, O God!
Cover the whole earth with your glory!

They booby-trapped my path;
I thought I was dead and done for.
They dug a mantrap to catch me,
and fell in headlong themselves.

I'm ready, God, so ready,
ready from head to toe,
Ready to sing, ready to raise a tune:
"Wake up, soul!
Wake up, harp! wake up, lute!
Wake up, you sleepyhead sun!"

I'm thanking you, GOD, out loud in the streets,
singing your praises in town and country.
The deeper your love, the higher it goes;
every cloud is a flag to your faithfulness.

Soar high in the skies, O God!
Cover the whole earth with your glory!

---

David is writing this psalm from a cave. As he crouches deep within its crags, he watches Saul and his army hunt for him as if they were the predators and he the prey. By traditional standards of the hunter and the hunted, David doesn't have a chance.

However, even when his enemies were near enough to pounce, David held on to his faith. When facing the snare of death, David still looked forward to God's deliverance.

> You will never know how much you believe something
> until it is a matter of life and death.

—C. S. Lewis

## A David Psalm

**58.** Is this any way to run a country?
Is there an honest politician in the house?
Behind the scenes you brew cauldrons of evil,
    behind closed doors you make deals with demons.

The wicked crawl from the wrong side of the cradle;
    their first words out of the womb are lies.
Poison, lethal rattlesnake poison,
    drips from their forked tongues—
Deaf to threats, deaf to charm,
    decades of wax built up in their ears.

God, smash their teeth to bits,
    leave them toothless tigers.
Let their lives be buckets of water spilled,
    all that's left, a damp stain in the sand.
Let them be trampled grass
    worn smooth by the traffic.
Let them dissolve into snail slime,
    be a miscarried fetus that never sees sunlight.
Before what they cook up is half-done, God,
    throw it out with the garbage!

The righteous will call up their friends
    when they see the wicked get their reward,
Serve up their blood in goblets
    as they toast one another,
Everyone cheering, "It's worth it to play by the rules!
    God's handing out trophies and tending the earth!"

**A David Psalm, When Saul Set a Watch on David's House in Order to Kill Him**

# 59.

My God! Rescue me from my enemies,
    defend me from these mutineers.
Rescue me from their dirty tricks,
    save me from their hit men.

Desperadoes have ganged up on me,
    they're hiding in ambush for me.
I did nothing to deserve this, GOD,
    crossed no one, wronged no one.
All the same, they're after me,
    determined to get me.

Wake up and see for yourself! You're GOD,
    GOD-of-Angel-Armies, Israel's God!
Get on the job and take care of these pagans,
    don't be soft on these hard cases.

They return when the sun goes down,
They howl like coyotes, ringing the city.
Then suddenly they're all at the gate,
Snarling invective, drawn daggers in their teeth.
They think they'll never get caught.

But you, GOD, break out laughing;
 you treat the godless nations like jokes.
Strong God, I'm watching you do it,
 I can always count on you.
God in dependable love shows up on time,
 shows me my enemies in ruin.

Don't make quick work of them, GOD,
 lest my people forget.
Bring them down in slow motion,
 take them apart piece by piece.
Let all their mean-mouthed arrogance
 catch up with them,
Catch them out and bring them down
 — every muttered curse
 — every barefaced lie.
Finish them off in fine style!
 Finish them off for good!
Then all the world will see
 that God rules well in Jacob,
 everywhere that God's in charge.

 They return when the sun goes down,
 They howl like coyotes, ringing the city.
 They scavenge for bones,
 And bite the hand that feeds them.

And me? I'm singing your prowess,
 shouting at cockcrow your largesse,
For you've been a safe place for me,
 a good place to hide.
Strong God, I'm watching you do it,
 I can always count on you —
 God, my dependable love.

## A David Psalm, When He Fought Against Aram-naharaim and Aram-zobah and Joab Killed Twelve Thousand Edomites at the Valley of Salt

**60.** God! you walked off and left us,
kicked our defenses to bits
And stalked off angry.
>Come back. Oh please, come back!

You shook earth to the foundations,
ripped open huge crevasses.
Heal the breaks! Everything's
coming apart at the seams.

You made your people look doom in the face,
then gave us cheap wine to drown our troubles.
Then you planted a flag to rally your people,
an unfurled flag to look to for courage.
Now do something quickly, answer right now,
so the one you love best is saved.

That's when God spoke in holy splendor,
"Bursting with joy,
I make a present of Shechem,
I hand out Succoth Valley as a gift.
Gilead's in my pocket,
to say nothing of Manasseh.
Ephraim's my hard hat,
Judah my hammer;
Moab's a scrub bucket,
I mop the floor with Moab,
Spit on Edom,
rain fireworks all over Philistia."

Who will take me to the thick of the fight?

Who'll show me the road to Edom?
You aren't giving up on us, are you, God?
    refusing to go out with our troops?

Give us help for the hard task;
    human help is worthless.
In God we'll do our very best;
    he'll flatten the opposition for good.

### A David Psalm

**61.** God, listen to me shout,
    bend an ear to my prayer.
When I'm far from anywhere,
    down to my last gasp,
I call out, "Guide me
    up High Rock Mountain!"

You've always given me breathing room,
    a place to get away from it all,
A lifetime pass to your safe-house,
    an open invitation as your guest.
You've always taken me seriously, God,
    made me welcome among those who know and love you.

Let the days of the king add up
    to years and years of good rule.
Set his throne in the full light of God;
    post Steady Love and Good Faith as lookouts,
And I'll be the poet who sings your glory—
    and live what I sing every day.

### Nothing Compares

I've heard all the stories
I've seen all the signs
Witnessed all the glory
Tasted all that's fine

Nothing compares to the greatness of knowing you, Lord
Nothing compares to the greatness of knowing you, Lord

I see all the people
Wasting all their time
Building up their riches
For a life that's fine

I find myself just living for today
'Cause I don't know what
Tomorrow's gonna bring
So no matter if I rise or fall
I'll never be alone, oh no

— Mac Powell, 2001

## A David Psalm

**62.** God, the one and only —
I'll wait as long as he says.
Everything I need comes from him,
   so why not?
He's solid rock under my feet,
   breathing room for my soul,
An impregnable castle:
   I'm set for life.

How long will you gang up on me?
   How long will you run with the bullies?

There's nothing to you, any of you —
    rotten floorboards, worm-eaten rafters,
Anthills plotting to bring down mountains,
    far gone in make-believe.
You talk a good line,
    but every "blessing" breathes a curse.

God, the one and only —
    I'll wait as long as he says.
Everything I hope for comes from him,
    so why not?
He's solid rock under my feet,
    breathing room for my soul,
An impregnable castle:
    I'm set for life.

My help and glory are in God
    — granite-strength and safe-harbor-God —
So trust him absolutely, people;
    lay your lives on the line for him.
    God is a safe place to be.

Man as such is smoke,
    woman as such, a mirage.
Put them together, they're nothing;
    two times nothing is nothing.

And a windfall, if it comes —
    don't make too much of it.

## SEARCHER ON THE WAY
*Fourteen Days*

During much of the tenth century AD, Abd-ar-Rahman III reigned as the most powerful prince of the Ummayad dynasty in Spain. He was known as the Emir of Cordoba from 912 to 929, and later as the Caliph of Cordoba from 929 to 961.

Abd-ar-Rahman III was a mighty ruler who unified a people plagued by tribal warfare and outside influence. First, he successfully established a centralized government in Spain and built a powerful army and navy. Then, through military action, he successfully broke ties with the aristocracy of the Arab world, the Fatimids of Egypt and North Africa, and the Christian kings of León.

After nearly twenty years of dramatic success, Abd-ar-Rahman III snubbed the caliphate tradition of Mecca and Medina and declared himself as caliph in Spain. Although rejected by some, this title gave Abd-ar-Rahman tremendous power and prestige throughout much of the Muslim world. He spent the next thirty-two years as a revered ruler of a peaceful and prosperous region.

When all was said and done, Abd-ar-Rahman III reflected on his life like other rulers before him. Remarkably, he came to the same basic conclusion as other mighty men of history:

> I have now reigned above fifty years in victory or peace; beloved by my subjects, dreaded by my enemies, and respected by my allies. Riches and honors, power and pleasure, have waited on my call, nor does any earthly blessing appear to have been wanting to my felicity. In this situation, I have diligently numbered the days of pure and genuine happiness which have fallen to my lot: they amount to Fourteen:—O man! place not thy confidence in this present world!

God said this once and for all;
>    how many times
Have I heard it repeated?
>    "Strength comes
Straight from God."

Love to you, Lord God!
>    You pay a fair wage for a good day's work!

## A David Psalm, When He Was out in the Judean Wilderness

**63.** God — you're my God!
>    I can't get enough of you!
I've worked up such hunger and thirst for God,
>    traveling across dry and weary deserts.

So here I am in the place of worship, eyes open,
>    drinking in your strength and glory.
In your generous love I am really living at last!
>    My lips brim praises like fountains.
I bless you every time I take a breath;
>    My arms wave like banners of praise to you.

I eat my fill of prime rib and gravy;
>    I smack my lips. It's time to shout praises!
If I'm sleepless at midnight,
>    I spend the hours in grateful reflection.
Because you've always stood up for me,
>    I'm free to run and play.
I hold on to you for dear life,
>    and you hold me steady as a post.

Those who are out to get me are marked for doom,
>    marked for death, bound for hell.
They'll die violent deaths;
>    jackals will tear them limb from limb.
But the king is glad in God;
>    his true friends spread the joy,
While small-minded gossips
>    are gagged for good.

**A David Psalm**

**64.** Listen and help, O God.
>    I'm reduced to a whine
And a whimper, obsessed
>    with feelings of doomsday.

Don't let them find me —
>    the conspirators out to get me,
Using their tongues as weapons,
>    flinging poison words,
>    poison-tipped arrow-words.
They shoot from ambush,
>    shoot without warning,
>    not caring who they hit.
They keep fit doing calisthenics
>    of evil purpose,
They keep lists of the traps
>    they've secretly set.
They say to each other,
>    "No one can catch us,
>    no one can detect our perfect crime."
The Detective detects the mystery
>    in the dark of the cellar heart.

The God of the Arrow shoots!
>    They double up in pain,
Fall flat on their faces
>    in full view of the grinning crowd.

Everyone sees it. God's
>    work is the talk of the town.
Be glad, good people! Fly to GOD!
>    Good-hearted people, make praise your habit.

## A David Psalm

**65.** Silence is praise to you,
>    Zion-dwelling God,
And also obedience.
>    You hear the prayer in it all.

During his reign, David conquered a Jebusite fortress near modern-day Jerusalem. The fortress was located on a hill in the southeastern region known as Mount Zion. As time went on, Zion became the ancient Jewish title for Jerusalem. Later, Solomon built the first Jewish Temple there, and Zion became the religious symbol of the Jewish homeland. After the Jews were dispersed throughout the world in the first century, Zion exemplified the long-term hope of the Jewish people—to return to their land and the holy city of God.

We all arrive at your doorstep sooner
>    or later, loaded with guilt,
Our sins too much for us —
>    but you get rid of them once and for all.
Blessed are the chosen! Blessed the guest
>    at home in your place!
We expect our fill of good things
>    in your house, your heavenly manse.

All your salvation wonders
    are on display in your trophy room.
Earth-Tamer, Ocean-Pourer,
    Mountain-Maker, Hill-Dresser,
Muzzler of sea storm and wave crash,
    of mobs in noisy riot —
Far and wide they'll come to a stop,
    they'll stare in awe, in wonder.
Dawn and dusk take turns
    calling, "Come and worship."

Oh, visit the earth,
    ask her to join the dance!
Deck her out in spring showers,
    fill the God-River with living water.
Paint the wheat fields golden.
    Creation was made for this!
Drench the plowed fields,
    soak the dirt clods
With rainfall as harrow and rake
    bring her to blossom and fruit.
Snow-crown the peaks with splendor,
    scatter rose petals down your paths,
All through the wild meadows, rose petals.
    Set the hills to dancing,
Dress the canyon walls with live sheep,
    a drape of flax across the valleys.
Let them shout, and shout, and shout!
    Oh, oh, let them sing!

**A David Psalm**

**68.** Up with God!
    Down with his enemies!

Adversaries, run for the hills!
Gone like a puff of smoke,
    like a blob of wax in the fire —
        one look at God and the wicked vanish.
When the righteous see God in action
    they'll laugh, they'll sing,
        they'll laugh and sing for joy.
Sing hymns to God;
    all heaven, sing out;
        clear the way for the coming of Cloud-Rider.
Enjoy GOD,
    cheer when you see him!

Father of orphans,
    champion of widows,
        is God in his holy house.
God makes homes for the homeless,
    leads prisoners to freedom,
        but leaves rebels to rot in hell.

God, when you took the lead with your people,
    when you marched out into the wild,
Earth shook, sky broke out in a sweat;
    God was on the march.
Even Sinai trembled at the sight of God on the move,
    at the sight of Israel's God.
You pour out rain in buckets, O God;
    thorn and cactus become an oasis
For your people to camp in and enjoy.
    You set them up in business;
    they went from rags to riches.

The Lord gave the word;
    thousands called out the good news:

"Kings of the armies
        are on the run, on the run!"
While housewives, safe and sound back home,
        divide up the plunder,
        the plunder of Canaanite silver and gold.
On that day that Shaddai scattered the kings,
        snow fell on Black Mountain.

You huge mountains, Bashan mountains,
        mighty mountains, dragon mountains.
All you mountains not chosen,
        sulk now, and feel sorry for yourselves,
For this is the mountain God has chosen to live on;
        he'll rule from this mountain forever.

The chariots of God, twice ten thousand,
        and thousands more besides,
The Lord in the lead, riding down Sinai —
        straight to the Holy Place!
You climbed to the High Place, captives in tow,
        your arms full of booty from rebels,
And now you sit there in state,
        GOD, sovereign GOD!

Blessed be the Lord —
        day after day he carries us along.
He's our Savior, our God, oh yes!
        He's God-for-us, he's God-who-saves-us.
Lord GOD knows all
        death's ins and outs.
What's more, he made heads roll,
        split the skulls of the enemy
As he marched out of heaven,
        saying, "I tied up the Dragon in knots,

put a muzzle on the Deep Blue Sea."
You can wade through your enemies' blood,
    and your dogs taste of your enemies from your boots.


See God on parade
    to the sanctuary, my God,
    my King on the march!
Singers out front, the band behind,
    maidens in the middle with castanets.
The whole choir blesses God.
    Like a fountain of praise, Israel blesses GOD.
Look — little Benjamin's out
    front and leading
Princes of Judah in their royal robes,
    princes of Zebulon, princes of Naphtali.
Parade your power, O God,
    the power, O God, that made us what we are.
Your temple, High God, is Jerusalem;
    kings bring gifts to you.
Rebuke that old crocodile, Egypt,
    with her herd of wild bulls and calves,
Rapacious in her lust for silver,
    crushing peoples, spoiling for a fight.
Let Egyptian traders bring blue cloth
    and Cush come running to God, her hands outstretched.


Sing, O kings of the earth!
    Sing praises to the Lord!
There he is: Sky-Rider,
    striding the ancient skies.
Listen — he's calling in thunder,
    rumbling, rolling thunder.
Call out "Bravo!" to God,
    the High God of Israel.

His splendor and strength
    rise huge as thunderheads.

A terrible beauty, O God,
    streams from your sanctuary.
It's Israel's strong God! He gives
    power and might to his people!
O you, his people — bless God!

**A David Psalm**

**69.** God, God, save me!
    I'm in over my head,

Quicksand under me, swamp water over me;
I'm going down for the third time.

I'm hoarse from calling for help,
Bleary-eyed from searching the sky for God.

I've got more enemies than hairs on my head;
Sneaks and liars are out to knife me in the back.

What I never stole
Must I now give back?

God, you know every sin I've committed;
My life's a wide-open book before you.

Don't let those who look to you in hope
Be discouraged by what happens to me,
Dear Lord! GOD of the armies!

Don't let those out looking for you

Come to a dead end by following me —
Please, dear God of Israel!

Because of you I look like an idiot,
I walk around ashamed to show my face.

My brothers shun me like a bum off the street;
My family treats me like an unwanted guest.

I love you more than I can say.
Because I'm madly in love with you,
They blame me for everything they dislike about you.

When I poured myself out in prayer and fasting,
All it got me was more contempt.

When I put on a sad face,
They treated me like a clown.

Now drunks and gluttons
Make up drinking songs about me.

And me? I pray.
GOD, it's time for a break!

God, answer in love!
Answer with your sure salvation!

Rescue me from the swamp,
Don't let me go under for good,

Pull me out of the clutch of the enemy;
This whirlpool is sucking me down.

Don't let the swamp be my grave, the Black Hole
Swallow me, its jaws clenched around me.

Now answer me, GOD, because you love me;
Let me see your great mercy full-face.

Don't look the other way; your servant can't take it.
I'm in trouble. Answer right now!

Come close, God; get me out of here.
Rescue me from this deathtrap.

You know how they kick me around —
Pin on me the donkey's ears, the dunce's cap.

I'm broken by their taunts,
Flat on my face, reduced to a nothing.

I looked in vain for one friendly face. Not one.
I couldn't find one shoulder to cry on.

They put poison in my soup,
Vinegar in my drink.

Let their supper be bait in a trap that snaps shut;
May their best friends be trappers who'll skin them alive.

Make them become blind as bats,
Give them the shakes from morning to night.

Let them know what you think of them,
Blast them with your red-hot anger.

Burn down their houses,

Leave them desolate with nobody at home.

They gossiped about the one you disciplined,
Made up stories about anyone wounded by God.

Pile on the guilt,
Don't let them off the hook.

Strike their names from the list of the living;
No rock-carved honor for them among the righteous.

I'm hurt and in pain;
Give me space for healing, and mountain air.

Let me shout God's name with a praising song,
Let me tell his greatness in a prayer of thanks.

For GOD, this is better than oxen on the altar,
Far better than blue-ribbon bulls.

The poor in spirit see and are glad —
Oh, you God-seekers, take heart!

For GOD listens to the poor,
He doesn't walk out on the wretched.

You heavens, praise him; praise him, earth;
Also ocean and all things that swim in it.

For God is out to help Zion,
Rebuilding the wrecked towns of Judah.

Guess who will live there —
The proud owners of the land?

No, the children of his servants will get it,
The lovers of his name will live in it.

## A David Prayer

**70.** God! Please hurry to my rescue!
          GOD, come quickly to my side!
Those who are out to get me —
      let them fall all over themselves.
Those who relish my downfall —
      send them down a blind alley.
Give them a taste of their own medicine,
      those gossips off clucking their tongues.

Let those on the hunt for you
      sing and celebrate.
Let all who love your saving way
      say over and over, "God is mighty!"

But I've lost it. I'm wasted.
      God — quickly, quickly!
Quick to my side, quick to my rescue!
      GOD, don't lose a minute.

## A Solomon Psalm

**72.** Give the gift of wise rule to the king, O God,
          the gift of just rule to the crown prince.
May he judge your people rightly,
      be honorable to your meek and lowly.
Let the mountains give exuberant witness;
      shape the hills with the contours of right living.
Please stand up for the poor,
      help the children of the needy,

come down hard on the cruel tyrants.
Outlast the sun, outlive the moon—
    age after age after age.
Be rainfall on cut grass,
    earth-refreshing rain showers.
Let righteousness burst into blossom
    and peace abound until the moon fades to nothing.
Rule from sea to sea,
    from the River to the Rim.


Foes will fall on their knees before God,
    his enemies lick the dust.
Kings remote and legendary will pay homage,
    kings rich and resplendent will turn over their wealth.
All kings will fall down and worship,
    and godless nations sign up to serve him,
Because he rescues the poor at the first sign of need,
    the destitute who have run out of luck.
He opens a place in his heart for the down-and-out,
    he restores the wretched of the earth.
He frees them from tyranny and torture—
    when they bleed, he bleeds;
    when they die, he dies.


And live! Oh, let him live!
    Deck him out in Sheba gold.
Offer prayers unceasing to him,
    bless him from morning to night.
Fields of golden grain in the land,
    cresting the mountains in wild exuberance,
Cornucopias of praise, praises
    springing from the city like grass from the earth.
May he never be forgotten,
    his fame shine on like sunshine.

May all godless people enter his circle of blessing
　　and bless the One who blessed them.

Blessed GOD, Israel's God,
　　the one and only wonder-working God!
Blessed always his blazing glory!
　　All earth brims with his glory.
Yes and Yes and Yes.

### A David Psalm

**86.** Bend an ear, GOD; answer me.
　　I'm one miserable wretch!
Keep me safe — haven't I lived a good life?
　　Help your servant — I'm depending on you!
You're my God; have mercy on me.
　　I count on you from morning to night.
Give your servant a happy life;
　　I put myself in your hands!
You're well-known as good and forgiving,
　　bighearted to all who ask for help.
Pay attention, GOD, to my prayer;
　　bend down and listen to my cry for help.
Every time I'm in trouble I call on you,
　　confident that you'll answer.

There's no one quite like you among the gods, O Lord,
　　and nothing to compare with your works.
All the nations you made are on their way,
　　ready to give honor to you, O Lord,
Ready to put your beauty on display,
　　parading your greatness,
And the great things you do —
　　God, you're the one, there's no one but you!

Train me, GOD, to walk straight;
    then I'll follow your true path.
Put me together, one heart and mind;
    then, undivided, I'll worship in joyful fear.

---

▶ **What does David mean by "one heart and mind; . . . undivided"?** Throughout the ancient Scriptures, the heart refers to the nonmaterial elements of the human being—the soul, the spirit, the mind. Whereas the brain is the material cause of neurological activity, the mind is the immaterial source of thought, reason, emotion, and conscience. That's what sets us apart from other animals—we have a soul at the heart of our being.

An undivided heart means that our thoughts and emotions (our immaterial source code) are pure, selfless, and forgiving—something that's impossible to attain by human effort. However, David understands that the first step toward achieving an undivided heart is a genuine focus on God and his ways.

---

From the bottom of my heart I thank you, dear Lord;
    I've never kept secret what you're up to.
You've always been great toward me — what love!
    You snatched me from the brink of disaster!
God, these bullies have reared their heads!
    A gang of thugs is after me —
    and they don't care a thing about you.
But you, O God, are both tender and kind,
    not easily angered, immense in love,
    and you never, never quit.
So look me in the eye and show kindness,
    give your servant the strength to go on,
    save your dear, dear child!
Make a show of how much you love me
    so the bullies who hate me will stand there slack-jawed,
As you, GOD, gently and powerfully
    put me back on my feet.

## A David Psalm

**101.** My theme song is God's love and justice,
    and I'm singing it right to you, GOD.
I'm finding my way down the road of right living,
    but how long before you show up?
I'm doing the very best I can,
    and I'm doing it at home, where it counts.
I refuse to take a second look
    at corrupting people and degrading things.
I reject made-in-Canaan gods,
    stay clear of contamination.
The crooked in heart keep their distance;
    I refuse to shake hands with those who plan evil.
I put a gag on the gossip
    who bad-mouths his neighbor;
I can't stand
    arrogance.
But I have my eye on salt-of-the-earth people —
    they're the ones I want working with me;
Men and women on the straight and narrow —
    these are the ones I want at my side.
But no one who traffics in lies
    gets a job with me; I have no patience with liars.
I've rounded up all the wicked like cattle
    and herded them right out of the country.
I purged GOD's city
    of all who make a business of evil.

## A David Psalm

**103.** O my soul, bless GOD.
    From head to toe, I'll bless his holy name!

O my soul, bless GOD,
>don't forget a single blessing!

>He forgives your sins — every one.
>He heals your diseases — every one.
>He redeems you from hell — saves your life!
>He crowns you with love and mercy — a paradise crown.
>He wraps you in goodness — beauty eternal.
>He renews your youth — you're always young in his presence.

GOD makes everything come out right;
>he puts victims back on their feet.

He showed Moses how he went about his work,
>opened up his plans to all Israel.

GOD is sheer mercy and grace;
>not easily angered, he's rich in love.

He doesn't endlessly nag and scold,
>nor hold grudges forever.

He doesn't treat us as our sins deserve,
>nor pay us back in full for our wrongs.

As high as heaven is over the earth,
>so strong is his love to those who fear him.

And as far as sunrise is from sunset,
>he has separated us from our sins.

As parents feel for their children,
>GOD feels for those who fear him.

He knows us inside and out,
>keeps in mind that we're made of mud.

Men and women don't live very long;
>like wildflowers they spring up and blossom,

But a storm snuffs them out just as quickly,
>leaving nothing to show they were here.

GOD's love, though, is ever and always,
>eternally present to all who fear him,

Making everything right for them and their children
     as they follow his Covenant ways
     and remember to do whatever he said.

GOD has set his throne in heaven;
     he rules over us all. He's the King!
So bless GOD, you angels,
     ready and able to fly at his bidding,
     quick to hear and do what he says.
Bless GOD, all you armies of angels,
     alert to respond to whatever he wills.
Bless GOD, all creatures, wherever you are —
     everything and everyone made by GOD.

And you, O my soul, bless GOD!

**A David Prayer**

# 108.
I'm ready, God, so ready,
     ready from head to toe.
Ready to sing,
     ready to raise a God-song:
"Wake, soul! Wake, lute!
     Wake up, you sleepyhead sun!"

I'm thanking you, GOD, out in the streets,
     singing your praises in town and country.
The deeper your love, the higher it goes;
     every cloud's a flag to your faithfulness.
Soar high in the skies, O God!
     Cover the whole earth with your glory!
And for the sake of the one you love so much,
     reach down and help me — answer me!

That's when God spoke in holy splendor:
    "Brimming over with joy,
I make a present of Shechem,
    I hand out Succoth Valley as a gift.
Gilead's in my pocket,
    to say nothing of Manasseh.
Ephraim's my hard hat,
    Judah my hammer.
Moab's a scrub bucket —
    I mop the floor with Moab,
Spit on Edom,
    rain fireworks all over Philistia."

Who will take me to the thick of the fight?
    Who'll show me the road to Edom?
You aren't giving up on us, are you, God?
    refusing to go out with our troops?

Give us help for the hard task;
    human help is worthless.
In God we'll do our very best;
    he'll flatten the opposition for good.

**A David Prayer**

**109.** My God, don't turn a deaf ear to my hallelujah prayer.
    Liars are pouring out invective on me;
Their lying tongues are like a pack of dogs out to get me,
    barking their hate, nipping my heels — and for no reason!
I loved them and now they slander me — yes, me! —
    and treat my prayer like a crime;
They return my good with evil,
    they return my love with hate.

Send the Evil One to accuse my accusing judge;
>   dispatch Satan to prosecute him.
When he's judged, let the verdict be "Guilty,"
>   and when he prays, let his prayer turn to sin.
Give him a short life,
>   and give his job to somebody else.
Make orphans of his children,
>   dress his wife in widow's weeds;
Turn his children into begging street urchins,
>   evicted from their homes — homeless.
May the bank foreclose and wipe him out,
>   and strangers, like vultures, pick him clean.
May there be no one around to help him out,
>   no one willing to give his orphans a break.
Chop down his family tree
>   so that nobody even remembers his name.
But erect a memorial to the sin of his father,
>   and make sure his mother's name is there, too —
Their sins recorded forever before GOD,
>   but they themselves sunk in oblivion.
That's all he deserves since he was never once kind,
>   hounded the afflicted and heartbroken to their graves.
Since he loved cursing so much,
>   let curses rain down;
Since he had no taste for blessing,
>   let blessings flee far from him.
He dressed up in curses like a fine suit of clothes;
>   he drank curses, took his baths in curses.
So give him a gift — a costume of curses;
>   he can wear curses every day of the week!
That's what they'll get, those out to get me —
>   an avalanche of just deserts from GOD.

Oh, GOD, my Lord, step in;
       work a miracle for me—you can do it!
Get me out of here—your love is so great!—
       I'm at the end of my rope, my life in ruins.
I'm fading away to nothing, passing away,
       my youth gone, old before my time.
I'm weak from hunger and can hardly stand up,
       my body a rack of skin and bones.
I'm a joke in poor taste to those who see me;
       they take one look and shake their heads.

Help me, oh help me, GOD, my God,
       save me through your wonderful love;
Then they'll know that your hand is in this,
       that you, GOD, have been at work.
Let them curse all they want;
       *you* do the blessing.
Let them be jeered by the crowd when they stand up,
       followed by cheers for me, your servant.
Dress my accusers in clothes dirty with shame,
       discarded and humiliating old ragbag clothes.

My mouth's full of great praise for GOD,
       I'm singing his hallelujahs surrounded by crowds,
For he's always at hand to take the side of the needy,
       to rescue a life from the unjust judge.

**A David Prayer**

**110.** The word of GOD to my Lord:
       "Sit alongside me here on my throne
              until I make your enemies a stool for your feet."
You were forged a strong scepter by GOD of Zion;
       now rule, though surrounded by enemies!
Your people will freely join you, resplendent in holy armor

on the great day of your conquest,
Join you at the fresh break of day,
    join you with all the vigor of youth.

GOD gave his word and he won't take it back:
    you're the permanent priest, the Melchizedek priest.
The Lord stands true at your side,
    crushing kings in his terrible wrath,
Bringing judgment on the nations,
    handing out convictions wholesale,
    crushing opposition across the wide earth.
The King-Maker put his King on the throne;
    the True King rules with head held high!

---

What is this all about? Is God asking David to sit alongside his throne? Or is this referring to someone else?

Remarkably, this passage literally starts with *Jehovah* said to *Adonai*. This is actually written as a conversation between God the Father and God the Son, and is known as one of the many "Messianic Psalms." A Messianic Psalm is a picture or prediction of a coming event related to the coming Messiah—the Savior of the world.

This psalm is quoted no less than twelve times in the New Testament texts written about 1,000 years after David. In Mark, Jesus uses this passage to set the religious teachers straight when they teach that the Messiah is the literal son of David. In Matthew, Jesus specifically applies this passage to himself claiming that he isn't just the son of David by lineage, but David's Lord (*Adonai*).

---

## A Pilgrim Song of David

**122.** When they said, "Let's go to the house of GOD,"
    my heart leaped for joy.
And now we're here, O Jerusalem,
    inside Jerusalem's walls!

Jerusalem, well-built city,
    built as a place for worship!

The city to which the tribes ascend,
     all GOD's tribes go up to worship,
To give thanks to the name of GOD —
     *this* is what it means to be Israel.
Thrones for righteous judgment
     are set there, famous David-thrones.

Pray for Jerusalem's peace!
     Prosperity to all you Jerusalem-lovers!
Friendly insiders, get along!
     Hostile outsiders, keep your distance!
For the sake of my family and friends,
     I say it again: live in peace!
For the sake of the house of our God, GOD,
     I'll do my very best for you.

## A Pilgrim Song of David

**124.** If GOD hadn't been for us
     — all together now, Israel, sing out! —
If GOD hadn't been for us
     when everyone went against us,
We would have been swallowed alive
     by their violent anger,
Swept away by the flood of rage,
     drowned in the torrent;
We would have lost our lives
     in the wild, raging water.

Oh, blessed be GOD!
     He didn't go off and leave us.
He didn't abandon us defenseless,
     helpless as a rabbit in a pack of snarling dogs.

We've flown free from their fangs,
　　free of their traps, free as a bird.
Their grip is broken;
　　we're free as a bird in flight.

GOD's strong name is our help,
　　the same GOD who made heaven and earth.


## A Pilgrim Song

**131.** GOD, I'm not trying to rule the roost,
　　　I don't want to be king of the mountain.
I haven't meddled where I have no business
　　or fantasized grandiose plans.

I've kept my feet on the ground,
　　I've cultivated a quiet heart.
Like a baby content in its mother's arms,
　　my soul is a baby content.

Wait, Israel, for GOD. Wait with hope.
　　Hope now; hope always!


## A Pilgrim Song of David

**133.** How wonderful, how beautiful,
　　　when brothers and sisters get along!
It's like costly anointing oil
　　flowing down head and beard,
Flowing down Aaron's beard,
　　flowing down the collar of his priestly robes.
It's like the dew on Mount Hermon
　　flowing down the slopes of Zion.

Yes, that's where GOD commands the blessing,
   ordains eternal life.


**A David Psalm**

**138.** Thank you! Everything in me says "Thank you!"
   Angels listen as I sing my thanks.
I kneel in worship facing your holy temple
   and say it again: "Thank you!"
Thank you for your love,
   thank you for your faithfulness;
Most holy is your name,
   most holy is your Word.
The moment I called out, you stepped in;
   you made my life large with strength.

When they hear what you have to say, GOD,
   all earth's kings will say "Thank you."
They'll sing of what you've done:
   "How great the glory of GOD!"
And here's why: GOD, high above, sees far below;
   no matter the distance, he knows everything about us.

When I walk into the thick of trouble,
   keep me alive in the angry turmoil.
With one hand
   strike my foes,
With your other hand
   save me.
Finish what you started in me, GOD.
   Your love is eternal — don't quit on me now.

## SEARCHER ON THE WAY

*A Legacy of Thanksgiving*

As a young colonel in the French and Indian War, George Washington faced a dramatic, life-changing event. During a fierce battle in 1755, Washington was one of dozens of officers who were singled-out by the Indian Chiefs as special targets. After a two-hour battle, Washington was the only officer on horseback not shot down.

After that bloody day, Washington made a practice of journaling his thanks to God. Similar to the psalmist, Washington wrote his heart to his Protector throughout his military and political career. Years later, after the successful creation of a new nation, President George Washington maintained his passion for *giving thanks where thanks are due*.

Although a rarely reported historical event, Washington called the people of the United States to a special day of Thanksgiving in 1789—the first of many Thanksgiving holidays to follow.

> Whereas it is the duty of all Nations to acknowledge the providence of Almighty God, to obey his will, to be grateful for his benefits, and humbly to implore his protection and favor—and whereas both Houses of Congress have by their joint Committee requested me "to recommend to the People of the United States a day of public thanksgiving and prayer to be observed by acknowledging with grateful hearts the many signal favors of Almighty God especially by affording them an opportunity peaceably to establish a form of government for their safety and happiness."
>
> Now therefore I do recommend and assign Thursday the 26th day of November next to be devoted by the People of these States to the service of that great and glorious Being, who is the

beneficent Author of all the good that was, that
is, or that will be—That we may then all unite in
rendering unto him our sincere and humble thanks.

## A David Psalm

**139.** GOD, investigate my life;
get all the facts firsthand.
I'm an open book to you;
even from a distance, you know what I'm thinking.
You know when I leave and when I get back;
I'm never out of your sight.
You know everything I'm going to say
before I start the first sentence.
I look behind me and you're there,
then up ahead and you're there, too—
your reassuring presence, coming and going.
This is too much, too wonderful—
I can't take it all in!

Is there anyplace I can go to avoid your Spirit?
to be out of your sight?
If I climb to the sky, you're there!
If I go underground, you're there!
If I flew on morning's wings
to the far western horizon,
You'd find me in a minute—
you're already there waiting!
Then I said to myself, "Oh, he even sees me in the dark!
At night I'm immersed in the light!"
It's a fact: darkness isn't dark to you;
night and day, darkness and light, they're all the same to you.

Oh yes, you shaped me first inside, then out;
    you formed me in my mother's womb.
I thank you, High God — you're breathtaking!
    Body and soul, I am marvelously made!
    I worship in adoration — what a creation!
You know me inside and out,
    you know every bone in my body;
You know exactly how I was made, bit by bit,
    how I was sculpted from nothing into something.
Like an open book, you watched me grow from conception to birth;
    all the stages of my life were spread out before you,
The days of my life all prepared
    before I'd even lived one day.

---

A fertilized human egg at the moment of conception looks like a simple, single-celled blob no bigger than a pinhead. However, we now know that amorphous blob contains information equivalent to 6 billion "chemical letters"—enough complex code to fill 1,000 books, 500 pages thick, with print so small that it would take a microscope to read it.

Through the marvel of DNA, every single human trait is established at the moment of conception. Within hours, that single cell starts reproducing and grows a cilia propulsion system to move the fertilized egg toward the uterus. Within six days, the original cell has reproduced its library of information over 100 times. Ultimately, that original blob of gelatin will divide into the 30 trillion cells that make up the human body.

Within four days of fertilization, the sex of a baby can be determined through microscopic techniques. Soon after one week of fertilization, the baby contains the beginning of all major body structures. Fetal circulation occurs by three weeks—complete with heart and major blood vessels coursing through its quarter-inch frame. And at five weeks, all basic body systems are developing, including the brain and nervous system.

---

Your thoughts — how rare, how beautiful!
    God, I'll never comprehend them!
I couldn't even begin to count them —
    any more than I could count the sand of the sea.
Oh, let me rise in the morning and live always with you!
    And please, God, do away with wickedness for good!

And you murderers — out of here! —
  all the men and women who belittle you, God,
  infatuated with cheap god-imitations.
See how I hate those who hate you, GOD,
  see how I loathe all this godless arrogance;
I hate it with pure, unadulterated hatred.
  Your enemies are my enemies!

Investigate my life, O God,
  find out everything about me;
Cross-examine and test me,
  get a clear picture of what I'm about;
See for yourself whether I've done anything wrong —
  then guide me on the road to eternal life.

## A David Psalm

**140.** GOD, get me out of here, away from this evil;
  protect me from these vicious people.
All they do is think up new ways to be bad;
  they spend their days plotting war games.
They practice the sharp rhetoric of hate and hurt,
  speak venomous words that maim and kill.
GOD, keep me out of the clutch of these wicked ones,
  protect me from these vicious people;
Stuffed with self-importance, they plot ways to trip me up,
  determined to bring me down.
These crooks invent traps to catch me
  and do their best to incriminate me.

I prayed, "GOD, you're my God!
  Listen, GOD! Mercy!
GOD, my Lord, Strong Savior,
  protect me when the fighting breaks out!

Don't let the wicked have their way, GOD,
  don't give them an inch!"

These troublemakers all around me —
  let them drown in their own verbal poison.
Let God pile hellfire on them,
  let him bury them alive in crevasses!
These loudmouths —
  don't let them be taken seriously;
These savages —
  let the Devil hunt them down!

I know that you, GOD, are on the side of victims,
  that you care for the rights of the poor.
And I know that the righteous personally thank you,
  that good people are secure in your presence.

## A David Psalm

**141.** GOD, come close. Come quickly!
  Open your ears — it's my voice you're hearing!
Treat my prayer as sweet incense rising;
  my raised hands are my evening prayers.

Post a guard at my mouth, GOD,
  set a watch at the door of my lips.
Don't let me so much as dream of evil
  or thoughtlessly fall into bad company.
And these people who only do wrong —
  don't let them lure me with their sweet talk!
May the Just One set me straight,
  may the Kind One correct me,
Don't let sin anoint my head.
  I'm praying hard against their evil ways!

Oh, let their leaders be pushed off a high rock cliff;
    make them face the music.
Like a rock pulverized by a maul,
    let their bones be scattered at the gates of hell.

But GOD, dear Lord,
    I only have eyes for you.
Since I've run for dear life to you,
    take good care of me.
Protect me from their evil scheming,
    from all their demonic subterfuge.
Let the wicked fall flat on their faces,
    while I walk off without a scratch.

## A David Prayer — When He Was in the Cave

**142.** I cry out loudly to GOD,
    loudly I plead with GOD for mercy.
I spill out all my complaints before him,
    and spell out my troubles in detail:

"As I sink in despair, my spirit ebbing away,
    you know how I'm feeling,
Know the danger I'm in,
    the traps hidden in my path.
Look right, look left —
    there's not a soul who cares what happens!
I'm up against it, with no exit —
    bereft, left alone.
I cry out, GOD, call out:
    'You're my last chance, my only hope for life!'
Oh listen, please listen;
    I've never been this low.
Rescue me from those who are hunting me down;

I'm no match for them.
Get me out of this dungeon
    so I can thank you in public.
Your people will form a circle around me
    and you'll bring me showers of blessing!

## SEARCHER ON THE WAY
*No Pit So Deep*

Corrie Ten Boom was born in the Netherlands in 1892. She worked as a watchmaker in the family business, living with her father and sister. When she was forty-eight, Holland fell to the Nazis. Her Christian family was very connected with the Jewish community in Holland, so she sought ways to support her friends with food and temporary shelter. Soon, this effort turned to full-scale involvement in the Dutch underground, where she hid people in a false wall in her home until secret locations could be found in the countryside.

After a year and a half, her family's kindness and courage were known throughout the Jewish community. However, in 1944, they were duped by a Nazi informant and turned over to the Gestapo. Corrie's father died within days, while Corrie and her sister, Betsie, started a horrific journey through a series of concentration camps in Holland and Germany.

Through it all, Corrie and Betsie stood on their faith—providing hope to their fellow inmates. They read from a secret Bible and held services whenever possible. Although Betsie died within a few months, she remained a spiritual rock to the end. Some of her last words were, "(We) must tell them what we have learned here. We must tell them that there is no pit so deep that He is not deeper still. They will listen to us, Corrie, because we have been here."

Due to an administrative oversight, Corrie was released one week before her portion of the camp was scheduled for death. She returned to her hometown but found nothing left for her there. Understanding her legacy, she began traveling and telling her story. She saw God in the depths of despair, and she spent the rest of her life sharing him with others.

## A David Psalm

**143.** Listen to this prayer of mine, GOD;
pay attention to what I'm asking.
Answer me — you're famous for your answers!
Do what's right for me.
But don't, please don't, haul me into court;
not a person alive would be acquitted there.

The enemy hunted me down;
he kicked me and stomped me within an inch of my life.
He put me in a black hole,
buried me like a corpse in that dungeon.
I sat there in despair, my spirit draining away,
my heart heavy, like lead.
I remembered the old days,
went over all you've done, pondered the ways you've worked,
Stretched out my hands to you,
as thirsty for you as a desert thirsty for rain.

Hurry with your answer, GOD!
I'm nearly at the end of my rope.
Don't turn away; don't ignore me!
That would be certain death.
If you wake me each morning with the sound of your loving voice,
I'll go to sleep each night trusting in you.
Point out the road I must travel;
I'm all ears, all eyes before you.
Save me from my enemies, GOD —
you're my only hope!
Teach me how to live to please you,
because you're my God.
Lead me by your blessed Spirit
into cleared and level pastureland.

Keep up your reputation, God — give me life!
    In your justice, get me out of this trouble!
In your great love, vanquish my enemies;
    make a clean sweep of those who harass me.
And why? Because I'm your servant.

## A David Psalm

**144.** Blessed be GOD, my mountain,
    who trains me to fight fair and well.
He's the bedrock on which I stand,
    the castle in which I live,
    my rescuing knight,
The high crag where I run for dear life,
    while he lays my enemies low.

I wonder why you care, GOD —
    why do you bother with us at all?
All we are is a puff of air;
    we're like shadows in a campfire.

Step down out of heaven, GOD;
    ignite volcanoes in the hearts of the mountains.
Hurl your lightnings in every direction;
    shoot your arrows this way and that.
Reach all the way from sky to sea:
    pull me out of the ocean of hate,
    out of the grip of those barbarians
Who lie through their teeth,
    who shake your hand
    then knife you in the back.

O God, let me sing a new song to you,
    let me play it on a twelve-string guitar —

A song to the God who saved the king,
    the God who rescued David, his servant.

Rescue me from the enemy sword,
    release me from the grip of those barbarians
Who lie through their teeth,
    who shake your hand
    then knife you in the back.

Make our sons in their prime
    like sturdy oak trees,
Our daughters as shapely and bright
    as fields of wildflowers.
Fill our barns with great harvest,
    fill our fields with huge flocks;
Protect us from invasion and exile —
    eliminate the crime in our streets.

How blessed the people who have all this!
How blessed the people who have GOD for God!

---

David was a musician at heart. It seems that most of his psalms were written for instruments. In fact, during his reign as king, David had an orchestra of 4,000 people who "played" the psalms as a form of public worship. The Chronicles of Israel provide us with a record of the six primary instruments used in ancient Jewish worship: the lyre, harp, flute, pipe, horn, trumpet, tambourine, and cymbal.

The stringed instruments consisted of the lyre and the harp. The lyre was a ten-stringed, rectangular zither, while the harp was a louder, lower-pitched, vertical instrument. The wind instruments consisted of the flute, pipe, horn, and trumpet. The flute was made of reeds and was also known as a shepherd's pipe. The pipe was similar to a modern oboe and was also known as a *chalil*. The horn was a simple ram's horn known as a *shofar*, which was used for long, ceremonial blasts. The trumpet was a more complicated instrument with a mouthpiece, straight tube, and bell shape at the end. The rhythm instruments consisted of the tambourine and cymbals. The tambourine was used primarily as a small drum, while small and large cymbals were used for dramatic percussion.

---

## David's Praise

**145.** I lift you high in praise, my God, O my King!
and I'll bless your name into eternity.

I'll bless you every day,
and keep it up from now to eternity.

GOD is magnificent; he can never be praised enough.
There are no boundaries to his greatness.

Generation after generation stands in awe of your work;
each one tells stories of your mighty acts.

Your beauty and splendor have everyone talking;
I compose songs on your wonders.

Your marvelous doings are headline news;
I could write a book full of the details of your greatness.

The fame of your goodness spreads across the country;
your righteousness is on everyone's lips.

GOD is all mercy and grace —
not quick to anger, is rich in love.

GOD is good to one and all;
everything he does is suffused with grace.

Creation and creatures applaud you, GOD;
your holy people bless you.

They talk about the glories of your rule,
they exclaim over your splendor,

Letting the world know of your power for good,

the lavish splendor of your kingdom.

Your kingdom is a kingdom eternal;
    you never get voted out of office.

GOD always does what he says,
    and is gracious in everything he does.

GOD gives a hand to those down on their luck,
    gives a fresh start to those ready to quit.

All eyes are on you, expectant;
    you give them their meals on time.

Generous to a fault,
    you lavish your favor on all creatures.

Everything GOD does is right —
    the trademark on all his works is love.

GOD's there, listening for all who pray,
    for all who pray and mean it.

He does what's best for those who fear him —
    hears them call out, and saves them.

GOD sticks by all who love him,
    but it's all over for those who don't.

My mouth is filled with GOD's praise.
    Let everything living bless him,
    bless his holy name from now to eternity!

Life is a passage of perplexity, and we all get through it in different ways. Here, David concludes his journey with praise. He takes all of his heartaches, lessons, and epiphanies and wraps them together in this final acrostic hymn. In the end, David praises God for his mighty acts throughout history, his ultimate sovereignty throughout eternity, and his miraculous response to those who truly seek him throughout humanity.

David brings us back to the simple conclusions of the other "journeyers" we read. Ultimately, all these participants in the *Great Pursuit* acknowledge their fallen and frustrated condition. They realize their rebellious nature and trust that everything God does is right.

In that place of understanding, God's patience, mercy, and grace start shining through on the dull finish of our being. In his patience, God allows us to make mistakes and turn from our selfish ways. In his mercy, God tempers his anger and holds back his ultimate wrath. In his grace, God knows that we can't do life on our own, so he showers us with his undeserved favor.

However, all of these journeys—all of these ancient accounts—seem to leave us hanging in some way. Do you see it? Each journeyer reaches the conclusion that there's got to be more than mere physical existence.

Alexander the Great conquered the known world of his time. When done, he wept, because "there were no more worlds to conquer."

Okay, here it is. When you come right down to it, the last thing to conquer is death itself—the meaningful survival of our own souls. David understands this when he says, "Investigate my life, O God, find out everything about me . . . then guide me on the road to eternal life."

Go back and read Ecclesiastes. The Quester's conclusion was "Fear God. Do what he tells you." Why? "Eventually God will bring everything that we do out into the open and judge it according to its hidden intent."

Reexamine Job. He came to the same conclusion via the path of suffering. He finally rested in the mystery of almighty God. He also trusted in his eternal redeemer, "the One who gives me back my life."

By different journeys and through different words, the pursuers ultimately realized their need for salvation outside of themselves. But how? But who?

David called him the Messiah. Other ancient writers called him Shiloh, Redeemer, Immanuel, Wonderful Counselor, Mighty God, the Prince of Peace, the coming Ruler, and the Son of God.

Hundreds of years pass, and then something remarkable happens.

# MARK

## INTRODUCTION TO MARK

Mark wastes no time in getting down to business—a single-sentence introduction, and not a digression to be found from beginning to end. An event has taken place that radically changes the way we look at and experience the world, and he can't wait to tell us about it. There's an air of breathless excitement in nearly every sentence he writes. The sooner we get the message, the better off we'll be, for the message is good, incredibly good: God is here, and he's on our side.

The bare announcement that God exists doesn't particularly qualify as news. Most people in most centuries have believed in the existence of God or gods. It may well be, in fact, that human beings in aggregate and through the centuries have given more attention and concern to divinity than to all their other concerns put together—food, housing, clothing, pleasure, work, family, whatever.

But that God is here right now, and on our side, actively seeking to help us in the way we most need help—*this* qualifies as news. For, common as belief in God is, there is also an enormous amount of guesswork and gossip surrounding the subject, which results in runaway superstition, anxiety, and exploitation. So Mark, understandably, is in a hurry to tell us what happened in the birth, life, death, and resurrection of Jesus—the Event that reveals the truth of God to us, so that we can live in reality and not illusion. He doesn't want us to waste a minute of these precious lives of ours ignorant of this most practical of all matters—that God is passionate to save us.

## John the Baptizer

**01.** The good news of Jesus Christ — the Message! — begins here, following to the letter the scroll of the prophet Isaiah.

Watch closely: I'm sending my preacher ahead of you;
He'll make the road smooth for you.
Thunder in the desert!
Prepare for God's arrival!
Make the road smooth and straight!

Beginning in 1947, the world discovered the ancient Jewish Scriptures, including texts and fragments from every book in our current Old Testament (except Esther), sitting miraculously intact in a cluster of desert caves near the Dead Sea in Israel. Now we have compelling proof that the Jewish prophecies of a coming Messiah predated Jesus. We now hold copies of great texts such as Isaiah, Daniel, and the Psalms that have been dated to at least 100 BC by a number of scientific methods (including paleographic, scribal, and carbon 14 dating). Why is this dramatic? Because the prophecies of a coming Messiah were not contrived or manipulated after the fact!

Here, John the Baptist refers to the scroll of Isaiah, which was originally penned by the prophet in the mid-700s BC. Remarkably, we can now view an entire manuscript copy of Isaiah at the Shrine of the Book Museum in Jerusalem, which paleographers date to between 150 and 125 BC, and radiocarbon labs date to between 335 and 122 BC. Thus, we have profound assurance that the book of Isaiah we read today is the same text that existed prior to the birth and ministry of Jesus Christ.

John the Baptizer appeared in the wild, preaching a baptism of life-change that leads to forgiveness of sins. People thronged to him from Judea and Jerusalem and, as they confessed their sins, were baptized by him in the Jordan River into a changed life. John wore a camel-hair habit, tied at the waist with a leather belt. He ate locusts and wild field honey.

As he preached he said, "The real action comes next: The star in this drama, to whom I'm a mere stagehand, will change your life. I'm baptizing you here in the river, turning your old life in for a kingdom life. His baptism — a holy baptism by the Holy Spirit — will change you from the inside out."

At this time, Jesus came from Nazareth in Galilee and was baptized by John in the Jordan. The moment he came out of the water, he saw the sky split open and God's Spirit, looking like a dove, come down on him. Along with the Spirit, a voice: "You are my Son, chosen and marked by my love, pride of my life."

## God's Kingdom Is Here

At once, this same Spirit pushed Jesus out into the wild. For forty wilderness days and nights he was tested by Satan. Wild animals were his companions, and angels took care of him.

After John was arrested, Jesus went to Galilee preaching the Message of God: "Time's up! God's kingdom is here. Change your life and believe the Message."

Passing along the beach of Lake Galilee, he saw Simon and his brother Andrew net-fishing. Fishing was their regular work. Jesus said to them, "Come with me. I'll make a new kind of fisherman out of you. I'll show you how to catch men and women instead of perch and bass." They didn't ask questions. They dropped their nets and followed.

A dozen yards or so down the beach, he saw the brothers James and John, Zebedee's sons. They were in the boat, mending their fishnets. Right off, he made the same offer. Immediately, they left their father Zebedee, the boat, and the hired hands, and followed.

## Confident Teaching

Then they entered Capernaum. When the Sabbath arrived, Jesus lost no time in getting to the meeting place. He spent the day there teaching. They were surprised at his teaching — so forthright, so confident — not quibbling and quoting like the religion scholars.

Suddenly, while still in the meeting place, he was interrupted by a man who was deeply disturbed and yelling out, "What business do you have here with us, Jesus? Nazarene! I know what you're up to! You're the Holy One of God, and you've come to destroy us!"

Jesus shut him up: "Quiet! Get out of him!" The afflicting spirit threw the man into spasms, protesting loudly — and got out.

Everyone there was incredulous, buzzing with curiosity. "What's going on here? A new teaching that does what it says? He shuts up defiling, demonic spirits and sends them packing!" News of this traveled fast and was soon all over Galilee.

Directly on leaving the meeting place, they came to Simon and Andrew's house, accompanied by James and John. Simon's mother-in-law was sick in bed, burning up with fever. They told Jesus. He went to her, took her hand, and raised her up. No sooner had the fever left than she was up fixing dinner for them.

That evening, after the sun was down, they brought sick and evil-afflicted people to him, the whole city lined up at his door! He cured their sick bodies and tormented spirits. Because the demons knew his true identity, he didn't let them say a word.

## The Leper

While it was still night, way before dawn, he got up and went out to a secluded spot and prayed. Simon and those with him went looking for him. They found him and said, "Everybody's looking for you."

Jesus said, "Let's go to the rest of the villages so I can preach there also. This is why I've come." He went to their meeting places all through Galilee, preaching and throwing out the demons.

A leper came to him, begging on his knees, "If you want to, you can cleanse me."

Deeply moved, Jesus put out his hand, touched him, and said, "I want to. Be clean." Then and there the leprosy was gone, his skin smooth and healthy. Jesus dismissed him with strict orders: "Say nothing to anyone. Take the offering for cleansing that Moses prescribed and present yourself to the priest. This will validate your healing to the people." But as soon as the man was out of earshot, he told everyone he met what had happened, spreading the news all over town. So Jesus kept to out-of-the-way places, no longer able to move freely in and out of the city. But people found him, and came from all over.

## A Paraplegic

**02.** After a few days, Jesus returned to Capernaum, and word got around that he was back home. A crowd gathered, jamming the entrance so no one could get in or out. He was teaching the Word. They brought a paraplegic to him, carried by four men. When they weren't able to get in because of the crowd, they removed part of the roof and lowered the paraplegic on his stretcher. Impressed by their bold belief, Jesus said to the paraplegic, "Son, I forgive your sins."

Some religion scholars sitting there started whispering among themselves, "He can't talk that way! That's blasphemy! God and only God can forgive sins."

Jesus knew right away what they were thinking, and said, "Why are you so skeptical? Which is simpler: to say to the paraplegic, 'I forgive your sins,' or say, 'Get up, take your stretcher, and start walking'? Well, just so it's clear that I'm the Son of Man and authorized to do either, or both . . ." (he looked now at the paraplegic), "Get up. Pick up your stretcher and go home." And the man did it — got up, grabbed his stretcher, and walked out, with everyone there watching him. They rubbed their eyes, incredulous — and then praised God, saying, "We've never seen anything like this!"

## The Tax Collector

Then Jesus went again to walk alongside the lake. Again a crowd came to him, and he taught them. Strolling along, he saw Levi, son of Alphaeus, at his work collecting taxes. Jesus said, "Come along with me." He came.

Later Jesus and his disciples were at home having supper with a collection of disreputable guests. Unlikely as it seems, more than a few of them had become followers. The religion scholars and Pharisees saw him keeping this kind of company and lit into his disciples: "What kind of example is this, acting cozy with the riffraff?"

Jesus, overhearing, shot back, "Who needs a doctor: the healthy or the sick? I'm here inviting the sin-sick, not the spiritually-fit."

---

▶ **Who were these religious scholars called the Pharisees? Why do they seem to pop up wherever Jesus is teaching and healing the people?**

The Pharisees were successors to the Jewish Hasidim, the religious elite who joined with the Maccabees during the revolt against Syrian control in 166-142 BC. The label "Pharisees" first surfaced during the reign of Hyrcanus sometime between 135-105 BC.

The Pharisees were the self-proclaimed keepers of the Jewish religion. Although some must have been godly men, most were known for their rigid rules and rituals. The core of their theology was that God only extends grace to those who keep his law. Guess what? The Pharisees were the men who often defined and redefined God's Law. Yes, they were the hypocrites of the day, and they saw Jesus as a threat to the machine.

---

## Feasting or Fasting?

The disciples of John and the disciples of the Pharisees made a practice of fasting. Some people confronted Jesus: "Why do the followers of John and the Pharisees take on the discipline of fasting, but your followers don't?"

Jesus said, "When you're celebrating a wedding, you don't skimp on the cake and wine. You feast. Later you may need to pull in your belt, but not now. As long as the bride and groom are with you, you have a good time. No one throws cold water on a friendly bonfire. This is Kingdom Come!"

He went on, "No one cuts up a fine silk scarf to patch old work clothes; you want fabrics that match. And you don't put your wine in cracked bottles."

One Sabbath day he was walking through a field of ripe grain. As his disciples made a path, they pulled off heads of grain. The Pharisees told on them to Jesus: "Look, your disciples are breaking Sabbath rules!"

Jesus said, "Really? Haven't you ever read what David did when he was hungry, along with those who were with him? How he entered the sanctuary and ate fresh bread off the altar, with the Chief Priest Abiathar right there watching — holy bread that no one but priests were allowed to eat — and handed it out to his companions?" Then Jesus said, "The Sabbath was made to serve us; we weren't made to serve the Sabbath. The Son of Man is no lackey to the Sabbath. He's in charge!"

### Doing Good on the Sabbath

**03.** Then he went back in the meeting place where he found a man with a crippled hand. The Pharisees had their eyes on Jesus to see if he would heal him, hoping to catch him in a Sabbath infraction. He said to the man with the crippled hand, "Stand here where we can see you."

Then he spoke to the people: "What kind of action suits the Sabbath best? Doing good or doing evil? Helping people or leaving them helpless?" No one said a word.

He looked them in the eye, one after another, angry now, furious at their hard-nosed religion. He said to the man, "Hold out your hand." He held it out — it was as good as new! The Pharisees got out as fast as they could, sputtering about how they would join forces with Herod's followers and ruin him.

### The Twelve Apostles

Jesus went off with his disciples to the sea to get away. But a huge crowd from Galilee trailed after them — also from Judea, Jerusalem, Idumea, across the Jordan, and around Tyre and Sidon — swarms of people who had heard the reports and had come to see for themselves. He told his disciples to get a boat ready so he wouldn't be trampled by the crowd. He had healed many people, and now everyone who had something wrong was pushing and shoving to get near and touch him.

Evil spirits, when they recognized him, fell down and cried out, "You are the Son of God!" But Jesus would have none of it. He shut them up, forbidding them to identify him in public.

He climbed a mountain and invited those he wanted with him. They climbed together. He settled on twelve, and designated them apostles. The plan was that they would be with him, and he would send them out to proclaim the Word and give them authority to banish demons. These are the Twelve:

Simon (Jesus later named him Peter, meaning "Rock"),
James, son of Zebedee,
John, brother of James (Jesus nicknamed the Zebedee
    brothers Boanerges, meaning "Sons of Thunder"),
Andrew,
Philip,
Bartholomew,
Matthew,
Thomas,
James, son of Alphaeus,
Thaddaeus,
Simon the Canaanite,
Judas Iscariot (who betrayed him).

Flavius Josephus (AD 37-100) was a Jewish general and member of the priestly aristocracy of the Jews. During the great Jewish revolt of AD 66-70, he decided to protect his own hide and turned to the side of the Roman Empire. Josephus spent the rest of his life in or around Rome as an advisor and historian to three emperors: Vespasian, Titus, and Domitian. For centuries, the works of Josephus were more widely read in Europe than any book other than the Bible.

Josephus is widely known for his invaluable accounts of ancient Jewish history. However, his works are also powerful sources of eyewitness testimony to the development of Western civilization, including the foundation and growth of Christianity in the first century.

Josephus was a Jew, writing as a Roman historian. He was simply a scribe of the historical record. Here's what he recorded in book 18 of his *Antiquities* (translated from a surviving Arabic manuscript):

> At this time there was a wise man who was called Jesus. And his conduct was good, and he was known to be virtuous. And many people from among the Jews and other nations became his disciples. Pilate condemned him to be crucified and to die. And those who had become his disciples did not abandon his discipleship. They reported that he had appeared to them three days after his crucifixion and that he was alive; accordingly, he was perhaps the Messiah concerning whom the prophets have recounted wonders.

Shlomo Pines, a well known Jewish scholar, discussed this reference to Jesus by Josephus in *The Testamonium Flavianum and Its Implications:*

> As far as probabilities go, no believing Christian

could have produced such a neutral text: for him
the only significant point about it could have been
its attesting the historical evidence of Jesus.

## Satan Fighting Satan?

Jesus came home and, as usual, a crowd gathered—so many making demands on him that there wasn't even time to eat. His friends heard what was going on and went to rescue him, by force if necessary. They suspected he was getting carried away with himself.

The religion scholars from Jerusalem came down spreading rumors that he was working black magic, using devil tricks to impress them with spiritual power. Jesus confronted their slander with a story: "Does it make sense to send a devil to catch a devil, to use Satan to get rid of Satan? A constantly squabbling family disintegrates. If Satan were fighting Satan, there soon wouldn't be any Satan left. Do you think it's possible in broad daylight to enter the house of an awake, able-bodied man, and walk off with his possessions unless you tie him up first? Tie him up, though, and you can clean him out.

"Listen to this carefully. I'm warning you. There's nothing done or said that can't be forgiven. But if you persist in your slanders against God's Holy Spirit, you are repudiating the very One who forgives, sawing off the branch on which you're sitting, severing by your own perversity all connection with the One who forgives." He gave this warning because they were accusing him of being in league with Evil.

## Jesus' Mother and Brothers

Just then his mother and brothers showed up. Standing outside, they relayed a message that they wanted a word with him. He was surrounded by the crowd when he was given the message, "Your mother and brothers and sisters are outside looking for you."

Jesus responded, "Who do you think are my mother and brothers?" Looking around, taking in everyone seated around him, he said, "Right here, right in front of you — my mother and my brothers. Obedience is thicker than blood. The person who obeys God's will is my brother and sister and mother."

### The Story of the Scattered Seed

**04.** He went back to teaching by the sea. A crowd built up to such a great size that he had to get into an offshore boat, using the boat as a pulpit as the people pushed to the water's edge. He taught by using stories, many stories.

"Listen. What do you make of this? A farmer planted seed. As he scattered the seed, some of it fell on the road and birds ate it. Some fell in the gravel; it sprouted quickly but didn't put down roots, so when the sun came up it withered just as quickly. Some fell in the weeds; as it came up, it was strangled among the weeds and nothing came of it. Some fell on good earth and came up with a flourish, producing a harvest exceeding his wildest dreams.

"Are you listening to this? Really listening?"

When they were off by themselves, those who were close to him, along with the Twelve, asked about the stories. He told them, "You've been given insight into God's kingdom — you know how it works. But to those who can't see it yet, everything comes in stories, creating readiness, nudging them toward receptive insight. These are people —

Whose eyes are open but don't see a thing,
Whose ears are open but don't understand a word,
Who avoid making an about-face and getting forgiven."

He continued, "Do you see how this story works? All my stories work this way.

"The farmer plants the Word. Some people are like the seed that falls on the hardened soil of the road. No sooner do they hear the Word than Satan snatches away what has been planted in them.

"And some are like the seed that lands in the gravel. When they first hear the Word, they respond with great enthusiasm. But there is such shallow soil of character that when the emotions wear off and some difficulty arrives, there is nothing to show for it.

"The seed cast in the weeds represents the ones who hear the kingdom news but are overwhelmed with worries about all the things they have to do and all the things they want to get. The stress strangles what they heard, and nothing comes of it.

"But the seed planted in the good earth represents those who hear the Word, embrace it, and produce a harvest beyond their wildest dreams."

### Giving, Not Getting

Jesus went on: "Does anyone bring a lamp home and put it under a wash-tub or beneath the bed? Don't you put it up on a table or on the mantel? We're not keeping secrets, we're telling them; we're not hiding things, we're bringing them out into the open.

"Are you listening to this? Really listening?

"Listen carefully to what I am saying—and be wary of the shrewd advice that tells you how to get ahead in the world on your own. Giving, not getting, is the way. Generosity begets generosity. Stinginess impoverishes."

### Never Without a Story

Then Jesus said, "God's kingdom is like seed thrown on a field by a man who then goes to bed and forgets about it. The seed sprouts and grows—he has no idea how it happens. The earth does it all without his help: first a green stem of grass, then a bud, then the ripened grain. When the grain is fully formed, he reaps—harvest time!

"How can we picture God's kingdom? What kind of story can we use? It's like a pine nut. When it lands on the ground it is quite small as seeds go, yet once it is planted it grows into a huge pine tree with thick branches. Eagles nest in it."

With many stories like these, he presented his message to them, fitting the stories to their experience and maturity. He was never without a story when he spoke. When he was alone with his disciples, he went over everything, sorting out the tangles, untying the knots.

### The Wind Ran Out of Breath

Late that day he said to them, "Let's go across to the other side." They took him in the boat as he was. Other boats came along. A huge storm came up. Waves poured into the boat, threatening to sink it. And Jesus was in the stern, head on a pillow, sleeping! They roused him, saying, "Teacher, is it nothing to you that we're going down?"

Awake now, he told the wind to pipe down and said to the sea, "Quiet! Settle down!" The wind ran out of breath; the sea became smooth as glass. Jesus reprimanded the disciples: "Why are you such cowards? Don't you have any faith at all?"

They were in absolute awe, staggered. "Who is this, anyway?" they asked. "Wind and sea at his beck and call!"

### The Madman

**05.** They arrived on the other side of the sea in the country of the Gerasenes. As Jesus got out of the boat, a madman from the cemetery came up to him. He lived there among the tombs and graves. No one could restrain him — he couldn't be chained, couldn't be tied down. He had been tied up many times with chains and ropes, but he broke the chains, snapped the ropes. No one was strong enough to tame him. Night and day he roamed through the graves and the hills, screaming out and slashing himself with sharp stones.

When he saw Jesus a long way off, he ran and bowed in worship before him — then bellowed in protest, "What business do you have, Jesus, Son of the High God, messing with me? I swear to God, don't give me a hard time!" (Jesus had just commanded the tormenting evil spirit, "Out! Get out of the man!")

Jesus asked him, "Tell me your name."

He replied, "My name is Mob. I'm a rioting mob." Then he desperately begged Jesus not to banish them from the country.

A large herd of pigs was browsing and rooting on a nearby hill. The demons begged him, "Send us to the pigs so we can live in them." Jesus gave the order. But it was even worse for the pigs than for the man. Crazed, they stampeded over a cliff into the sea and drowned.

Those tending the pigs, scared to death, bolted and told their story in town and country. Everyone wanted to see what had happened. They came up to Jesus and saw the madman sitting there wearing decent clothes and making sense, no longer a walking madhouse of a man.

Those who had seen it told the others what had happened to the demon-possessed man and the pigs. At first they were in awe — and then they were upset, upset over the drowned pigs. They demanded that Jesus leave and not come back.

As Jesus was getting into the boat, the demon-delivered man begged to go along, but he wouldn't let him. Jesus said, "Go home to your own people. Tell them your story — what the Master did, how he had mercy on you." The man went back and began to preach in the Ten Towns area about what Jesus had done for him. He was the talk of the town.

## A Risk of Faith

After Jesus crossed over by boat, a large crowd met him at the seaside. One of the meeting-place leaders named Jairus came. When he saw Jesus, he fell to his knees, beside himself as he begged, "My dear daughter is at death's door. Come and lay hands on her so she will get well and live." Jesus went with him, the whole crowd tagging along, pushing and jostling him.

A woman who had suffered a condition of hemorrhaging for twelve years — a long succession of physicians had treated her, and treated her badly, taking all her money and leaving her worse off than before — had heard about Jesus. She slipped in from behind and touched his robe. She was thinking to herself, "If I can put a finger on his robe, I can get well." The moment she did it, the flow of blood dried up. She could feel the change and knew her plague was over and done with.

At the same moment, Jesus felt energy discharging from him. He turned around to the crowd and asked, "Who touched my robe?"

His disciples said, "What are you talking about? With this crowd pushing and jostling you, you're asking, 'Who touched me?' Dozens have touched you!"

But he went on asking, looking around to see who had done it. The woman, knowing what had happened, knowing she was the one, stepped up in fear and trembling, knelt before him, and gave him the whole story.

Jesus said to her, "Daughter, you took a risk of faith, and now you're healed and whole. Live well, live blessed! Be healed of your plague."

———

While he was still talking, some people came from the leader's house and told him, "Your daughter is dead. Why bother the Teacher any more?"

Jesus overheard what they were talking about and said to the leader, "Don't listen to them; just trust me."

He permitted no one to go in with him except Peter, James, and John. They entered the leader's house and pushed their way through the gossips looking for a story and neighbors bringing in casseroles. Jesus was abrupt: "Why all this busybody grief and gossip? This child isn't dead; she's sleeping." Provoked to sarcasm, they told him he didn't know what he was talking about.

But when he had sent them all out, he took the child's father and mother, along with his companions, and entered the child's room. He clasped the girl's hand and said, "*Talitha koum*," which means, "Little girl, get up." At that, she was up and walking around! This girl was twelve years of age. They, of course, were all beside themselves with joy. He gave them strict orders that no one was to know what had taken place in that room. Then he said, "Give her something to eat."

### Just a Carpenter

**06.** He left there and returned to his hometown. His disciples came along. On the Sabbath, he gave a lecture in the meeting place. He made a real hit, impressing everyone. "We had no idea he was this good!" they said. "How did he get so wise all of a sudden, get such ability?"

But in the next breath they were cutting him down: "He's just a carpenter—Mary's boy. We've known him since he was a kid. We know his brothers, James, Justus, Jude, and Simon, and his sisters. Who does he think he is?" They tripped over what little they knew about him and fell, sprawling. And they never got any further.

Jesus told them, "A prophet has little honor in his hometown, among his relatives, on the streets he played in as a child." Jesus wasn't able to do much of anything there—he laid hands on a few sick people and healed them, that's all. He couldn't get over their stubbornness. He left and made a circuit of the other villages, teaching.

### The Twelve

Jesus called the Twelve to him, and sent them out in pairs. He gave them authority and power to deal with the evil opposition. He sent them off with these instructions:

"Don't think you need a lot of extra equipment for this. *You* are the equipment. No special appeals for funds. Keep it simple.

"And no luxury inns. Get a modest place and be content there until you leave.

"If you're not welcomed, not listened to, quietly withdraw. Don't make a scene. Shrug your shoulders and be on your way."

Then they were on the road. They preached with joyful urgency that life can be radically different; right and left they sent the demons packing; they brought wellness to the sick, anointing their bodies, healing their spirits.

## The Death of John

King Herod heard of all this, for by this time the name of Jesus was on everyone's lips. He said, "This has to be John the Baptizer come back from the dead — that's why he's able to work miracles!"

Others said, "No, it's Elijah."

Others said, "He's a prophet, just like one of the old-time prophets."

But Herod wouldn't budge: "It's John, sure enough. I cut off his head, and now he's back, alive."

Herod was the one who had ordered the arrest of John, put him in chains, and sent him to prison at the nagging of Herodias, his brother Philip's wife. For John had provoked Herod by naming his relationship with Herodias "adultery." Herodias, smoldering with hate, wanted to kill him, but didn't dare because Herod was in awe of John. Convinced that he was a holy man, he gave him special treatment. Whenever he listened to him he was miserable with guilt — and yet he couldn't stay away. Something in John kept pulling him back.

But a portentous day arrived when Herod threw a birthday party, inviting all the brass and bluebloods in Galilee. Herodias's daughter entered the banquet hall and danced for the guests. She dazzled Herod and the guests.

The king said to the girl, "Ask me anything. I'll give you

anything you want." Carried away, he kept on, "I swear, I'll split my kingdom with you if you say so!"

She went back to her mother and said, "What should I ask for?"

"Ask for the head of John the Baptizer."

Excited, she ran back to the king and said, "I want the head of John the Baptizer served up on a platter. And I want it now!"

That sobered the king up fast. But unwilling to lose face with his guests, he caved in and let her have her wish. The king sent the executioner off to the prison with orders to bring back John's head. He went, cut off John's head, brought it back on a platter, and presented it to the girl, who gave it to her mother. When John's disciples heard about this, they came and got the body and gave it a decent burial.

## Supper for Five Thousand

The apostles then rendezvoused with Jesus and reported on all that they had done and taught. Jesus said, "Come off by yourselves; let's take a break and get a little rest." For there was constant coming and going. They didn't even have time to eat.

So they got in the boat and went off to a remote place by themselves. Someone saw them going and the word got around. From the surrounding towns people went out on foot, running, and got there ahead of them. When Jesus arrived, he saw this huge crowd. At the sight of them, his heart broke — like sheep with no shepherd they were. He went right to work teaching them.

When his disciples thought this had gone on long enough — it was now quite late in the day — they interrupted: "We are a long way out in the country, and it's very late. Pronounce a benediction and send these folks off so they can get some supper."

Jesus said, "You do it. Fix supper for them."

They replied, "Are you serious? You want us to go spend a fortune on food for their supper?"

But he was quite serious. "How many loaves of bread do you have? Take an inventory."

That didn't take long. "Five," they said, "plus two fish."

Jesus got them all to sit down in groups of fifty or a hundred — they looked like a patchwork quilt of wildflowers spread out on the green grass! He took the five loaves and two fish, lifted his face to heaven in prayer, blessed, broke, and gave the bread to the disciples, and the disciples in turn gave it to the people. He did the same with the fish. They all ate their fill. The disciples gathered twelve baskets of leftovers. More than five thousand were at the supper.

## Walking on the Sea

As soon as the meal was finished, Jesus insisted that the disciples get in the boat and go on ahead across to Bethsaida while he dismissed the congregation. After sending them off, he climbed a mountain to pray.

Late at night, the boat was far out at sea; Jesus was still by himself on land. He could see his men struggling with the oars, the wind having come up against them. At about four o'clock in the morning, Jesus came toward them, walking on the sea. He intended to go right by them. But when they saw him walking on the sea, they thought it was a ghost and screamed, scared out of their wits.

Jesus was quick to comfort them: "Courage! It's me. Don't be afraid." As soon as he climbed into the boat, the wind died down. They were stunned, shaking their heads, wondering what was going on. They didn't understand what he had done at the supper. None of this had yet penetrated their hearts.

They beached the boat at Gennesaret and tied up at the landing. As soon as they got out of the boat, word got around fast. People ran this way and that, bringing their sick on stretchers to where they heard he was. Wherever he went, village or town or country crossroads, they brought their sick to the marketplace and begged him to let them touch the edge of his coat — that's all. And whoever touched him became well.

During a major drought on the Sea of Galilee in 1986, two brothers noticed a distinct oval shape in the recently-revealed mud. Representatives of the Israel Department of Antiquities, who were mapping previously unknown harbors along the drought-stricken shoreline, including biblical Gennesaret and Tabgha, checked it out and confirmed that it was the remains of an ancient fishing vessel.

What happened next was remarkable. Working around the clock, the so-called "Galilee Boat" was exhumed from the mud over an eleven-day period in a painstaking process that preserved the fragile remains. The boat was wrapped in a polyurethane shell and then immersed in a special tank of water to avoid quick disintegration. Finally, over a period of years, the rotten wood was replaced, underwater, with a special wax. Ultimately, through a months-long process of gradually raising the water temperature, the wax-filled shell was removed from the tank and placed on display.

To date, multiple studies have placed the ancient vessel at 100 BC to AD 100. The structure and features of the boat are consistent with the fishing boats mentioned throughout the accounts of Mark, John, and the other New Testament writers.

## The Source of Your Pollution

**07.** The Pharisees, along with some religion scholars who had come from Jerusalem, gathered around him. They noticed that some of his disciples weren't being careful with ritual washings before meals. The Pharisees — Jews in general, in fact — would never eat a meal without going through the motions of a ritual hand-washing, with an especially vigorous scrubbing if they had just come from the market (to say nothing of the scourings they'd give jugs and pots and pans).

The Pharisees and religion scholars asked, "Why do your disciples flout the rules, showing up at meals without washing their hands?"

Jesus answered, "Isaiah was right about frauds like you, hit the bull's-eye in fact:

These people make a big show of saying the right thing,
but their heart isn't in it.

They act like they are worshiping me,
    but they don't mean it.
They just use me as a cover
    for teaching whatever suits their fancy,
Ditching God's command
    and taking up the latest fads."

He went on, "Well, good for you. You get rid of God's command so you won't be inconvenienced in following the religious fashions! Moses said, 'Respect your father and mother,' and, 'Anyone denouncing father or mother should be killed.' But you weasel out of that by saying that it's perfectly acceptable to say to father or mother, 'Gift! What I owed you I've given as a gift to God,' thus relieving yourselves of obligation to father or mother. You scratch out God's Word and scrawl a whim in its place. You do a lot of things like this."

Jesus called the crowd together again and said, "Listen now, all of you — take this to heart. It's not what you swallow that pollutes your life; it's what you vomit — that's the real pollution."

When he was back home after being with the crowd, his disciples said, "We don't get it. Put it in plain language."

Jesus said, "Are you being willfully stupid? Don't you see that what you swallow can't contaminate you? It doesn't enter your heart but your stomach, works its way through the intestines, and is finally flushed." (That took care of dietary quibbling; Jesus was saying that *all* foods are fit to eat.)

He went on: "It's what comes out of a person that pollutes: obscenities, lusts, thefts, murders, adulteries, greed, depravity, deceptive dealings, carousing, mean looks, slander, arrogance, foolishness — all these are vomit from the heart. *There* is the source of your pollution."

———

From there Jesus set out for the vicinity of Tyre. He entered a house there where he didn't think he would be found, but he couldn't escape notice. He was barely inside when a woman who had a disturbed daughter heard where he was. She came and knelt at his feet, begging for help. The woman was Greek, Syro-Phoenician by birth. She asked him to cure her daughter.

He said, "Stand in line and take your turn. The children get fed first. If there's any left over, the dogs get it."

She said, "Of course, Master. But don't dogs under the table get scraps dropped by the children?"

Jesus was impressed. "You're right! On your way! Your daughter is no longer disturbed. The demonic affliction is gone." She went home and found her daughter relaxed on the bed, the torment gone for good.

Then he left the region of Tyre, went through Sidon back to Galilee Lake and over to the district of the Ten Towns. Some people brought a man who could neither hear nor speak and asked Jesus to lay a healing hand on him. He took the man off by himself, put his fingers in the man's ears and some spit on the man's tongue. Then Jesus looked up in prayer, groaned mightily, and commanded, "*Ephphatha!* — Open up!" And it happened. The man's hearing was clear and his speech plain — just like that.

Jesus urged them to keep it quiet, but they talked it up all the more, beside themselves with excitement. "He's done it all and done it well. He gives hearing to the deaf, speech to the speechless."

### A Meal for Four Thousand

**08.** At about this same time he again found himself with a hungry crowd on his hands. He called his disciples together and said, "This crowd is breaking my heart. They have stuck with me for three days, and now they have nothing to eat. If I send them home hungry, they'll faint along the way — some of them have come a long distance."

His disciples responded, "What do you expect us to do about it? Buy food out here in the desert?"

He asked, "How much bread do you have?"

"Seven loaves," they said.

So Jesus told the crowd to sit down on the ground. After giving thanks, he took the seven bread loaves, broke them into pieces, and gave them to his disciples so they could hand them out to the crowd. They also had a few fish. He pronounced a blessing over the fish and told his disciples to hand them out as well. The crowd ate its fill. Seven sacks of leftovers were collected. There were well over four thousand at the meal. Then he sent them home. He himself went straight to the boat with his disciples and set out for Dalmanoutha.

When they arrived, the Pharisees came out and started in on him, badgering him to prove himself, pushing him up against the wall. Provoked, he said, "Why does this generation clamor for miraculous guarantees? If I have anything to say about it, you'll not get so much as a hint of a guarantee."

### Contaminating Yeast

He then left them, got back in the boat, and headed for the other side. But the disciples forgot to pack a lunch. Except for a single loaf of bread, there wasn't a crumb in the boat. Jesus warned, "Be very careful. Keep a sharp eye out for the contaminating yeast of Pharisees and the followers of Herod."

Meanwhile, the disciples were finding fault with each other because they had forgotten to bring bread. Jesus overheard and said, "Why are you fussing because you forgot bread? Don't you see the point of all this? Don't you get it at all? Remember the five loaves I broke for the five thousand? How many baskets of leftovers did you pick up?"

They said, "Twelve."

"And the seven loaves for the four thousand — how many bags full of leftovers did you get?"

"Seven."

He said, "Do you still not get it?"

They arrived at Bethsaida. Some people brought a sightless man and begged Jesus to give him a healing touch. Taking him by the hand, he led him out of the village. He put spit in the man's eyes, laid hands on him, and asked, "Do you see anything?"

He looked up. "I see men. They look like walking trees." So Jesus laid hands on his eyes again. The man looked hard and realized that he had recovered perfect sight, saw everything in bright, twenty-twenty focus. Jesus sent him straight home, telling him, "Don't enter the village."

## The Messiah

Jesus and his disciples headed out for the villages around Caesarea Philippi. As they walked, he asked, "Who do the people say I am?"

"Some say 'John the Baptizer,'" they said. "Others say 'Elijah.' Still others say 'one of the prophets.'"

He then asked, "And you — what are you saying about me? Who am I?"

Peter gave the answer: "You are the Christ, the Messiah."

Jesus warned them to keep it quiet, not to breathe a word of it to anyone. He then began explaining things to them: "It is necessary that the Son of Man proceed to an ordeal of suffering, be tried and found guilty by the elders, high priests, and religion scholars, be killed, and after three days rise up alive." He said this simply and clearly so they couldn't miss it.

But Peter grabbed him in protest. Turning and seeing his disciples wavering, wondering what to believe, Jesus confronted Peter. "Peter, get out of my way! Satan, get lost! You have no idea how God works."

Calling the crowd to join his disciples, he said, "Anyone who intends to come with me has to let me lead. You're not in the driver's seat; *I* am. Don't run from suffering; embrace it. Follow me and I'll show you how. Self-help is no help at all. Self-sacrifice is the way, my way, to saving yourself, your true self. What good would it do to get everything you want and lose you, the real you? What could you ever trade your soul for?

"If any of you are embarrassed over me and the way I'm leading you when you get around your fickle and unfocused friends, know that you'll be an even greater embarrassment to the Son of Man when he arrives in all the splendor of God, his Father, with an army of the holy angels."

---

▶ We all pursue different things at different times in our lives. We try the latest diets, exercises, and motivation techniques. We dabble in philosophy, yoga, and charismatic crusades. However, once we've tried it all and picked our selections from the spiritual buffet, we're ultimately confronted with the same basic question Jesus asked his disciples. He didn't want to hear the various theories of others. He didn't want the "religious line." He wanted an answer directly from the heart: "Who am I?"

You see, Caesarea Philippi was a hub for various spiritual movements and pantheistic cults. The place was located at the head of the springs that fed the Sea of Galilee in Israel, and various gods of fertility and nature were worshiped there. As Jesus glanced at all the religious clutter of the day, he wanted a direct and simple answer from his followers.

Peter replied, "You are the Christ, the Messiah."

Yes, all rules, rituals, and religion were stripped away with six powerful words.

---

**09.** Then he drove it home by saying, "This isn't pie in the sky by and by. Some of you who are standing here are going to see it happen, see the kingdom of God arrive in full force."

### In a Light-Radiant Cloud

Six days later, three of them *did* see it. Jesus took Peter, James, and John and led them up a high mountain. His appearance changed from the inside out, right before their eyes. His clothes shimmered, glistening white, whiter than any bleach could make them. Elijah, along with Moses, came into view, in deep conversation with Jesus.

Peter interrupted, "Rabbi, this is a great moment! Let's build three memorials — one for you, one for Moses, one for Elijah." He blurted this out without thinking, stunned as they all were by what they were seeing.

Just then a light-radiant cloud enveloped them, and from deep in the cloud, a voice: "This is my Son, marked by my love. Listen to him."

The next minute the disciples were looking around, rubbing their eyes, seeing nothing but Jesus, only Jesus.

Coming down the mountain, Jesus swore them to secrecy. "Don't tell a soul what you saw. After the Son of Man rises from the dead, you're free to talk." They puzzled over that, wondering what on earth "rising from the dead" meant.

Meanwhile they were asking, "Why do the religion scholars say that Elijah has to come first?"

Jesus replied, "Elijah does come first and get everything ready for the coming of the Son of Man. They treated this Elijah like dirt, much like they will treat the Son of Man, who will, according to Scripture, suffer terribly and be kicked around contemptibly."

### There Are No Ifs

When they came back down the mountain to the other disciples, they saw a huge crowd around them, and the religion scholars cross-examining them. As soon as the people in the crowd saw Jesus, admiring excitement stirred them. They ran and greeted him. He asked, "What's going on? What's all the commotion?"

A man out of the crowd answered, "Teacher, I brought my mute son, made speechless by a demon, to you. Whenever it seizes him, it throws him to the ground. He foams at the mouth, grinds his teeth, and goes stiff as a board. I told your disciples, hoping they could deliver him, but they couldn't."

Jesus said, "What a generation! No sense of God! How many times do I have to go over these things? How much longer do I have to put up with this? Bring the boy here." They brought him. When the demon saw Jesus, it threw the boy into a seizure, causing him to writhe on the ground and foam at the mouth.

He asked the boy's father, "How long has this been going on?"

"Ever since he was a little boy. Many times it pitches him into fire or the river to do away with him. If you can do anything, do it. Have a heart and help us!"

Jesus said, "If? There are no 'ifs' among believers. Anything can happen."

No sooner were the words out of his mouth than the father cried, "Then I believe. Help me with my doubts!"

Seeing that the crowd was forming fast, Jesus gave the vile spirit its marching orders: "Dumb and deaf spirit, I command you — Out of him, and stay out!" Screaming, and with much thrashing about, it left. The boy was pale as a corpse, so people started saying, "He's dead." But Jesus, taking his hand, raised him. The boy stood up.

After arriving back home, his disciples cornered Jesus and asked, "Why couldn't we throw the demon out?"

He answered, "There is no way to get rid of this kind of demon except by prayer."

Leaving there, they went through Galilee. He didn't want anyone to know their whereabouts, for he wanted to teach his disciples. He told them, "The Son of Man is about to be betrayed to some people who want nothing to do with God. They will murder him. Three days after his murder, he will rise, alive." They didn't know what he was talking about, but were afraid to ask him about it.

## So You Want First Place?

They came to Capernaum. When he was safe at home, he asked them, "What were you discussing on the road?"

The silence was deafening — they had been arguing with one another over who among them was greatest.

He sat down and summoned the Twelve. "So you want first place? Then take the last place. Be the servant of all."

He put a child in the middle of the room. Then, cradling the little one in his arms, he said, "Whoever embraces one of these children as I do embraces me, and far more than me — God who sent me."

---

John spoke up, "Teacher, we saw a man using your name to expel demons and we stopped him because he wasn't in our group."

Jesus wasn't pleased. "Don't stop him. No one can use my name to do something good and powerful, and in the next breath cut me down. If he's not an enemy, he's an ally. Why, anyone by just giving you a cup of water in my name is on our side. Count on it that God will notice.

"On the other hand, if you give one of these simple, childlike believers a hard time, bullying or taking advantage of their simple trust, you'll soon wish you hadn't. You'd be better off dropped in the middle of the lake with a millstone around your neck.

"If your hand or your foot gets in God's way, chop it off and throw it away. You're better off maimed or lame and alive than the proud owner of two hands and two feet, godless in a furnace of eternal fire. And if your eye distracts you from God, pull it out and throw it away. You're better off one-eyed and alive than exercising your twenty-twenty vision from inside the fire of hell.

"Everyone's going through a refining fire sooner or later, but you'll be well-preserved, protected from the *eternal* flames. Be preservatives yourselves. Preserve the peace."

### Divorce

**10.** From there he went to the area of Judea across the Jordan. A crowd of people, as was so often the case, went along, and he, as he so often did, taught them. Pharisees came up, intending to give him a hard time. They asked, "Is it legal for a man to divorce his wife?"

Jesus said, "What did Moses command?"

They answered, "Moses gave permission to fill out a certificate of dismissal and divorce her."

Jesus said, "Moses wrote this command only as a concession to your hardhearted ways. In the original creation, God made male and female to be together. Because of this, a man leaves father and mother, and in marriage he becomes one flesh with a woman — no longer two individuals, but forming a new unity. Because God created this organic union of the two sexes, no one should desecrate his art by cutting them apart."

When they were back home, the disciples brought it up again. Jesus gave it to them straight: "A man who divorces his wife so he can marry someone else commits adultery against her. And a woman who divorces her husband so she can marry someone else commits adultery."

———

The people brought children to Jesus, hoping he might touch them. The disciples shooed them off. But Jesus was irate and let them know it: "Don't push these children away. Don't ever get between them and me. These children are at the very center of life in the kingdom. Mark this: Unless you accept God's kingdom in the simplicity of a child, you'll never get in." Then, gathering the children up in his arms, he laid his hands of blessing on them.

But all things shall be ours! Up, heart, and sing.
All things were made for us — we are God's heirs —
Moon, sun, and wildest comets that do trail
A crowd of small worlds for a swiftness-tail!
Up from thy depths in me, my child-heart bring —
The child alone inherits everything:
God's little children-gods — all things are theirs!

—George MacDonald

## To Enter God's Kingdom

As he went out into the street, a man came running up, greeted him with great reverence, and asked, "Good Teacher, what must I do to get eternal life?"

Jesus said, "Why are you calling me good? No one is good, only God. You know the commandments: Don't murder, don't commit adultery, don't steal, don't lie, don't cheat, honor your father and mother."

He said, "Teacher, I have — from my youth — kept them all!"

Jesus looked him hard in the eye — and loved him! He said, "There's one thing left: Go sell whatever you own and give it to the poor. All your wealth will then be heavenly wealth. And come follow me."

The man's face clouded over. This was the last thing he expected to hear, and he walked off with a heavy heart. He was holding on tight to a lot of things, and not about to let go.

Looking at his disciples, Jesus said, "Do you have any idea how difficult it is for people who 'have it all' to enter God's kingdom?" The disciples couldn't believe what they were hearing, but Jesus kept on: "You can't imagine how difficult. I'd say it's easier for a camel to go through a needle's eye than for the rich to get into God's kingdom."

*That* set the disciples back on their heels. "Then who has any chance at all?" they asked.

Jesus was blunt: "No chance at all if you think you can pull it off by yourself. Every chance in the world if you let God do it."

Peter tried another angle: "We left everything and followed you."

Jesus said, "Mark my words, no one who sacrifices house, brothers, sisters, mother, father, children, land — whatever — because of me and the Message will lose out. They'll get it all back, but multiplied many times in homes, brothers, sisters, mothers, children, and land — but also in troubles. And then the bonus of eternal life! This is once again the Great Reversal: Many who are first will end up last, and the last first."

Back on the road, they set out for Jerusalem. Jesus had a head start on them, and they were following, puzzled and not just a little afraid. He took the Twelve and began again to go over what to expect next. "Listen to me carefully. We're on our way up to Jerusalem. When we get there, the Son of Man will be betrayed to the religious leaders and scholars. They will sentence him to death. Then they will hand him over to the Romans, who will mock and spit on him, give him the third degree, and kill him. After three days he will rise alive."

## The Highest Places of Honor

James and John, Zebedee's sons, came up to him. "Teacher, we have something we want you to do for us."

"What is it? I'll see what I can do."

Arrange it," they said, "so that we will be awarded the highest places of honor in your glory — one of us at your right, the other at your left."

Jesus said, "You have no idea what you're asking. Are you capable of drinking the cup I drink, of being baptized in the baptism I'm about to be plunged into?"

"Sure," they said. "Why not?"

Jesus said, "Come to think of it, you *will* drink the cup I drink, and be baptized in my baptism. But as to awarding places of honor, that's not my business. There are other arrangements for that."

When the other ten heard of this conversation, they lost their tempers with James and John. Jesus got them together to settle things down. "You've observed how godless rulers throw their weight around," he said, "and when people get a little power how quickly it goes to their heads. It's not going to be that way with you. Whoever wants to be great must become a servant. Whoever wants to be first among you must be your slave. That is what the Son of Man has done: He came to serve, not to be served — and then to give away his life in exchange for many who are held hostage."

———

They spent some time in Jericho. As Jesus was leaving town, trailed by his disciples and a parade of people, a blind beggar by the name of Bartimaeus, son of Timaeus, was sitting alongside the road. When he heard that Jesus the Nazarene was passing by, he began to cry out, "Son of David, Jesus! Mercy, have mercy on me!" Many tried to hush him up, but he yelled all the louder, "Son of David! Mercy, have mercy on me!"

Jesus stopped in his tracks. "Call him over."

They called him. "It's your lucky day! Get up! He's calling you to come!" Throwing off his coat, he was on his feet at once and came to Jesus.

Jesus said, "What can I do for you?"

The blind man said, "Rabbi, I want to see."

"On your way," said Jesus. "Your faith has saved and healed you."

In that very instant he recovered his sight and followed Jesus down the road.

### Entering Jerusalem on a Colt

**11.** When they were nearing Jerusalem, at Bethphage and Bethan on Mount Olives, he sent off two of the disciples with instructions: "Go to the village across from you. As soon as you enter, you'll find a colt tethered, one that has never yet been ridden. Untie it and bring it. If anyone asks, 'What are you doing?' say, 'The Master needs him, and will return him right away.'"

They went and found a colt tied to a door at the street corner and untied it. Some of those standing there said, "What are you doing untying that colt?" The disciples replied exactly as Jesus had instructed them, and the people let them alone. They brought the colt to Jesus, spread their coats on it, and he mounted.

The people gave him a wonderful welcome, some throwing their coats on the street, others spreading out rushes they had cut in the fields. Running ahead and following after, they were calling out,

Hosanna!
Blessed is he who comes in God's name!
Blessed the coming kingdom of our father David!
Hosanna in highest heaven!

He entered Jerusalem, then entered the Temple. He looked around, taking it all in. But by now it was late, so he went back to Bethany with the Twelve.

## The Cursed Fig Tree

As they left Bethany the next day, he was hungry. Off in the distance he saw a fig tree in full leaf. He came up to it expecting to find something for breakfast, but found nothing but fig leaves. (It wasn't yet the season for figs.) He addressed the tree: "No one is going to eat fruit from you again — ever!" And his disciples overheard him.

They arrived at Jerusalem. Immediately on entering the Temple Jesus started throwing out everyone who had set up shop there, buying and selling. He kicked over the tables of the bankers and the stalls of the pigeon merchants. He didn't let anyone even carry a basket through the Temple. And then he taught them, quoting this text:

My house was designated a house of prayer for the nations;
You've turned it into a hangout for thieves.

The high priests and religion scholars heard what was going on and plotted how they might get rid of him. They panicked, for the entire crowd was carried away by his teaching.

At evening, Jesus and his disciples left the city.

In the morning, walking along the road, they saw the fig tree, shriveled to a dry stick. Peter, remembering what had happened the previous day, said to him, "Rabbi, look — the fig tree you cursed is shriveled up!"

Jesus was matter-of-fact: "Embrace this God-life. Really embrace it, and nothing will be too much for you. This mountain, for instance: Just say, 'Go jump in the lake' — no shuffling or shilly-shallying — and it's as good as done. That's why I urge you to pray for absolutely everything, ranging from small to large. Include everything as you embrace this God-life, and you'll get God's everything. And when you assume the posture of prayer, remember that it's not all *asking*. If you have anything against someone, *forgive* — only then will your heavenly Father be inclined to also wipe your slate clean of sins."

### His Credentials

Then when they were back in Jerusalem once again, as they were walking through the Temple, the high priests, religion scholars, and leaders came up and demanded, "Show us your credentials. Who authorized you to speak and act like this?"

Jesus responded, "First let me ask you a question. Answer my question and then I'll present my credentials. About the baptism of John — who authorized it: heaven or humans? Tell me."

They were on the spot, and knew it. They pulled back into a huddle and whispered, "If we say 'heaven,' he'll ask us why we didn't believe John; if we say 'humans,' we'll be up against it with the people because they all hold John up as a prophet." They decided to concede that round to Jesus. "We don't know," they said.

Jesus replied, "Then I won't answer your question either."

### The Story About a Vineyard

**12.** Then Jesus started telling them stories. "A man planted a vineyard. He fenced it, dug a winepress, erected a watchtower, turned it over to the farmhands, and went off on a trip. At the time for harvest, he sent a servant back to the farmhands to collect his profits.

"They grabbed him, beat him up, and sent him off empty-handed. So he sent another servant. That one they tarred and feathered. He sent another and that one they killed. And on and on, many others. Some they beat up, some they killed.

"Finally there was only one left: a beloved son. In a last-ditch effort, he sent him, thinking, 'Surely they will respect my son.'

"But those farmhands saw their chance. They rubbed their hands together in greed and said, 'This is the heir! Let's kill him and have it all for ourselves.' They grabbed him, killed him, and threw him over the fence.

"What do you think the owner of the vineyard will do? Right. He'll come and clean house. Then he'll assign the care of the vineyard to others. Read it for yourselves in Scripture:

> That stone the masons threw out
>> is now the cornerstone!
> This is God's work;
>> we rub our eyes — we can hardly believe it!"

They wanted to lynch him then and there but, intimidated by public opinion, held back. They knew the story was about them. They got away from there as fast as they could.

## Paying Taxes to Caesar

They sent some Pharisees and followers of Herod to bait him, hoping to catch him saying something incriminating. They came up and said, "Teacher, we know you have integrity, that you are indifferent to public opinion, don't pander to your students, and teach the way of God accurately. Tell us: Is it lawful to pay taxes to Caesar or not?"

He knew it was a trick question, and said, "Why are you playing these games with me? Bring me a coin and let me look at it." They handed him one.

"This engraving—who does it look like? And whose name is on it?"

"Caesar," they said.

Jesus said, "Give Caesar what is his, and give God what is his."

Their mouths hung open, speechless.

## Our Intimacies Will Be with God

Some Sadducees, the party that denies any possibility of resurrection, came up and asked, "Teacher, Moses wrote that if a man dies and leaves a wife but no child, his brother is obligated to marry the widow and have children. Well, there once were seven brothers. The first took a wife. He died childless. The second married her. He died, and still no child. The same with the third. All seven took their turn, but no child. Finally the wife died. When they are raised at the resurrection, whose wife is she? All seven were her husband."

Jesus said, "You're way off base, and here's why: One, you don't know your Bibles; two, you don't know how God works. After the dead are raised up, we're past the marriage business. As it is with angels now, all our ecstasies and intimacies then will be with God. And regarding the dead, whether or not they are raised, don't you ever read the Bible? How God at the bush said to Moses, 'I am—not *was*—the God of Abraham, the God of Isaac, and the God of Jacob'? The living God is God of the *living*, not the dead. You're way, way off base."

## The Most Important Commandment

One of the religion scholars came up. Hearing the lively exchanges of question and answer and seeing how sharp Jesus was in his answers, he put in his question: "Which is most important of all the commandments?"

Jesus said, "The first in importance is, 'Listen, Israel: The Lord your God is one; so love the Lord God with all your passion and prayer and intelligence and energy.' And here is the second: 'Love others as well as you love yourself.' There is no other commandment that ranks with these."

The religion scholar said, "A wonderful answer, Teacher! So lucid and accurate — that God is one and there is no other. And loving him with all passion and intelligence and energy, and loving others as well as you love yourself. Why, that's better than all offerings and sacrifices put together!"

---

The Ten Commandments are found in chapter 20 of Exodus. They were given directly by God to the people of Israel at Mount Sinai after he delivered them from slavery in Egypt. In summary, here they are:

(1) No other gods, only me; (2) no carved gods of any size, shape, or form; (3) no using the name of God in curses or silly banter; (4) observe the Sabbath day, to keep it holy; (5) honor your father and mother; (6) no murder; (7) no adultery; (8) no stealing; (9) no lies; and (10) no lusting after your neighbor's stuff.

Here in Mark, about 1,400 years later, Jesus took the opportunity to wrap up the Ten Commandments in an even tighter bundle: *Love God and love others*.

---

When Jesus realized how insightful he was, he said, "You're almost there, right on the border of God's kingdom."

After that, no one else dared ask a question.

---

While he was teaching in the Temple, Jesus asked, "How is it that the religion scholars say that the Messiah is David's 'son,' when we all know that David, inspired by the Holy Spirit, said,

God said to my Master,
> "Sit here at my right hand
> until I put your enemies under your feet."

"David here designates the Messiah 'my Master' — so how can the Messiah also be his 'son'?"

The large crowd was delighted with what they heard.

He continued teaching. "Watch out for the religion scholars. They love to walk around in academic gowns, preening in the radiance of public flattery, basking in prominent positions, sitting at the head table at every church function. And all the time they are exploiting the weak and helpless. The longer their prayers, the worse they get. But they'll pay for it in the end."

Sitting across from the offering box, he was observing how the crowd tossed money in for the collection. Many of the rich were making large contributions. One poor widow came up and put in two small coins — a measly two cents. Jesus called his disciples over and said, "The truth is that this poor widow gave more to the collection than all the others put together. All the others gave what they'll never miss; she gave extravagantly what she couldn't afford — she gave her all."

**Doomsday Deceivers**

**13.** As he walked away from the Temple, one of his disciples said, "Teacher, look at that stonework! Those buildings!"

Jesus said, "You're impressed by this grandiose architecture? There's not a stone in the whole works that is not going to end up in a heap of rubble."

Later, as he was sitting on Mount Olives in full view of the Temple, Peter, James, John, and Andrew got him off by himself and asked, "Tell us, when is this going to happen? What sign will we get that things are coming to a head?"

Jesus began, "Watch out for doomsday deceivers. Many leaders are going to show up with forged identities claiming, 'I'm the One.' They will deceive a lot of people. When you hear of wars and rumored wars, keep your head and don't panic. This is routine history, and no sign of the end. Nation will fight nation and ruler fight ruler, over and over. Earthquakes will occur in various places. There will be famines. But these things are nothing compared to what's coming.

"And watch out! They're going to drag you into court. And then it will go from bad to worse, dog-eat-dog, everyone at your throat because you carry my name. You're placed there as sentinels to truth. The Message has to be preached all across the world.

"When they bring you, betrayed, into court, don't worry about what you'll say. When the time comes, say what's on your heart — the Holy Spirit will make his witness in and through you.

"It's going to be brother killing brother, father killing child, children killing parents. There's no telling who will hate you because of me.

"Stay with it — that's what is required. Stay with it to the end. You won't be sorry; you'll be saved.

### Run for the Hills

"But be ready to run for it when you see the monster of desecration set up where it should *never* be. You who can read, make sure you understand what I'm talking about. If you're living in Judea at the time, run for the hills; if you're working in the yard, don't go back to the house to get anything; if you're out in the field, don't go back to get your coat. Pregnant and nursing mothers will have it especially hard. Hope and pray this won't happen in the middle of winter.

"These are going to be hard days — nothing like it from the time God made the world right up to the present. And there'll be nothing like it again. If he let the days of trouble run their course, nobody would make it. But because of God's chosen people, those he personally chose, he has already intervened.

### No One Knows the Day or Hour

"If anyone tries to flag you down, calling out, 'Here's the Messiah!' or points, 'There he is!' don't fall for it. Fake Messiahs and lying preachers are going to pop up everywhere. Their impressive credentials and dazzling performances will pull the wool over the eyes of even those who ought to know better. So watch out. I've given you fair warning.

"Following those hard times,

Sun will fade out,
    moon cloud over,
Stars fall out of the sky,
    cosmic powers tremble.

"And then they'll see the Son of Man enter in grand style, his Arrival filling the sky — no one will miss it! He'll dispatch the angels; they will pull in the chosen from the four winds, from pole to pole.

"Take a lesson from the fig tree. From the moment you notice its buds form, the merest hint of green, you know summer's just around the corner. And so it is with you. When you see all these things, you know he is at the door. Don't take this lightly. I'm not just saying this for some future generation, but for this one, too — these things will happen. Sky and earth will wear out; my words won't wear out.

"But the exact day and hour? No one knows that, not even heaven's angels, not even the Son. Only the Father. So keep a sharp lookout, for you don't know the timetable. It's like a man who takes a trip, leaving home and putting his servants in charge, each assigned a task, and commanding the gatekeeper to stand watch. So, stay at your post, watching. You have no idea when the homeowner is returning, whether evening, midnight, cockcrow, or morning. You don't want him showing up unannounced, with you asleep on the job. I say it to you, and I'm saying it to all: Stay at your post. Keep watch."

## Anointing His Head

**14.** In only two days the eight-day Festival of Passover and the Feast of Unleavened Bread would begin. The high priests and religion scholars were looking for a way they could seize Jesus by stealth and kill him. They agreed that it should not be done during Passover Week. "We don't want the crowds up in arms," they said.

> ▶ The Passover was the Jewish festival commemorating the final blow to Pharaoh and the Egyptians, which allowed the Israelites to escape slavery in Egypt. This is the event where the angel of the Lord killed the firstborn of the Egyptians, but passed over any house that placed lamb's blood on the wood frame of the door.
>
> During the Passover celebration, unblemished lambs were killed for the feast on the fourteenth of Nisan in the Jewish calendar (March-April). The meal was eaten the same day after sundown. Since the Jewish day began at sundown, the Passover feast actually took place on the fifteenth of Nisan. The Feast of Unleavened Bread was a seven-day celebration that immediately followed the Passover. During this time, the normal population of Jerusalem would swell by several hundred thousand Jewish pilgrims.
>
> A few years earlier, when John the Baptist saw Jesus for the first time, he cried out, "Here he is, God's Passover Lamb! He forgives the sins of the world!"

Jesus was at Bethany, a guest of Simon the Leper. While he was eating dinner, a woman came up carrying a bottle of very expensive perfume. Opening the bottle, she poured it on his head. Some of the guests became furious among themselves. "That's criminal! A sheer waste! This perfume could have been sold for well over a year's wages and handed out to the poor." They swelled up in anger, nearly bursting with indignation over her.

But Jesus said, "Let her alone. Why are you giving her a hard time? She has just done something wonderfully significant for me. You will have the poor with you every day for the rest of your lives. Whenever you feel like it, you can do something for them. Not so with me. She did what she could when she could — she pre-anointed my body for burial. And you can be sure that wherever in the whole world the Message is preached, what she just did is going to be talked about admiringly."

Judas Iscariot, one of the Twelve, went to the cabal of high priests, determined to betray him. They couldn't believe their ears, and promised to pay him well. He started looking for just the right moment to hand him over.

## Traitor to the Son of Man

On the first of the Days of Unleavened Bread, the day they prepare the Passover sacrifice, his disciples asked him, "Where do you want us to go and make preparations so you can eat the Passover meal?"

He directed two of his disciples, "Go into the city. A man carrying a water jug will meet you. Follow him. Ask the owner of whichever house he enters, 'The Teacher wants to know, Where is my guest room where I can eat the Passover meal with my disciples?' He will show you a spacious second-story room, swept and ready. Prepare for us there."

The disciples left, came to the city, found everything just as he had told them, and prepared the Passover meal.

After sunset he came with the Twelve. As they were at the supper table eating, Jesus said, "I have something hard but important to say to you: One of you is going to hand me over to the conspirators, one who at this moment is eating with me."

Stunned, they started asking, one after another, "It isn't me, is it?"

He said, "It's one of the Twelve, one who eats with me out of the same bowl. In one sense, it turns out that the Son of Man is entering into a way of treachery well-marked by the Scriptures — no surprises here. In another sense, the man who turns him in, turns traitor to the Son of Man — better never to have been born than do this!"

## "This Is My Body"

In the course of their meal, having taken and blessed the bread, he broke it and gave it to them. Then he said,

Take, this is my body.

Taking the chalice, he gave it to them, thanking God, and they all drank from it. He said,

This is my blood,
God's new covenant,
Poured out for many people.

"I'll not be drinking wine again until the new day when I drink it in the kingdom of God."

They sang a hymn and then went directly to Mount Olives.

———

Jesus told them, "You're all going to feel that your world is falling apart and that it's my fault. There's a Scripture that says,

I will strike the shepherd;
The sheep will go helter-skelter.

"But after I am raised up, I will go ahead of you, leading the way to Galilee."

Peter blurted out, "Even if everyone else is ashamed of you when things fall to pieces, I won't be."

Jesus said, "Don't be so sure. Today, this very night in fact, before the rooster crows twice, you will deny me three times."

He blustered in protest, "Even if I have to die with you, I will never deny you." All the others said the same thing.

## Gethsemane

They came to an area called Gethsemane. Jesus told his disciples, "Sit here while I pray." He took Peter, James, and John with him. He plunged into a sinkhole of dreadful agony. He told them, "I feel bad enough right now to die. Stay here and keep vigil with me."

Going a little ahead, he fell to the ground and prayed for a way out: "Papa, Father, you can — can't you? — get me out of this. Take this cup away from me. But please, not what I want — what do *you* want?"

He came back and found them sound asleep. He said to Peter, "Simon, you went to sleep on me? Can't you stick it out with me a single hour? Stay alert, be in prayer, so you don't enter the danger zone without even knowing it. Don't be naive. Part of you is eager, ready for anything in God; but another part is as lazy as an old dog sleeping by the fire."

He then went back and prayed the same prayer. Returning, he again found them sound asleep. They simply couldn't keep their eyes open, and they didn't have a plausible excuse.

He came back a third time and said, "Are you going to sleep all night? No — you've slept long enough. Time's up. The Son of Man is about to be betrayed into the hands of sinners. Get up. Let's get going. My betrayer has arrived."

### A Gang of Ruffians

No sooner were the words out of his mouth when Judas, the one out of the Twelve, showed up, and with him a gang of ruffians, sent by the high priests, religion scholars, and leaders, brandishing swords and clubs. The betrayer had worked out a signal with them: "The one I kiss, that's the one — seize him. Make sure he doesn't get away." He went straight to Jesus and said, "Rabbi!" and kissed him. The others then grabbed him and roughed him up. One of the men standing there unsheathed his sword, swung, and came down on the Chief Priest's servant, lopping off the man's ear.

Jesus said to them, "What is this, coming after me with swords and clubs as if I were a dangerous criminal? Day after day I've been sitting in the Temple teaching, and you never so much as lifted a hand against me. What you in fact have done is confirm the prophetic writings." All the disciples cut and ran.

A young man was following along. All he had on was a bedsheet. Some of the men grabbed him but he got away, running off naked, leaving them holding the sheet.

## Condemned to Death

They led Jesus to the Chief Priest, where the high priests, religious leaders, and scholars had gathered together. Peter followed at a safe distance until they got to the Chief Priest's courtyard, where he mingled with the servants and warmed himself at the fire.

The high priests conspiring with the Jewish Council looked high and low for evidence against Jesus by which they could sentence him to death. They found nothing. Plenty of people were willing to bring in false charges, but nothing added up, and they ended up canceling each other out. Then a few of them stood up and lied: "We heard him say, 'I am going to tear down this Temple, built by hard labor, and in three days build another without lifting a hand.'" But even they couldn't agree exactly.

In the middle of this, the Chief Priest stood up and asked Jesus, "What do you have to say to the accusation?" Jesus was silent. He said nothing.

The Chief Priest tried again, this time asking, "Are you the Messiah, the Son of the Blessed?"

Jesus said, "Yes, I am, and you'll see it yourself:

The Son of Man seated
At the right hand of the Mighty One,
Arriving on the clouds of heaven."

The Chief Priest lost his temper. Ripping his clothes, he yelled, "Did you hear that? After that do we need witnesses? You heard the blasphemy. Are you going to stand for it?"

They condemned him, one and all. The sentence: death.

Some of them started spitting at him. They blindfolded his eyes, then hit him, saying, "Who hit you? Prophesy!" The guards, punching and slapping, took him away.

---

▶ After the religious leaders arrested Jesus, they looked for evidence and witnesses against him, but found none. So they went after Jesus himself and confronted him for a confession.

The Chief Priest asked, "Are you the Messiah, the Son of the Blessed?"

In response, Jesus said, "I am."

As we've seen throughout the ancient Scriptures, "I-AM" is the very name of God to the Hebrews. Thus, Jesus was not only declaring himself the Christ—Savior of the world—but the eternal, self-existing, creator God.

If there's any question as to what Jesus said and what his council of accusers heard, look at what happened next. His testimony of "I AM" was followed with shrieks of blasphemy and a sentence of death. Jesus had declared himself the Christ—the God-in-the-flesh version.

---

## The Rooster Crowed

While all this was going on, Peter was down in the courtyard. One of the Chief Priest's servant girls came in and, seeing Peter warming himself there, looked hard at him and said, "You were with the Nazarene, Jesus."

He denied it: "I don't know what you're talking about." He went out on the porch. A rooster crowed.

The girl spotted him and began telling the people standing around, "He's one of them." He denied it again.

After a little while, the bystanders brought it up again. "You've *got* to be one of them. You've got 'Galilean' written all over you."

Now Peter got really nervous and swore, "I never laid eyes on this man you're talking about." Just then the rooster crowed a second time. Peter remembered how Jesus had said, "Before a rooster crows twice, you'll deny me three times." He collapsed in tears.

## Standing Before Pilate

**15.** At dawn's first light, the high priests, with the religious leaders and scholars, arranged a conference with the entire Jewish Council. After tying Jesus securely, they took him out and presented him to Pilate.

Pilate asked him, "Are you the 'King of the Jews'?"

He answered, "If you say so." The high priests let loose a barrage of accusations.

Pilate asked again, "Aren't you going to answer anything? That's quite a list of accusations." Still, he said nothing. Pilate was impressed, really impressed.

It was a custom at the Feast to release a prisoner, anyone the people asked for. There was one prisoner called Barabbas, locked up with the insurrectionists who had committed murder during the uprising against Rome. As the crowd came up and began to present its petition for him to release a prisoner, Pilate anticipated them: "Do you want me to release the King of the Jews to you?" Pilate knew by this time that it was through sheer spite that the high priests had turned Jesus over to him.

But the high priests by then had worked up the crowd to ask for the release of Barabbas. Pilate came back, "So what do I do with this man you call King of the Jews?"

They yelled, "Nail him to a cross!"

Pilate objected, "But for what crime?"

But they yelled all the louder, "Nail him to a cross!"

Pilate gave the crowd what it wanted, set Barabbas free and turned Jesus over for whipping and crucifixion.

The soldiers took Jesus into the palace (called Praetorium) and called together the entire brigade. They dressed him up in purple and put a crown plaited from a thornbush on his head. Then they began their mockery: "Bravo, King of the Jews!" They banged on his head with a club, spit on him, and knelt down in mock worship. After they had had their fun, they took off the purple cape and put his own clothes back on him. Then they marched out to nail him to the cross.

## The Crucifixion

There was a man walking by, coming from work, Simon from Cyrene, the father of Alexander and Rufus. They made him carry Jesus' cross.

The soldiers brought Jesus to Golgotha, meaning "Skull Hill." They offered him a mild painkiller (wine mixed with myrrh), but he wouldn't take it. And they nailed him to the cross. They divided up his clothes and threw dice to see who would get them.

They nailed him up at nine o'clock in the morning. The charge against him — THE KING OF THE JEWS — was printed on a poster. Along with him, they crucified two criminals, one to his right, the other to his left. People passing along the road jeered, shaking their heads in mock lament: "You bragged that you could tear down the Temple and then rebuild it in three days — so show us your stuff! Save yourself! If you're really God's Son, come down from that cross!"

The high priests, along with the religion scholars, were right there mixing it up with the rest of them, having a great time poking fun at him: "He saved others — but he can't save himself! Messiah, is he? King of Israel? Then let him climb down from that cross. We'll *all* become believers then!" Even the men crucified alongside him joined in the mockery.

At noon the sky became extremely dark. The darkness lasted three hours. At three o'clock, Jesus groaned out of the depths, crying loudly, "*Eloi, Eloi, lama sabachthani?*" which means, "My God, my God, why have you abandoned me?"

Why did Jesus cry out, "My God, my God, why have you abandoned me?" The primary reason is that he was fulfilling prophecy from approximately 1,000 years earlier. Turn back to Psalm 22 and note that the whole Scripture presents a suffering Messiah, starting with the same cry to God.

Some of the bystanders who heard him said, "Listen, he's calling for Elijah." Someone ran off, soaked a sponge in sour wine, put it on a stick, and gave it to him to drink, saying, "Let's see if Elijah comes to take him down."

But Jesus, with a loud cry, gave his last breath. At that moment the Temple curtain ripped right down the middle. When the Roman captain standing guard in front of him saw that he had quit breathing, he said, "This has to be the Son of God!"


### Taken to a Tomb

There were women watching from a distance, among them Mary Magdalene, Mary the mother of the younger James and Joses, and Salome. When Jesus was in Galilee, these women followed and served him, and had come up with him to Jerusalem.

Late in the afternoon, since it was the Day of Preparation (that is, Sabbath eve), Joseph of Arimathea, a highly respected member of the Jewish Council, came. He was one who lived expectantly, on the lookout for the kingdom of God. Working up his courage, he went to Pilate and asked for Jesus' body. Pilate questioned whether he could be dead that soon and called for the captain to verify that he was really dead. Assured by the captain, he gave Joseph the corpse.

Having already purchased a linen shroud, Joseph took him down, wrapped him in the shroud, placed him in a tomb that had been cut into the rock, and rolled a large stone across the opening. Mary Magdalene and Mary, mother of Joses, watched the burial.

## The Resurrection

**16.** When the Sabbath was over, Mary Magdalene, Mary the mother of James, and Salome bought spices so they could embalm him. Very early on Sunday morning, as the sun rose, they went to the tomb. They worried out loud to each other, "Who will roll back the stone from the tomb for us?"

Then they looked up, saw that it had been rolled back — it was a huge stone — and walked right in. They saw a young man sitting on the right side, dressed all in white. They were completely taken aback, astonished.

He said, "Don't be afraid. I know you're looking for Jesus the Nazarene, the One they nailed on the cross. He's been raised up; he's here no longer. You can see for yourselves that the place is empty. Now — on your way. Tell his disciples and Peter that he is going on ahead of you to Galilee. You'll see him there, exactly as he said."

They got out as fast as they could, beside themselves, their heads swimming. Stunned, they said nothing to anyone.

[After rising from the dead, Jesus appeared early on Sunday morning to Mary Magdalene, whom he had delivered from seven demons. She went to his former companions, now weeping and carrying on, and told them. When they heard her report that she had seen him alive and well, they didn't believe her.

Later he appeared, but in a different form, to two of them out walking in the countryside. They went back and told the rest, but they weren't believed either.

Still later, as the Eleven were eating supper, he appeared and took them to task most severely for their stubborn unbelief, refusing to believe those who had seen him raised up. Then he said, "Go into the world. Go everywhere and announce the Message of God's good news to one and all. Whoever believes and is baptized is saved; whoever refuses to believe is damned.

"These are some of the signs that will accompany believers: They will throw out demons in my name, they will speak in new tongues, they will take snakes in their hands, they will drink poison and not be hurt, they will lay hands on the sick and make them well."

Then the Master Jesus, after briefing them, was taken up to heaven, and he sat down beside God in the place of honor. And the disciples went everywhere preaching, the Master working right with them, validating the Message with indisputable evidence.]

Note: Mark 16:9-20 [the portion in brackets] is contained only in later manuscripts.

## SEARCHER ON THE WAY
*Karma vs. Grace*

Bono, the singer-songwriter for the monster-selling rock group *U2*, was the son of a Protestant father and Catholic mother in Ireland—a country at battle over religion during his entire youth. In a 2006 speech before Christians, Muslims, and Jews in Washington, DC, Bono shared,

> One of the things that I picked up from my father
> and mother was the sense that religion often gets in
> the way of God.
>
> Seeing what religious people, in the name of
> God, did to my native land . . . and in this country;
> seeing God's second-hand car salesmen on the
> cable TV channels . . . seeing the self-righteousness
> roll down like a mighty stream from certain corners
> of the religious establishment—I must confess, I
> changed the channel. I wanted my MTV.
>
> Even though I was a believer. Perhaps
> because I was a believer. I was cynical . . . not
> about God, but about God's politics.

So, what does Bono believe in? In an interview with Michka Assayas (Bono: In Conversation, 2005), Bono made his "nonreligion" very clear.:

> At the center of all religions is the idea of Karma.
> You know, what you put out comes back to you: an
> eye for an eye, a tooth for a tooth, or in physics—
> every action is met by an equal or opposite one.
>
> And yet, along comes this idea called Grace
> to upend all that. . . . Love interrupts, if you like, the
> consequences of your actions, which in my case is
> very good news indeed, because I've done a lot of
> stupid stuff.

I'd be in big trouble if Karma was going to finally be my judge. It doesn't excuse my mistakes, but I'm holding out for Grace. I'm holding out that Jesus took my sins onto the Cross, because I know who I am, and I hope I don't have to depend on my own religiosity.

# JOHN

In Genesis, the first book of the Bible, God is presented as speaking the creation into existence. God speaks the word and it happens: heaven and earth, ocean and stream, trees and grass, birds and fish, animals and humans. Everything, seen and unseen, called into being by God's spoken word.

In deliberate parallel to the opening words of Genesis, John presents God as speaking salvation into existence. This time God's word takes on human form and enters history in the person of Jesus. Jesus speaks the word and it happens: forgiveness and judgment, healing and illumination, mercy and grace, joy and love, freedom and resurrection. Everything broken and fallen, sinful and diseased, called into salvation by God's spoken word.

For, somewhere along the line things went wrong (Genesis tells that story, too) and are in desperate need of fixing. The fixing is all accomplished by speaking—God speaking salvation into being in the person of Jesus. Jesus, in this account, not only speaks the word of God; he *is* the Word of God.

Keeping company with these words, we begin to realize that our words are more important than we ever supposed. Saying "I believe," for instance, marks the difference between life and death. Our words accrue dignity and gravity in conversations with Jesus. For Jesus doesn't impose salvation as a solution; he *narrates* salvation into being through leisurely conversation, intimate personal relationships, compassionate responses, passionate prayer, and—putting it all together—a sacrificial death. We don't casually walk away from words like that.

## The Life-Light

**01.** The Word was first,
the Word present to God,
God present to the Word.
The Word was God,
in readiness for God from day one.

Everything was created through him;
nothing — not one thing! —
came into being without him.

> In the decades since Einstein, observational discoveries in the areas of cosmology, astronomy, and physics have shown beyond a reasonable doubt that our universe did in fact have a beginning. Science now declares that prior to a certain moment in history there was nothing; during and after that certain moment in history there was something— our fantastic cosmos. The Big Bang is one effort to explain what happened during and after that singular moment. The theory states that in the beginning, all time, space, and matter came into being, from nowhere, all of a sudden, for no apparent reason. John starts from a slightly different perspective.

What came into existence was Life,
and the Life was Light to live by.
The Life-Light blazed out of the darkness;
the darkness couldn't put it out.

There once was a man, his name John, sent by God to point out the way to the Life-Light. He came to show everyone where to look, who to believe in. John was not himself the Light; he was there to show the way to the Light.

The Life-Light was the real thing:
>     Every person entering Life
>     he brings into Light.
He was in the world,
>     the world was there through him,
>     and yet the world didn't even notice.
He came to his own people,
>     but they didn't want him.
But whoever did want him,
>     who believed he was who he claimed
>     and would do what he said,
He made to be their true selves,
>     their child-of-God selves.
These are the God-begotten,
>     not blood-begotten,
>     not flesh-begotten,
>     not sex-begotten.

The Word became flesh and blood,
>     and moved into the neighborhood.
We saw the glory with our own eyes,
>     the one-of-a-kind glory,
>     like Father, like Son,
Generous inside and out,
>     true from start to finish.

---

"The Word" comes from the Greek *Logos*. Greek philosophers such as Plato used *Logos* not only of the spoken word but also of the unspoken word—the word still in the mind, the reason. When applied to the universe, Greeks were speaking to the rational principle that governs all things.

A Greek philosopher named Heraclitus first used the term *Logos* around 600 BC to designate the divine reason or plan that coordinates the entire universe. Monotheistic Jews used *Logos* to refer to God, since he was the rational mind—reason—behind the creation and coordination of the universe.

John pointed him out and called, "This is the One! The One I told you was coming after me but in fact was ahead of me. He has always been ahead of me, has always had the first word."

We all live off his generous bounty,
    gift after gift after gift.
We got the basics from Moses,
    and then this exuberant giving and receiving,
This endless knowing and understanding—
    all this came through Jesus, the Messiah.
No one has ever seen God,
    not so much as a glimpse.
This one-of-a-kind God-Expression,
    who exists at the very heart of the Father,
    has made him plain as day.

## Thunder in the Desert

When Jews from Jerusalem sent a group of priests and officials to ask John who he was, he was completely honest. He didn't evade the question. He told the plain truth: "I am not the Messiah."

They pressed him, "Who, then? Elijah?"

"I am not."

"The Prophet?"

"No."

Exasperated, they said, "Who, then? We need an answer for those who sent us. Tell us something—anything!—about yourself."

"I'm thunder in the desert: 'Make the road straight for God!' I'm doing what the prophet Isaiah preached."

Those sent to question him were from the Pharisee party. Now they had a question of their own: "If you're neither the Messiah, nor Elijah, nor the Prophet, why do you baptize?"

John answered, "I only baptize using water. A person you don't recognize has taken his stand in your midst. He comes after me, but he is not in second place to me. I'm not even worthy to hold his coat for him."

These conversations took place in Bethany on the other side of the Jordan, where John was baptizing at the time.

### The God-Revealer

The very next day John saw Jesus coming toward him and yelled out, "Here he is, God's Passover Lamb! He forgives the sins of the world! This is the man I've been talking about, 'the One who comes after me but is really ahead of me.' I knew nothing about who he was — only this: that my task has been to get Israel ready to recognize him as the God-Revealer. That is why I came here baptizing with water, giving you a good bath and scrubbing sins from your life so you can get a fresh start with God."

John clinched his witness with this: "I watched the Spirit, like a dove flying down out of the sky, making himself at home in him. I repeat, I know nothing about him except this: The One who authorized me to baptize with water told me, 'The One on whom you see the Spirit come down and stay, this One will baptize with the Holy Spirit.' That's exactly what I saw happen, and I'm telling you, there's no question about it: *This* is the Son of God."

### Come, See for Yourself

The next day John was back at his post with two disciples, who were watching. He looked up, saw Jesus walking nearby, and said, "Here he is, God's Passover Lamb."

The two disciples heard him and went after Jesus. Jesus looked over his shoulder and said to them, "What are you after?"

They said, "Rabbi" (which means "Teacher"), "where are you staying?"

He replied, "Come along and see for yourself."

They came, saw where he was living, and ended up staying with him for the day. It was late afternoon when this happened.

Andrew, Simon Peter's brother, was one of the two who heard John's witness and followed Jesus. The first thing he did after finding where Jesus lived was find his own brother, Simon, telling him, "We've found the Messiah" (that is, "Christ"). He immediately led him to Jesus.

Jesus took one look up and said, "You're John's son, Simon? From now on your name is Cephas" (or Peter, which means "Rock").

The next day Jesus decided to go to Galilee. When he got there, he ran across Philip and said, "Come, follow me." (Philip's hometown was Bethsaida, the same as Andrew and Peter.)

Philip went and found Nathanael and told him, "We've found the One Moses wrote of in the Law, the One preached by the prophets. It's *Jesus*, Joseph's son, the one from Nazareth!" Nathanael said, "Nazareth? You've got to be kidding."

But Philip said, "Come, see for yourself."

When Jesus saw him coming he said, "There's a real Israelite, not a false bone in his body."

Nathanael said, "Where did you get that idea? You don't know me."

Jesus answered, "One day, long before Philip called you here, I saw you under the fig tree."

Nathanael exclaimed, "Rabbi! You are the Son of God, the King of Israel!"

Jesus said, "You've become a believer simply because I say I saw you one day sitting under the fig tree? You haven't seen anything yet! Before this is over you're going to see heaven open and God's angels descending to the Son of Man and ascending again."

## From Water to Wine

**02.** Three days later there was a wedding in the village of Cana in Galilee. Jesus' mother was there. Jesus and his disciples were guests also. When they started running low on wine at the wedding banquet, Jesus' mother told him, "They're just about out of wine."

Jesus said, "Is that any of our business, Mother—yours or mine? This isn't my time. Don't push me."

She went ahead anyway, telling the servants, "Whatever he tells you, do it."

Six stoneware water pots were there, used by the Jews for ritual washings. Each held twenty to thirty gallons. Jesus ordered the servants, "Fill the pots with water." And they filled them to the brim.

"Now fill your pitchers and take them to the host," Jesus said, and they did.

When the host tasted the water that had become wine (he didn't know what had just happened but the servants, of course, knew), he called out to the bridegroom, "Everybody I know begins with their finest wines and after the guests have had their fill brings in the cheap stuff. But you've saved the best till now!"

This act in Cana of Galilee was the first sign Jesus gave, the first glimpse of his glory. And his disciples believed in him.

After this he went down to Capernaum along with his mother, brothers, and disciples, and stayed several days.

## Tear Down This Temple . . .

When the Passover Feast, celebrated each spring by the Jews, was about to take place, Jesus traveled up to Jerusalem. He found the Temple teeming with people selling cattle and sheep and doves. The loan sharks were also there in full strength.

Jesus put together a whip out of strips of leather and chased them out of the Temple, stampeding the sheep and cattle, upending the tables of the loan sharks, spilling coins left and right. He told the dove merchants, "Get your things out of here! Stop turning my Father's house into a shopping mall!" That's when his disciples remembered the Scripture, "Zeal for your house consumes me."

> Jesus embodies religious truth, and he has no time for deceptive religion. When religion gets clogged with money, power, greed, and hypocrisy, Jesus is the first to declare his righteous rage. In fact, Jesus took a bullwhip out on religion—he cleared Jerusalem's Temple in a powerful display of anger and strength.
>
> I wonder how many of us need to reexamine our so-called religious life. Are we caught up in the marketing of a machine, or are we seeking to know and worship God?

But the Jews were upset. They asked, "What credentials can you present to justify this?" Jesus answered, "Tear down this Temple and in three days I'll put it back together."

They were indignant: "It took forty-six years to build this Temple, and you're going to rebuild it in three days?" But Jesus was talking about his body as the Temple. Later, after he was raised from the dead, his disciples remembered he had said this. They then put two and two together and believed both what was written in Scripture and what Jesus had said.

During the time he was in Jerusalem, those days of the Passover Feast, many people noticed the signs he was displaying and, seeing they pointed straight to God, entrusted their lives to him. But Jesus didn't entrust his life to them. He knew them inside and out, knew how untrustworthy they were. He didn't need any help in seeing right through them.

### Born from Above

**03.** There was a man of the Pharisee sect, Nicodemus, a prominent leader among the Jews. Late one night he visited Jesus and said, "Rabbi, we all know you're a teacher straight from God. No one could do all the God-pointing, God-revealing acts you do if God weren't in on it."

Jesus said, "You're absolutely right. Take it from me: Unless a person is born from above, it's not possible to see what I'm pointing to — to God's kingdom."

"How can anyone," said Nicodemus, "be born who has already been born and grown up? You can't re-enter your mother's womb and be born again. What are you saying with this 'born-from-above' talk?"

Jesus said, "You're not listening. Let me say it again. Unless a person submits to this original creation — the 'wind-hovering-over-the-water' creation, the invisible moving the visible, a baptism into a new life — it's not possible to enter God's kingdom. When you look at a baby, it's just that: a body you can look at and touch. But the person who takes shape within is formed by something you can't see and touch — the Spirit — and becomes a living spirit.

"So don't be so surprised when I tell you that you have to be 'born from above' — out of this world, so to speak. You know well enough how the wind blows this way and that. You hear it rustling through the trees, but you have no idea where it comes from or where it's headed next. That's the way it is with everyone 'born from above' by the wind of God, the Spirit of God."

Nicodemus asked, "What do you mean by this? How does this happen?"

Jesus said, "You're a respected teacher of Israel and you don't know these basics? Listen carefully. I'm speaking sober truth to you. I speak only of what I know by experience; I give witness only to what I have seen with my own eyes. There is nothing secondhand here, no hearsay. Yet instead of facing the evidence and accepting it, you procrastinate with questions. If I tell you things that are plain as the hand before your face and you don't believe me, what use is there in telling you of things you can't see, the things of God?

"No one has ever gone up into the presence of God except the One who came down from that Presence, the Son of Man. In the same way that Moses lifted the serpent in the desert so people could have something to see and then believe, it is necessary for the Son of

Man to be lifted up — and everyone who looks up to him, trusting and expectant, will gain a real life, eternal life.

"This is how much God loved the world: He gave his Son, his one and only Son. And this is why: so that no one need be destroyed; by believing in him, anyone can have a whole and lasting life. God didn't go to all the trouble of sending his Son merely to point an accusing finger, telling the world how bad it was. He came to help, to put the world right again. Anyone who trusts in him is acquitted; anyone who refuses to trust him has long since been under the death sentence without knowing it. And why? Because of that person's failure to believe in the one-of-a-kind Son of God when introduced to him.

---

Imagine a colony of ants. The worker ants are out scavenging for food fit for a queen. Imagine yourself above the ants as an "ant-loving" human who would rather have the entire colony move into your personally designed ant farm. You see the trail of ants on its quest heading directly for ant bait, which is destined to return to the nest and ultimately the queen, causing death and destruction to the entire colony. But you know a better way . . . a way that they can be saved from death and destruction. But how are you going to communicate that to them? You are so much larger. You speak a different language. There is no way for you to come down to their level and redirect them to your ant farm. But, you come upon an idea . . . "What if I were to become an ant? Then I would be able to relate to the ants, communicate with the ants, and warn the ants of the impending disaster ahead. I could tell them that I have a better way that leads them from death unto life . . . and all they have to do is believe in my plan, follow me, and turn from their former path!"

---

"This is the crisis we're in: God-light streamed into the world, but men and women everywhere ran for the darkness. They went for the darkness because they were not really interested in pleasing God. Everyone who makes a practice of doing evil, addicted to denial and illusion, hates God-light and won't come near it, fearing a painful exposure. But anyone working and living in truth and reality welcomes God-light so the work can be seen for the God-work it is."

## The Bridegroom's Friend

After this conversation, Jesus went on with his disciples into the Judean countryside and relaxed with them there. He was also baptizing. At the same time, John was baptizing over at Aenon near Salim, where water was abundant. This was before John was thrown into jail. John's disciples got into an argument with the establishment Jews over the nature of baptism. They came to John and said, "Rabbi, you know the one who was with you on the other side of the Jordan? The one you authorized with your witness? Well, he's now competing with us. He's baptizing, too, and everyone's going to him instead of us."

John answered, "It's not possible for a person to succeed — I'm talking about *eternal* success — without heaven's help. You yourselves were there when I made it public that I was not the Messiah but simply the one sent ahead of him to get things ready. The one who gets the bride is, by definition, the bridegroom. And the bridegroom's friend, his 'best man' — that's me — in place at his side where he can hear every word, is genuinely happy. How could he be jealous when he knows that the wedding is finished and the marriage is off to a good start?

"That's why my cup is running over. This is the assigned moment for him to move into the center, while I slip off to the sidelines.

"The One who comes from above is head and shoulders over other messengers from God. The earthborn is earthbound and speaks earth language; the heavenborn is in a league of his own. He sets out the evidence of what he saw and heard in heaven. No one wants to deal with these facts. But anyone who examines this evidence will come to stake his life on this: that God himself is the truth.

"The One that God sent speaks God's words. And don't think he rations out the Spirit in bits and pieces. The Father loves the Son extravagantly. He turned everything over to him so he could give it away — a lavish distribution of gifts. That is why whoever accepts and trusts the Son gets in on everything, life complete and forever! And that is also why the person who avoids and distrusts the Son is in the dark and doesn't see life. All he experiences of God is darkness, and an angry darkness at that."

## The Woman at the Well

**04.** Jesus realized that the Pharisees were keeping count of the baptisms that he and John performed (although his disciples, not Jesus, did the actual baptizing). They had posted the score that Jesus was ahead, turning him and John into rivals in the eyes of the people. So Jesus left the Judean countryside and went back to Galilee.

To get there, he had to pass through Samaria. He came into Sychar, a Samaritan village that bordered the field Jacob had given his son Joseph. Jacob's well was still there. Jesus, worn out by the trip, sat down at the well. It was noon.

A woman, a Samaritan, came to draw water. Jesus said, "Would you give me a drink of water?" (His disciples had gone to the village to buy food for lunch.)

The Samaritan woman, taken aback, asked, "How come you, a Jew, are asking me, a Samaritan woman, for a drink?" (Jews in those days wouldn't be caught dead talking to Samaritans.)

Jesus answered, "If you knew the generosity of God and who I am, you would be asking *me* for a drink, and I would give you fresh, living water."

The woman said, "Sir, you don't even have a bucket to draw with, and this well is deep. So how are you going to get this 'living water'? Are you a better man than our ancestor Jacob, who dug this well and drank from it, he and his sons and livestock, and passed it down to us?"

Jesus said, "Everyone who drinks this water will get thirsty again and again. Anyone who drinks the water I give will never thirst — not ever. The water I give will be an artesian spring within, gushing fountains of endless life."

The woman said, "Sir, give me this water so I won't ever get thirsty, won't ever have to come back to this well again!"

He said, "Go call your husband and then come back."

"I have no husband," she said.

"That's nicely put: 'I have no husband.' You've had five husbands, and the man you're living with now isn't even your husband. You spoke the truth there, sure enough."

"Oh, so you're a prophet! Well, tell me this: Our ancestors worshiped God at this mountain, but you Jews insist that Jerusalem is the only place for worship, right?"

"Believe me, woman, the time is coming when you Samaritans will worship the Father neither here at this mountain nor there in Jerusalem. You worship guessing in the dark; we Jews worship in the clear light of day. God's way of salvation is made available through the Jews. But the time is coming — it has, in fact, come — when what you're called will not matter and where you go to worship will not matter.

"It's who you are and the way you live that count before God. Your worship must engage your spirit in the pursuit of truth. That's the kind of people the Father is out looking for: those who are simply and honestly *themselves* before him in their worship. God is sheer being itself — Spirit. Those who worship him must do it out of their very being, their spirits, their true selves, in adoration."

The woman said, "I don't know about that. I do know that the Messiah is coming. When he arrives, we'll get the whole story."

"I am he," said Jesus. "You don't have to wait any longer or look any further."

Just then his disciples came back. They were shocked. They couldn't believe he was talking with that kind of a woman. No one said what they were all thinking, but their faces showed it.

The woman took the hint and left. In her confusion she left her water pot. Back in the village she told the people, "Come see a man who knew all about the things I did, who knows me inside and out. Do you think this could be the Messiah?" And they went out to see for themselves.

## It's Harvest Time

In the meantime, the disciples pressed him, "Rabbi, eat. Aren't you going to eat?"

He told them, "I have food to eat you know nothing about."

The disciples were puzzled. "Who could have brought him food?"

Jesus said, "The food that keeps me going is that I do the will of the One who sent me, finishing the work he started. As you look around right now, wouldn't you say that in about four months it will be time to harvest? Well, I'm telling you to open your eyes and take a good look at what's right in front of you. These Samaritan fields are ripe. It's harvest time!

"The Harvester isn't waiting. He's taking his pay, gathering in this grain that's ripe for eternal life. Now the Sower is arm in arm with the Harvester, triumphant. That's the truth of the saying, 'This one sows, that one harvests.' I sent you to harvest a field you never worked. Without lifting a finger, you have walked in on a field worked long and hard by others."

Many of the Samaritans from that village committed themselves to him because of the woman's witness: "He knew all about the things I did. He knows me inside and out!" They asked him to stay on, so Jesus stayed two days. A lot more people entrusted their lives to him when they heard what he had to say. They said to the woman, "We're no longer taking this on your say-so. We've heard it for ourselves and know it for sure. He's the Savior of the world!"

———

### Your Grace Is Enough

Great is your faithfulness, oh God.
You wrestle with the sinner's heart,
You lead us by still waters
Into mercy,
And nothing can keep us apart.

Great is your love and justice, God.
You use the weak to lead the strong,
You lead us in the song of
Your salvation,
And all Your people sing along.

Your grace is enough,
Heaven reaching down to us.
Your grace is enough for me.
God, I see your grace is enough;
I'm covered in Your love.
Your grace is enough for me, For me.

— Matt Maher & Chris Tomlin, 2003

After the two days he left for Galilee. Now, Jesus knew well from experience that a prophet is not respected in the place where he grew up. So when he arrived in Galilee, the Galileans welcomed him, but only because they were impressed with what he had done in Jerusalem during the Passover Feast, not that they really had a clue about who he was or what he was up to.

Now he was back in Cana of Galilee, the place where he made the water into wine. Meanwhile in Capernaum, there was a certain official from the king's court whose son was sick. When he heard that Jesus had come from Judea to Galilee, he went and asked that he come down and heal his son, who was on the brink of death. Jesus put him off: "Unless you people are dazzled by a miracle, you refuse to believe."

But the court official wouldn't be put off. "Come down! It's life or death for my son."

Jesus simply replied, "Go home. Your son lives."

The man believed the bare word Jesus spoke and headed home. On his way back, his servants intercepted him and announced, "Your son lives!"

He asked them what time he began to get better. They said, "The fever broke yesterday afternoon at one o'clock." The father knew that that was the very moment Jesus had said, "Your son lives."

That clinched it. Not only he but his entire household believed. This was now the second sign Jesus gave after having come from Judea into Galilee.

## Even on the Sabbath

**05.** Soon another Feast came around and Jesus was back in Jerusalem. Near the Sheep Gate in Jerusalem there was a pool, in Hebrew called *Bethesda*, with five alcoves. Hundreds of sick people — blind, crippled, paralyzed — were in these alcoves. One man had been an invalid there for thirty-eight years. When Jesus saw him stretched out by the pool and knew how long he had been there, he said, "Do you want to get well?"

The sick man said, "Sir, when the water is stirred, I don't have anybody to put me in the pool. By the time I get there, somebody else is already in."

Jesus said, "Get up, take your bedroll, start walking." The man was healed on the spot. He picked up his bedroll and walked off.

That day happened to be the Sabbath. The Jews stopped the healed man and said, "It's the Sabbath. You can't carry your bedroll around. It's against the rules."

But he told them, "The man who made me well told me to. He said, 'Take your bedroll and start walking.'"

They asked, "Who gave you the order to take it up and start walking?" But the healed man didn't know, for Jesus had slipped away into the crowd.

A little later Jesus found him in the Temple and said, "You look wonderful! You're well! Don't return to a sinning life or something worse might happen."

The man went back and told the Jews that it was Jesus who had made him well. That is why the Jews were out to get Jesus — because he did this kind of thing on the Sabbath.

But Jesus defended himself. "My Father is working straight through, even on the Sabbath. So am I."

That really set them off. The Jews were now not only out to expose him; they were out to *kill* him. Not only was he breaking the Sabbath, but he was calling God his own Father, putting himself on a level with God.

## What the Father Does, the Son Does

So Jesus explained himself at length. "I'm telling you this straight. The Son can't independently do a thing, only what he sees the Father doing. What the Father does, the Son does. The Father loves the Son and includes him in everything he is doing.

"But you haven't seen the half of it yet, for in the same way that the Father raises the dead and creates life, so does the Son. The Son gives life to anyone he chooses. Neither he nor the Father shuts anyone out. The Father handed all authority to judge over to the Son so that the Son will be honored equally with the Father. Anyone who dishonors the Son, dishonors the Father, for it was the Father's decision to put the Son in the place of honor.

"It's urgent that you listen carefully to this: Anyone here who believes what I am saying right now and aligns himself with the Father, who has in fact put me in charge, has at this very moment the real, lasting life and is no longer condemned to be an outsider. This person has taken a giant step from the world of the dead to the world of the living.

"It's urgent that you get this right: The time has arrived — I mean right now! — when dead men and women will hear the voice of the

Son of God and, hearing, will come alive. Just as the Father has life in himself, he has conferred on the Son life in himself. And he has given him the authority, simply because he is the Son of Man, to decide and carry out matters of Judgment.

"Don't act so surprised at all this. The time is coming when everyone dead and buried will hear his voice. Those who have lived the right way will walk out into a resurrection Life; those who have lived the wrong way, into a resurrection Judgment.

"I can't do a solitary thing on my own: I listen, then I decide. You can trust my decision because I'm not out to get my own way but only to carry out orders. If I were simply speaking on my own account, it would be an empty, self-serving witness. But an independent witness confirms me, the most reliable Witness of all. Furthermore, you all saw and heard John, and he gave expert and reliable testimony about me, didn't he?

"But my purpose is not to get your vote, and not to appeal to mere human testimony. I'm speaking to you this way so that you will be saved. John was a torch, blazing and bright, and you were glad enough to dance for an hour or so in his bright light. But the witness that really confirms me far exceeds John's witness. It's the work the Father gave me to complete. These very tasks, as I go about completing them, confirm that the Father, in fact, sent me. The Father who sent me, confirmed me. And you missed it. You never heard his voice, you never saw his appearance. There is nothing left in your memory of his Message because you do not take his Messenger seriously.

———

"You have your heads in your Bibles constantly because you think you'll find eternal life there. But you miss the forest for the trees. These Scriptures are all about *me*! And here I am, standing right before you, and you aren't willing to receive from me the life you say you want.

▶ In the Jewish Scriptures there are over three hundred predictions about the future Messiah. These predictions were written by multiple authors over about one thousand years. Dramatically, Jesus is declaring himself that promised Messiah. He's saying, "Wake up! What are the odds that I could accidentally fulfill or purposefully manipulate over three hundred predictions written hundreds of years before my birth?"

Professor Peter Stoner (1888-1980) asked the same question. Stoner was Chairman of the Departments of Mathematics and Astronomy at Pasadena City College until 1953, and Chairman of the Science Division of Westmont College from 1953 to 1957. Stoner calculated the probability of one man fulfilling only a handful of the over three hundred messianic prophecies. In 1944, he published his research results in *Science Speaks: Scientific Proof of the Accuracy of Prophecy and the Bible*. Stoner concluded that the probability of one person fulfilling just eight of the specific prophecies was one chance in $10^{17}$ (one followed by seventeen zeros). How about one person fulfilling just forty-eight of the over three hundred prophecies? Stoner calculated these odds at one chance in $10^{157}$—way beyond statistical impossibility!

Someone once said that the Old Testament is the New Testament concealed, and the New Testament is the Old Testament revealed. Here, Jesus is saying, "How much clearer can it get?"

---

"I'm not interested in crowd approval. And do you know why? Because I know you and your crowds. I know that love, especially God's love, is not on your working agenda. I came with the authority of my Father, and you either dismiss me or avoid me. If another came, acting self-important, you would welcome him with open arms. How do you expect to get anywhere with God when you spend all your time jockeying for position with each other, ranking your rivals and ignoring God?

"But don't think I'm going to accuse you before my Father. Moses, in whom you put so much stock, is your accuser. If you believed, really believed, what Moses said, you would believe me. He wrote of me. If you won't take seriously what *he* wrote, how can I expect you to take seriously what *I* speak?"

### Bread and Fish for All

**06.** After this, Jesus went across the Sea of Galilee (some call it Tiberias). A huge crowd followed him, attracted by the miracles they had seen him do among the sick. When he got to the other side, he climbed a hill and sat down, surrounded by his disciples. It was nearly time for the Feast of Passover, kept annually by the Jews.

When Jesus looked out and saw that a large crowd had arrived, he said to Philip, "Where can we buy bread to feed these people?" He said this to stretch Philip's faith. He already knew what he was going to do.

Philip answered, "Two hundred silver pieces wouldn't be enough to buy bread for each person to get a piece."

One of the disciples — it was Andrew, brother to Simon Peter — said, "There's a little boy here who has five barley loaves and two fish. But that's a drop in the bucket for a crowd like this."

Jesus said, "Make the people sit down." There was a nice carpet of green grass in this place. They sat down, about five thousand of them. Then Jesus took the bread and, having given thanks, gave it to those who were seated. He did the same with the fish. All ate as much as they wanted.

When the people had eaten their fill, he said to his disciples, "Gather the leftovers so nothing is wasted." They went to work and filled twelve large baskets with leftovers from the five barley loaves.

The people realized that God was at work among them in what Jesushad just done. They said, "This is the Prophet for sure, God's Prophet right here in Galilee!" Jesus saw that in their enthusiasm, they were about to grab him and make him king, so he slipped off and went back up the mountain to be by himself.

In the evening his disciples went down to the sea, got in the boat, and headed back across the water to Capernaum. It had grown quite dark and Jesus had not yet returned. A huge wind blew up, churning the sea. They were maybe three or four miles out when they saw Jesus walking on the sea, quite near the boat. They were scared senseless, but he reassured them, "It's me. It's all right. Don't be afraid." So they took him on board. In no time they reached land — the exact spot they were headed to.

# SEARCHER ON THE WAY
*Amazing Grace*

John Newton was born in London in 1725. At a young age, he went to sea with his father, the commander of a merchant ship in the Mediterranean Sea. In 1744, Newton was conscripted into service on a British naval vessel. He deserted, was recaptured, and relegated to lower deck duties after a public flogging. Ultimately, he was transferred to a slave ship near Sierra Leone, where he served a slave trader under abusive conditions. In 1748, Newton escaped the ship, but then returned to the African shores as the captain of his own slave-trading vessel.

John Newton was not a religious man. However, on May 10, 1748, while he was piloting his ship through a fierce storm, Newton experienced his self-described moment of "great deliverance." His journals reveal that all seemed lost and the vessel was doomed to sink. Out of nowhere, he shouted for all to hear, "Lord, have mercy upon us."

The ship survived the storm, and Newton believed that's where God's grace began working in his life. He realized his wretched nature, and that he was saved by God's amazing grace. Newton soon entered the ministry, and started writing hymns.

Amazing grace! (how sweet the sound)
That sav'd a wretch like me!
I once was lost, but now am found,
Was blind, but now I see.

'Twas grace that taught my heart to fear,
And grace my fears reliev'd;
How precious did that grace appear,
The hour I first believ'd!

Thro' many dangers, toils and snares,
I have already come;

'Tis grace has brought me safe thus far,
And grace will lead me home.

Yes, when this flesh and heart shall fail,
And mortal life shall cease;
I shall possess, within the veil,
A life of joy and peace.

The next day the crowd that was left behind realized that there had been only one boat, and that Jesus had not gotten into it with his disciples. They had seen them go off without him. By now boats from Tiberias had pulled up near where they had eaten the bread blessed by the Master. So when the crowd realized he was gone and wasn't coming back, they piled into the Tiberias boats and headed for Capernaum, looking for Jesus.

When they found him back across the sea, they said, "Rabbi, when did you get here?" Jesus answered, "You've come looking for me not because you saw God in my actions but because I fed you, filled your stomachs — and for free.

**The Bread of Life**

"Don't waste your energy striving for perishable food like that. Work for the food that sticks with you, food that nourishes your lasting life, food the Son of Man provides. He and what he does are guaranteed by God the Father to last."

To that they said, "Well, what do we do then to get in on God's works?"

Jesus said, "Throw your lot in with the One that God has sent. That kind of a commitment gets you in on God's works."

They waffled: "Why don't you give us a clue about who you are, just a hint of what's going on? When we see what's up, we'll commit ourselves. Show us what you can do. Moses fed our ancestors with bread in the desert. It says so in the Scriptures: 'He gave them bread from heaven to eat.'"

Jesus responded, "The real significance of that Scripture is not that Moses gave you bread from heaven but that my Father is right now offering you bread from heaven, the *real* bread. The Bread of God came down out of heaven and is giving life to the world."

They jumped at that: "Master, give us this bread, now and forever!"

Jesus said, "I am the Bread of Life. The person who aligns with me hungers no more and thirsts no more, ever. I have told you this explicitly because even though you have seen me in action, you don't really believe me. Every person the Father gives me eventually comes running to me. And once that person is with me, I hold on and don't let go. I came down from heaven not to follow my own whim but to accomplish the will of the One who sent me.

"This, in a nutshell, is that will: that everything handed over to me by the Father be completed — not a single detail missed — and at the wrap-up of time I have everything and everyone put together, upright and whole. This is what my Father wants: that anyone who sees the Son and trusts who he is and what he does and then aligns with him will enter *real* life, *eternal* life. My part is to put them on their feet alive and whole at the completion of time."

At this, because he said, "I am the Bread that came down from heaven," the Jews started arguing over him: "Isn't this the son of Joseph? Don't we know his father? Don't we know his mother? How can he now say, 'I came down out of heaven' and expect anyone to believe him?"

Jesus said, "Don't bicker among yourselves over me. You're not in charge here. The Father who sent me is in charge. He draws people to me — that's the only way you'll ever come. Only then do I do my work, putting people together, setting them on their feet, ready for the End. This is what the prophets meant when they wrote, 'And then they will all be personally taught by God.' Anyone who has spent any time at all listening to the Father, really listening and therefore learning, comes to me to be taught personally — to see it with his own eyes, hear it with his own ears, from me, since I have it firsthand from the Father. No one has seen the Father except the One who has his Being alongside the Father — and you can see *me*.

"I'm telling you the most solemn and sober truth now: Whoever believes in me has real life, eternal life. I am the Bread of Life. Your ancestors ate the manna bread in the desert and died. But now here is Bread that truly comes down out of heaven. Anyone eating this Bread will not die, ever. I am the Bread — living Bread! — who came down out of heaven. Anyone who eats this Bread will live — and forever! The Bread that I present to the world so that it can eat and live is myself, this flesh-and-blood self."

At this, the Jews started fighting among themselves: "How can this man serve up his flesh for a meal?"

But Jesus didn't give an inch. "Only insofar as you eat and drink flesh and blood, the flesh and blood of the Son of Man, do you have life within you. The one who brings a hearty appetite to this eating and drinking has eternal life and will be fit and ready for the Final Day. My flesh is real food and my blood is real drink. By eating my flesh and drinking my blood you enter into me and I into you. In the same way that the fully alive Father sent me here and I live because of him, so the one who makes a meal of me lives because of me. This is the Bread from heaven. Your ancestors ate bread and later died. Whoever eats this Bread will live always."

He said these things while teaching in the meeting place in Capernaum.

## Too Tough to Swallow

Many among his disciples heard this and said, "This is tough teaching, too tough to swallow."

Jesus sensed that his disciples were having a hard time with this and said, "Does this throw you completely? What would happen if you saw the Son of Man ascending to where he came from? The Spirit can make life. Sheer muscle and willpower don't make anything happen. Every word I've spoken to you is a Spirit-word, and so it is life-making. But some of you are resisting, refusing to have any part in this." (Jesus knew from the start that some weren't going to risk themselves with him. He knew also who would betray him.) He went on to say, "This is why I told you earlier that no one is capable of coming to me on his own. You get to me only as a gift from the Father."

After this a lot of his disciples left. They no longer wanted to be associated with him. Then Jesus gave the Twelve their chance: "Do you also want to leave?"

Peter replied, "Master, to whom would we go? You have the words of real life, eternal life. We've already committed ourselves, confident that you are the Holy One of God."

Jesus responded, "Haven't I handpicked you, the Twelve? Still, one of you is a devil!" He was referring to Judas, son of Simon Iscariot. This man — one from the Twelve! — was even then getting ready to betray him.

**07.** Later Jesus was going about his business in Galilee. He didn't want to travel in Judea because the Jews there were looking for a chance to kill him. It was near the time of Tabernacles, a feast observed annually by the Jews.

His brothers said, "Why don't you leave here and go up to the Feast so your disciples can get a good look at the works you do? No one who intends to be publicly known does everything behind the scenes. If you're serious about what you are doing, come out in the open and show the world." His brothers were pushing him like this because they didn't believe in him either.

Jesus came back at them, "Don't crowd me. This isn't my time. It's your time — it's *always* your time; you have nothing to lose. The world has nothing against you, but it's up in arms against me. It's against me because I expose the evil behind its pretensions. You go ahead, go up to the Feast. Don't wait for me. I'm not ready. It's not the right time for me."

He said this and stayed on in Galilee. But later, after his family had gone up to the Feast, he also went. But he kept out of the way, careful not to draw attention to himself. The Jews were already out looking for him, asking around, "Where is that man?"

There was a lot of contentious talk about him circulating through the crowds. Some were saying, "He's a good man." But others said, "Not so. He's selling snake oil." This kind of talk went on in guarded whispers because of the intimidating Jewish leaders.

## Could It Be the Messiah?

With the Feast already half over, Jesus showed up in the Temple, teaching. The Jews were impressed, but puzzled: "How does he know so much without being schooled?"

Jesus said, "I didn't make this up. What I teach comes from the One who sent me. Anyone who wants to do his will can test this teaching and know whether it's from God or whether I'm making it up. A person making things up tries to make himself look good. But someone trying to honor the one who sent him sticks to the facts and doesn't tamper with reality. It was Moses, wasn't it, who gave you God's Law? But none of you are living it. So why are you trying to kill me?"

The crowd said, "You're crazy! Who's trying to kill you? You're demon-possessed."

Jesus said, "I did one miraculous thing a few months ago, and you're still standing around getting all upset, wondering what I'm up to. Moses prescribed circumcision — originally it came not from Moses but from his ancestors — and so you circumcise a man, dealing with one part of his body, even if it's the Sabbath. You do this in order to preserve one item in the Law of Moses. So why are you upset with me because I made a man's whole body well on the Sabbath? Don't be nitpickers; use your head — and heart! — to discern what is right, to test what is authentically right."

That's when some of the people of Jerusalem said, "Isn't this the one they were out to kill? And here he is out in the open, saying whatever he pleases, and no one is stopping him. Could it be that the rulers know that he is, in fact, the Messiah? And yet we know where this man came from. The Messiah is going to come out of nowhere. Nobody is going to know where he comes from."

That provoked Jesus, who was teaching in the Temple, to cry out, "Yes, you think you know me and where I'm from, but that's not where I'm from. I didn't set myself up in business. My true origin is in the One who sent me, and you don't know him at all. I come from him — that's how I know him. He sent me here."

They were looking for a way to arrest him, but not a hand was laid on him because it wasn't yet God's time. Many from the crowd committed themselves in faith to him, saying, "Will the Messiah, when he comes, provide better or more convincing evidence than this?"

The Pharisees, alarmed at this seditious undertow going through the crowd, teamed up with the high priests and sent their police to arrest him. Jesus rebuffed them: "I am with you only a short time. Then I go on to the One who sent me. You will look for me, but you won't find me. Where I am, you can't come."

The Jews put their heads together. "Where do you think he is going that we won't be able to find him? Do you think he is about to travel to the Greek world to teach the Jews? What is he talking about, anyway: 'You will look for me, but you won't find me,' and 'Where I am, you can't come'?"

On the final and climactic day of the Feast, Jesus took his stand. He cried out, "If anyone thirsts, let him come to me and drink. Rivers of living water will brim and spill out of the depths of anyone who believes in me this way, just as the Scripture says." (He said this in regard to the Spirit, whom those who believed in him were about to receive. The Spirit had not yet been given because Jesus had not yet been glorified.)

Those in the crowd who heard these words were saying, "This has to be the Prophet." Others said, "He is the Messiah!" But others were saying, "The Messiah doesn't come from Galilee, does he?

Don't the Scriptures tell us that the Messiah comes from David's line and from Bethlehem, David's village?" So there was a split in the crowd over him. Some went so far as wanting to arrest him, but no one laid a hand on him.

That's when the Temple police reported back to the high priests and Pharisees, who demanded, "Why didn't you bring him with you?"

The police answered, "Have you heard the way he talks? We've never heard anyone speak like this man."

The Pharisees said, "Are you carried away like the rest of the rabble? You don't see any of the leaders believing in him, do you? Or any from the Pharisees? It's only this crowd, ignorant of God's Law, that is taken in by him — and damned."

Nicodemus, the man who had come to Jesus earlier and was both a ruler and a Pharisee, spoke up. "Does our Law decide about a man's guilt without first listening to him and finding out what he is doing?"

But they cut him off. "Are you also campaigning for the Galilean? Examine the evidence. See if any prophet ever comes from Galilee."

Then they all went home.

### To Throw the Stone

**08.** Jesus went across to Mount Olives, but he was soon back in the Temple again. Swarms of people came to him. He sat down and taught them.

The religion scholars and Pharisees led in a woman who had been caught in an act of adultery. They stood her in plain sight of everyone and said, "Teacher, this woman was caught red-handed in the act of adultery. Moses, in the Law, gives orders to stone such persons. What do you say?" They were trying to trap him into saying something incriminating so they could bring charges against him.

Jesus bent down and wrote with his finger in the dirt. They kept at him, badgering him. He straightened up and said, "The sinless one among you, go first: Throw the stone." Bending down again, he wrote some more in the dirt.

Hearing that, they walked away, one after another, beginning with the oldest. The woman was left alone. Jesus stood up and spoke to her. "Woman, where are they? Does no one condemn you?"

"No one, Master."

"Neither do I," said Jesus. "Go on your way. From now on, don't sin."

### You're Missing God in All This

Jesus once again addressed them: "I am the world's Light. No one who follows me stumbles around in the darkness. I provide plenty of light to live in."

The Pharisees objected, "All we have is your word on this. We need more than this to go on."

Jesus replied, "You're right that you only have my word. But you can depend on it being true. I know where I've come from and where I go next. You don't know where I'm from or where I'm headed. You decide according to what you can see and touch. I don't make judgments like that. But even if I did, my judgment would be true because I wouldn't make it out of the narrowness of my experience but in the largeness of the One who sent me, the Father. That fulfills the conditions set down in God's Law: that you can count on the testimony of two witnesses. And that is what you have: You have my word and you have the word of the Father who sent me."

They said, "Where is this so-called Father of yours?"

Jesus said, "You're looking right at me and you don't see me. How do you expect to see the Father? If you knew me, you would at the same time know the Father."

He gave this speech in the Treasury while teaching in the Temple. No one arrested him because his time wasn't yet up.

Then he went over the same ground again. "I'm leaving and

you are going to look for me, but you're missing God in this and are headed for a dead end. There is no way you can come with me."

The Jews said, "So, is he going to kill himself? Is that what he means by 'You can't come with me'?"

Jesus said, "You're tied down to the mundane; I'm in touch with what is beyond your horizons. You live in terms of what you see and touch. I'm living on other terms. I told you that you were missing God in all this. You're at a dead end. If you won't believe I am who I say I am, you're at the dead end of sins. You're missing God in your lives."

They said to him, "Just who are you anyway?"

Jesus said, "What I've said from the start. I have so many things to say that concern you, judgments to make that affect you, but if you don't accept the trustworthiness of the One who commanded my words and acts, none of it matters. That is who you are questioning — not me but the One who sent me."

They still didn't get it, didn't realize that he was referring to the Father. So Jesus tried again. "When you raise up the Son of Man, then you will know who I am — that I'm not making this up, but speaking only what the Father taught me. The One who sent me stays with me. He doesn't abandon me. He sees how much joy I take in pleasing him."

When he put it in these terms, many people decided to believe.

### If the Son Sets You Free

Then Jesus turned to the Jews who had claimed to believe in him. "If you stick with this, living out what I tell you, you are my disciples for sure. Then you will experience for yourselves the truth, and the truth will free you."

Surprised, they said, "But we're descendants of Abraham. We've never been slaves to anyone. How can you say, 'The truth will free you'?"

Jesus said, "I tell you most solemnly that anyone who chooses a life of sin is trapped in a dead-end life and is, in fact, a slave. A slave is a transient, who can't come and go at will. The Son, though, has an established position, the run of the house. So if the Son sets you free, you are free through and through. I know you are Abraham's descendants. But I also know that you are trying to kill me because my message hasn't yet penetrated your thick skulls. I'm talking about things I have seen while keeping company with the Father, and you just go on doing what you have heard from your father."

They were indignant. "Our father is Abraham!"

Jesus said, "If you were Abraham's children, you would have been doing the things Abraham did. And yet here you are trying to kill me, a man who has spoken to you the truth he got straight from God! Abraham never did that sort of thing. You persist in repeating the works of your father."

They said, "We're not bastards. We have a legitimate father: the one and only God."

"If God were your father," said Jesus, "you would love me, for I came from God and arrived here. I didn't come on my own. He sent me. Why can't you understand one word I say? Here's why: You can't handle it. You're from your father, the Devil, and all you want to do is please him. He was a killer from the very start. He couldn't stand the truth because there wasn't a shred of truth in him. When the Liar speaks, he makes it up out of his lying nature and fills the world with lies. I arrive on the scene, tell you the plain truth, and you refuse to have a thing to do with me. Can any one of you convict me of a single misleading word, a single sinful act? But if I'm telling the truth, why don't you believe me? Anyone on God's side listens to God's words. This is why you're not listening — because you're not on God's side."

### I Am Who I Am

The Jews then said, "That clinches it. We were right all along when we called you a Samaritan and said you were crazy — demon-possessed!"

Jesus said, "I'm not crazy. I simply honor my Father, while you dishonor me. I am not trying to get anything for myself. God intends something gloriously grand here and is making the decisions that will bring it about. I say this with absolute confidence. If you practice what I'm telling you, you'll never have to look death in the face."

At this point the Jews said, "Now we *know* you're crazy. Abraham died. The prophets died. And you show up saying, 'If you practice what I'm telling you, you'll never have to face death, not even a taste.' Are you greater than Abraham, who died? And the prophets died! Who do you think you are!"

Jesus said, "If I turned the spotlight on myself, it wouldn't amount to anything. But my Father, the same One you say is your Father, put me here at this time and place of splendor. You haven't recognized him in this. But I have. If I, in false modesty, said I didn't know what was going on, I would be as much of a liar as you are. But I do know, and I am doing what he says. Abraham — your 'father' — with jubilant faith looked down the corridors of history and saw my day coming. He saw it and cheered."

The Jews said, "You're not even fifty years old — and Abraham saw you?"

"Believe me," said Jesus, "*I am who I am* long before Abraham was anything."

That did it — pushed them over the edge. They picked up rocks to throw at him. But Jesus slipped away, getting out of the Temple.

### True Blindness

**09.** Walking down the street, Jesus saw a man blind from birth. His disciples asked, "Rabbi, who sinned: this man or his parents, causing him to be born blind?"

Jesus said, "You're asking the wrong question. You're looking for someone to blame. There is no such cause-effect here. Look instead for what God can do. We need to be energetically at work for the One who sent me here, working while the sun shines. When night falls, the workday is over. For as long as I am in the world, there is plenty of light. I am the world's Light."

He said this and then spit in the dust, made a clay paste with the saliva, rubbed the paste on the blind man's eyes, and said, "Go, wash at the Pool of Siloam" (Siloam means "Sent"). The man went and washed — and saw.

---

▶ The Pool of Siloam is the ancient termination point for King Hezekiah's famous tunnel that brought water from the Gihon Spring at the floor of the Kidron Valley into the city of Jerusalem. The 1,750 foot tunnel was dug by two separate teams that miraculously met in the middle. The famous Siloam Inscription commemorates the engineering marvel that brought water to the Pool of Siloam and protected Jerusalem's water supply in the event of siege.

In 2004, archaeologists stumbled upon this same Pool of Siloam when sewer engineers uncovered ancient steps during pipe maintenance near the mouth of Hezekiah's ancient water tunnel. The bulldozers were immediately stopped, and by the summer of 2005, archaeologists carefully revealed the huge pool. Pottery indicates that this was indeed the Pool of Siloam used during the time of Jesus.

---

Soon the town was buzzing. His relatives and those who year after year had seen him as a blind man begging were saying, "Why, isn't this the man we knew, who sat here and begged?"

Others said, "It's him all right!"

But others objected, "It's not the same man at all. It just looks like him."

He said, "It's me, the very one."

They said, "How did your eyes get opened?"

"A man named Jesus made a paste and rubbed it on my eyes and told me, 'Go to Siloam and wash.' I did what he said. When I washed, I saw."

"So where is he?"

"I don't know."

They marched the man to the Pharisees. This day when Jesus made the paste and healed his blindness was the Sabbath. The

Pharisees grilled him again on how he had come to see. He said, "He put a clay paste on my eyes, and I washed, and now I see."

Some of the Pharisees said, "Obviously, this man can't be from God. He doesn't keep the Sabbath."

Others countered, "How can a bad man do miraculous, God-revealing things like this?" There was a split in their ranks.

They came back at the blind man, "You're the expert. He opened *your* eyes. What do you say about him?"

He said, "He is a prophet."

The Jews didn't believe it, didn't believe the man was blind to begin with. So they called the parents of the man now bright-eyed with sight. They asked them, "Is this your son, the one you say was born blind? So how is it that he now sees?"

His parents said, "We know he is our son, and we know he was born blind. But we don't know how he came to see — haven't a clue about who opened his eyes. Why don't you ask him? He's a grown man and can speak for himself." (His parents were talking like this because they were intimidated by the Jewish leaders, who had already decided that anyone who took a stand that this was the Messiah would be kicked out of the meeting place. That's why his parents said, "Ask him. He's a grown man.")

They called the man back a second time — the man who had been blind — and told him, "Give credit to God. We know this man is an impostor."

He replied, "I know nothing about that one way or the other. But I know one thing for sure: I was blind . . . I now see."

They said, "What did he do to you? How did he open your eyes?"

"I've told you over and over and you haven't listened. Why do you want to hear it again? Are you so eager to become his disciples?"

With that they jumped all over him. "*You* might be a disciple of that man, but we're disciples of Moses. We know for sure that God spoke to Moses, but we have no idea where this man even comes from."

The man replied, "This is amazing! You claim to know nothing about him, but the fact is, he opened my eyes! It's well known that God isn't at the beck and call of sinners, but listens carefully to anyone who lives in reverence and does his will. That someone opened the eyes of a man born blind has never been heard of—ever. If this man didn't come from God, he wouldn't be able to do anything."

They said, "You're nothing but dirt! How dare you take that tone with us!" Then they threw him out in the street.

Jesus heard that they had thrown him out, and went and found him. He asked him, "Do you believe in the Son of Man?"

The man said, "Point him out to me, sir, so that I can believe in him."

Jesus said, "You're looking right at him. Don't you recognize my voice?"

"Master, I believe," the man said, and worshiped him.

Jesus then said, "I came into the world to bring everything into the clear light of day, making all the distinctions clear, so that those who have never seen will see, and those who have made a great pretense of seeing will be exposed as blind."

Some Pharisees overheard him and said, "Does that mean you're calling us blind?"

Jesus said, "If you were really blind, you would be blameless, but since you claim to see everything so well, you're accountable for every fault and failure."

### He Calls His Sheep by Name

**10.** "Let me set this before you as plainly as I can. If a person climbs over or through the fence of a sheep pen instead of going through the gate, you know he's up to no good—a sheep rustler! The shepherd walks right up to the gate. The gatekeeper opens the gate to him and the sheep recognize his voice. He calls his own sheep by name and leads them out. When he gets them all out, he leads them and they follow because they are familiar with his voice.

They won't follow a stranger's voice but will scatter because they aren't used to the sound of it."

Jesus told this simple story, but they had no idea what he was talking about. So he tried again. "I'll be explicit, then. I am the Gate for the sheep. All those others are up to no good — sheep stealers, every one of them. But the sheep didn't listen to them. I am the Gate. Anyone who goes through me will be cared for — will freely go in and out, and find pasture. A thief is only there to steal and kill and destroy. I came so they can have real and eternal life, more and better life than they ever dreamed of.

"I am the Good Shepherd. The Good Shepherd puts the sheep before himself, sacrifices himself if necessary. A hired man is not a real shepherd. The sheep mean nothing to him. He sees a wolf come and runs for it, leaving the sheep to be ravaged and scattered by the wolf. He's only in it for the money. The sheep don't matter to him.

"I am the Good Shepherd. I know my own sheep and my own sheep know me. In the same way, the Father knows me and I know the Father. I put the sheep before myself, sacrificing myself if necessary. You need to know that I have other sheep in addition to those in this pen. I need to gather and bring them, too. They'll also recognize my voice. Then it will be one flock, one Shepherd. This is why the Father loves me: because I freely lay down my life. And so I am free to take it up again. No one takes it from me. I lay it down of my own free will. I have the right to lay it down; I also have the right to take it up again. I received this authority personally from my Father."

This kind of talk caused another split in the Jewish ranks. A lot of them were saying, "He's crazy, a maniac — out of his head completely. Why bother listening to him?" But others weren't so sure: "These aren't the words of a crazy man. Can a 'maniac' open blind eyes?"

———

They were celebrating Hanukkah just then in Jerusalem. It was winter. Jesus was strolling in the Temple across Solomon's Porch. The Jews, circling him, said, "How long are you going to keep us guessing? If you're the Messiah, tell us straight out."

Jesus answered, "I told you, but you don't believe. Everything I have done has been authorized by my Father, actions that speak louder than words. You don't believe because you're not my sheep. My sheep recognize my voice. I know them, and they follow me. I give them real and eternal life. They are protected from the Destroyer for good. No one can steal them from out of my hand. The Father who put them under my care is so much greater than the Destroyer and Thief. No one could ever get them away from him. I and the Father are one heart and mind."

Again the Jews picked up rocks to throw at him. Jesus said, "I have made a present to you from the Father of a great many good actions. For which of these acts do you stone me?"

The Jews said, "We're not stoning you for anything good you did, but for what you said — this blasphemy of calling yourself God."

Jesus said, "I'm only quoting your inspired Scriptures, where God said, 'I tell you — you are gods.' If God called your ancestors 'gods' — and Scripture doesn't lie — why do you yell, 'Blasphemer! Blasphemer!' at the unique One the Father consecrated and sent into the world, just because I said, 'I am the Son of God'? If I don't do the things my Father does, well and good; don't believe me. But if I am doing them, put aside for a moment what you hear me say about myself and just take the evidence of the actions that are right before your eyes. Then perhaps things will come together for you, and you'll see that not only are we doing the same thing, we *are* the same — Father and Son. He is in me; I am in him."

▶ Why has the name "Jesus Christ" caused more division, agitation, and controversy than any other name in history? If God comes up in a coffee-shop discussion, nobody is really offended. If we speak about Buddha or Brahman, Moses or Mohammed, we really

They tried yet again to arrest him, but he slipped through their fingers. He went back across the Jordan to the place where John first baptized, and stayed there. A lot of people followed him over. They were saying, "John did no miracles, but everything he said about this man has come true." Many believed in him then and there.

## The Death of Lazarus

**11** A man was sick, Lazarus of Bethany, the town of Mary and her sister Martha. This was the same Mary who massaged the Lord's feet with aromatic oils and then wiped them with her hair. It was her brother Lazarus who was sick. So the sisters sent word to Jesus, "Master, the one you love so very much is sick."

When Jesus got the message, he said, "This sickness is not fatal. It will become an occasion to show God's glory by glorifying God's Son."

Jesus loved Martha and her sister and Lazarus, but oddly, when he heard that Lazarus was sick, he stayed on where he was for two more days. After the two days, he said to his disciples, "Let's go back to Judea."

They said, "Rabbi, you can't do that. The Jews are out to kill you, and you're going back?"

Jesus replied, "Are there not twelve hours of daylight? Anyone who walks in daylight doesn't stumble because there's plenty of light from the sun. Walking at night, he might very well stumble because he can't see where he's going."

He said these things, and then announced, "Our friend Lazarus has fallen asleep. I'm going to wake him up."

The disciples said, "Master, if he's gone to sleep, he'll get a good rest and wake up feeling fine." Jesus was talking about death, while his disciples thought he was talking about taking a nap.

Then Jesus became explicit: "Lazarus died. And I am glad for your sakes that I wasn't there. You're about to be given new grounds for believing. Now let's go to him."

That's when Thomas, the one called the Twin, said to his companions, "Come along. We might as well die with him."

When Jesus finally got there, he found Lazarus already four days dead. Bethany was near Jerusalem, only a couple of miles away, and many of the Jews were visiting Martha and Mary, sympathizing with them over their brother. Martha heard Jesus was coming and went out to meet him. Mary remained in the house.

Martha said, "Master, if you'd been here, my brother wouldn't have died. Even now, I know that whatever you ask God he will give you."

Jesus said, "Your brother will be raised up."

Martha replied, "I know that he will be raised up in the resurrection at the end of time."

"You don't have to wait for the End. I am, right now, Resurrection and Life. The one who believes in me, even though he or she dies, will live. And everyone who lives believing in me does not ultimately die at all. Do you believe this?"

"Yes, Master. All along I have believed that you are the Messiah, the Son of God who comes into the world."

After saying this, she went to her sister Mary and whispered in her ear, "The Teacher is here and is asking for you."

The moment she heard that, she jumped up and ran out to him. Jesus had not yet entered the town but was still at the place where Martha had met him. When her sympathizing Jewish friends saw Mary run off, they followed her, thinking she was on her way to the tomb to weep there. Mary came to where Jesus was waiting and fell at his feet, saying, "Master, if only you had been here, my brother would not have died."

When Jesus saw her sobbing and the Jews with her sobbing, a deep anger welled up within him. He said, "Where did you put him?"

"Master, come and see," they said. Now Jesus wept.

The Jews said, "Look how deeply he loved him."

Others among them said, "Well, if he loved him so much, why didn't he do something to keep him from dying? After all, he opened the eyes of a blind man."

Then Jesus, the anger again welling up within him, arrived at the tomb. It was a simple cave in the hillside with a slab of stone laid against it. Jesus said, "Remove the stone."

The sister of the dead man, Martha, said, "Master, by this time there's a stench. He's been dead four days!"

Jesus looked her in the eye. "Didn't I tell you that if you believed, you would see the glory of God?"

Then, to the others, "Go ahead, take away the stone."

They removed the stone. Jesus raised his eyes to heaven and prayed, "Father, I'm grateful that you have listened to me. I know you always do listen, but on account of this crowd standing here I've spoken so that they might believe that you sent me."

Then he shouted, "Lazarus, come out!" And he came out, a cadaver, wrapped from head to toe, and with a kerchief over his face.

Jesus told them, "Unwrap him and let him loose."

### The Man Who Creates God-Signs

That was a turnaround for many of the Jews who were with Mary. They saw what Jesus did, and believed in him. But some went back to the Pharisees and told on Jesus. The high priests and Pharisees called a meeting of the Jewish ruling body. "What do we do now?" they asked. "This man keeps on doing things, creating God-signs. If we let him go on, pretty soon everyone will be believing in him and the Romans will come and remove what little power and privilege we still have."

Then one of them — it was Caiaphas, the designated Chief Priest that year — spoke up, "Don't you know anything? Can't you see that it's to our advantage that one man dies for the people rather than the whole nation be destroyed?" He didn't say this of his own accord, but as Chief Priest that year he unwittingly prophesied that Jesus was about to die sacrificially for the nation, and not only for the nation but so that all God's exile-scattered children might be gathered together into one people.

From that day on, they plotted to kill him. So Jesus no longer went out in public among the Jews. He withdrew into the country bordering the desert to a town called Ephraim and secluded himself there with his disciples.

The Jewish Passover was coming up. Crowds of people were making their way from the country up to Jerusalem to get themselves ready for the Feast. They were curious about Jesus. There was a lot of talk of him among those standing around in the Temple: "What do you think? Do you think he'll show up at the Feast or not?"

Meanwhile, the high priests and Pharisees gave out the word that anyone getting wind of him should inform them. They were all set to arrest him.

### Anointing His Feet

**12.** Six days before Passover, Jesus entered Bethany where Lazarus, so recently raised from the dead, was living. Lazarus and his sisters invited Jesus to dinner at their home. Martha served. Lazarus was one of those sitting at the table with them. Mary came in with a jar of very expensive aromatic oils, anointed and massaged Jesus' feet, and then wiped them with her hair. The fragrance of the oils filled the house.

Judas Iscariot, one of his disciples, even then getting ready to betray him, said, "Why wasn't this oil sold and the money given to the poor? It would have easily brought three hundred silver pieces." He said this not because he cared two cents about the poor but because he was a thief. He was in charge of their common funds, but also embezzled them.

Jesus said, "Let her alone. She's anticipating and honoring the day of my burial. You always have the poor with you. You don't always have me."

Word got out among the Jews that he was back in town. The people came to take a look, not only at Jesus but also at Lazarus, who had been raised from the dead. So the high priests plotted to kill Lazarus because so many of the Jews were going over and believing in Jesus on account of him.

## See How Your King Comes

The next day the huge crowd that had arrived for the Feast heard that Jesus was entering Jerusalem. They broke off palm branches and went out to meet him. And they cheered:

> Hosanna!
> Blessed is he who comes in God's name!
> Yes! The King of Israel!

Jesus got a young donkey and rode it, just as the Scripture has it:

> No fear, Daughter Zion:
>> See how your king comes,
>> riding a donkey's colt.

The disciples didn't notice the fulfillment of many Scriptures at the time, but after Jesus was glorified, they remembered that what was written about him matched what was done to him.

The crowd that had been with him when he called Lazarus from the tomb, raising him from the dead, was there giving eyewitness accounts. It was because they had spread the word of this latest God-sign that the crowd swelled to a welcoming parade. The Pharisees took one look and threw up their hands: "It's out of control. The world's in a stampede after him."

### A Grain of Wheat Must Die

There were some Greeks in town who had come up to worship at the Feast. They approached Philip, who was from Bethsaida in Galilee: "Sir, we want to see Jesus. Can you help us?"

Philip went and told Andrew. Andrew and Philip together told Jesus. Jesus answered, "Time's up. The time has come for the Son of Man to be glorified.

"Listen carefully: Unless a grain of wheat is buried in the ground, dead to the world, it is never any more than a grain of wheat. But if it is buried, it sprouts and reproduces itself many times over. In the same way, anyone who holds on to life just as it is destroys that life. But if you let it go, reckless in your love, you'll have it forever, real and eternal.

"If any of you wants to serve me, then follow me. Then you'll be where I am, ready to serve at a moment's notice. The Father will honor and reward anyone who serves me.

"Right now I am storm-tossed. And what am I going to say? 'Father, get me out of this'? No, this is why I came in the first place. I'll say, 'Father, put your glory on display.'"

A voice came out of the sky: "I have glorified it, and I'll glorify it again."

The listening crowd said, "Thunder!"

Others said, "An angel spoke to him!"

Jesus said, "The voice didn't come for me but for you. At this moment the world is in crisis. Now Satan, the ruler of this world, will be thrown out. And I, as I am lifted up from the earth, will attract everyone to me and gather them around me." He put it this way to show how he was going to be put to death.

Voices from the crowd answered, "We heard from God's Law that the Messiah lasts forever. How can it be necessary, as you put it, that the Son of Man 'be lifted up'? Who is this 'Son of Man'?"

Jesus said, "For a brief time still, the light is among you. Walk by the light you have so darkness doesn't destroy you. If you walk in darkness, you don't know where you're going. As you have the light, believe in the light. Then the light will be within you, and shining through your lives. You'll be children of light."

### Their Eyes Are Blinded

Jesus said all this, and then went into hiding. All these God-signs he had given them and they still didn't get it, still wouldn't trust him. This proved that the prophet Isaiah was right:

> God, who believed what we preached?
> Who recognized God's arm, outstretched and ready to act?

First they wouldn't believe, then they *couldn't* — again, just as

Isaiah said:

> Their eyes are blinded,
> > their hearts are hardened,
> So that they wouldn't see with their eyes
> > and perceive with their hearts,
> And turn to me, God,
> > so I could heal them.

Isaiah said these things after he got a glimpse of God's cascading brightness that would pour through the Messiah.

On the other hand, a considerable number from the ranks of the leaders did believe. But because of the Pharisees, they didn't come out in the open with it. They were afraid of getting kicked out of the meeting place. When push came to shove they cared more for human approval than for God's glory.

Jesus summed it all up when he cried out, "Whoever believes in me, believes not just in me but in the One who sent me. Whoever looks at me is looking, in fact, at the One who sent me. I am Light that has come into the world so that all who believe in me won't have to stay any longer in the dark.

"If anyone hears what I am saying and doesn't take it seriously, I don't reject him. I didn't come to reject the world; I came to save the world. But you need to know that whoever puts me off, refusing to take in what I'm saying, is willfully choosing rejection. The Word, the Word-made-flesh that I have spoken and that I am, *that* Word and no other is the last word. I'm not making any of this up on my own. The Father who sent me gave me orders, told me what to say and how to say it. And I know exactly what his command produces: real and eternal life. That's all I have to say. What the Father told me, I tell you."

## Washing His Disciples' Feet

**13.** Just before the Passover Feast, Jesus knew that the time had come to leave this world to go to the Father. Having loved his dear companions, he continued to love them right to the end. It was suppertime. The Devil by now had Judas, son of Simon the Iscariot, firmly in his grip, all set for the betrayal.

Jesus knew that the Father had put him in complete charge of everything, that he came from God and was on his way back to God. So he got up from the supper table, set aside his robe, and put on an apron. Then he poured water into a basin and began to wash the feet of the disciples, drying them with his apron. When he got to Simon Peter, Peter said, "Master, *you* wash *my* feet?"

Jesus answered, "You don't understand now what I'm doing, but it will be clear enough to you later."

Peter persisted, "You're not going to wash my feet — ever!"

Jesus said, "If I don't wash you, you can't be part of what I'm doing."

"Master!" said Peter. "Not only my feet, then. Wash my hands! Wash my head!"

Jesus said, "If you've had a bath in the morning, you only need your feet washed now and you're clean from head to toe. My concern, you understand, is holiness, not hygiene. So now you're clean. But not every one of you." (He knew who was betraying him. That's why he said, "Not every one of you.") After he had finished washing their feet, he took his robe, put it back on, and went back to his place at the table.

Then he said, "Do you understand what I have done to you? You address me as 'Teacher' and 'Master,' and rightly so. That is what I am. So if I, the Master and Teacher, washed your feet, you must now wash each other's feet. I've laid down a pattern for you. What I've done, you do. I'm only pointing out the obvious. A servant is not ranked above his master; an employee doesn't give orders to the employer. If you understand what I'm telling you, act like it — and live a blessed life.

## The One Who Ate Bread at My Table

"I'm not including all of you in this. I know precisely whom I've selected, so as not to interfere with the fulfillment of this Scripture:

> The one who ate bread at my table
> Turned on his heel against me.

"I'm telling you all this ahead of time so that when it happens you will believe that I am who I say I am. Make sure you get this right: Receiving someone I send is the same as receiving me, just as receiving me is the same as receiving the One who sent me."

After he said these things, Jesus became visibly upset, and then he told them why. "One of you is going to betray me."

The disciples looked around at one another, wondering who on earth he was talking about. One of the disciples, the one Jesus loved dearly, was reclining against him, his head on his shoulder. Peter motioned to him to ask who Jesus might be talking about. So, being the closest, he said, "Master, who?"

Jesus said, "The one to whom I give this crust of bread after I've dipped it." Then he dipped the crust and gave it to Judas, son of Simon the Iscariot. As soon as the bread was in his hand, Satan entered him.

"What you must do," said Jesus, "do. Do it and get it over with."

No one around the supper table knew why he said this to him. Some thought that since Judas was their treasurer, Jesus was telling him to buy what they needed for the Feast, or that he should give something to the poor.

Judas, with the piece of bread, left. It was night.

## A New Command

When he had left, Jesus said, "Now the Son of Man is seen for who he is, and God seen for who he is in him. The moment God is seen in him, God's glory will be on display. In glorifying him, he himself is glorified — glory all around!

"Children, I am with you for only a short time longer. You are going to look high and low for me. But just as I told the Jews, I'm telling you: 'Where I go, you are not able to come.'

"Let me give you a new command: Love one another. In the same way I loved you, you love one another. This is how everyone will recognize that you are my disciples — when they see the love you have for each other."

Simon Peter asked, "Master, just where are you going?"

Jesus answered, "You can't now follow me where I'm going. You will follow later."

"Master," said Peter, "why can't I follow now? I'll lay down my life for you!"

"Really? You'll lay down your life for me? The truth is that before the rooster crows, you'll deny me three times."

## The Road

**14.** "Don't let this throw you. You trust God, don't you? Trust me. There is plenty of room for you in my Father's home. If that weren't so, would I have told you that I'm on my way to get a room ready for you? And if I'm on my way to get your room ready, I'll come back and get you so you can live where I live. And you already know the road I'm taking."

Thomas said, "Master, we have no idea where you're going. How do you expect us to know the road?"

Jesus said, "I am the Road, also the Truth, also the Life. No one gets to the Father apart from me. If you really knew me, you would know my Father as well. From now on, you do know him. You've even seen him!"

Philip said, "Master, show us the Father; then we'll be content."

"You've been with me all this time, Philip, and you still don't understand? To see me is to see the Father. So how can you ask, 'Where is the Father?' Don't you believe that I am in the Father and the Father is in me? The words that I speak to you aren't mere words. I don't just make them up on my own. The Father who resides in me crafts each word into a divine act.

"Believe me: I am in my Father and my Father is in me. If you can't believe that, believe what you see — these works. The person who trusts me will not only do what I'm doing but even greater things, because I, on my way to the Father, am giving you the same work to do that I've been doing. You can count on it. From now on, whatever you request along the lines of who I am and what I am doing, I'll do it. That's how the Father will be seen for who he is in the Son. I mean it. Whatever you request in this way, I'll do.

### The Spirit of Truth

"If you love me, show it by doing what I've told you. I will talk to the Father, and he'll provide you another Friend so that you will always have someone with you. This Friend is the Spirit of Truth. The godless world can't take him in because it doesn't have eyes to see him, doesn't know what to look for. But you know him already because he has been staying with you, and will even be *in* you!

"I will not leave you orphaned. I'm coming back. In just a little while the world will no longer see me, but you're going to see me because I am alive and you're about to come alive. At that moment you will know absolutely that I'm in my Father, and you're in me, and I'm in you.

"The person who knows my commandments and keeps them, that's who loves me. And the person who loves me will be loved by my Father, and I will love him and make myself plain to him."

Judas (not Iscariot) said, "Master, why is it that you are about to make yourself plain to us but not to the world?"

"Because a loveless world," said Jesus, "is a sightless world. If anyone loves me, he will carefully keep my word and my Father will love him—we'll move right into the neighborhood! Not loving me means not keeping my words. The message you are hearing isn't mine. It's the message of the Father who sent me.

"I'm telling you these things while I'm still living with you. The Friend, the Holy Spirit whom the Father will send at my request, will make everything plain to you. He will remind you of all the things I have told you. I'm leaving you well and whole. That's my parting gift to you. Peace. I don't leave you the way you're used to being left—feeling abandoned, bereft. So don't be upset. Don't be distraught.

---

> The Holy Spirit is one of the three persons of God—Father, Son, and Holy Spirit. For many of us, this is a difficult concept to grasp. The Scriptures declare that there is only one living God, yet we learn from these same Scriptures that he comprises three separate personages. One way to partially visualize this concept is to examine the nature of water ($H_2O$). Water is one element, but it can take on the form of three distinct properties—liquid, ice, and vapor. An egg is another picture. It is comprised of the white, the yolk, and the shell, yet it is still one egg. Of course, by no means do these examples paint a complete picture of God, but they are illustrative of the fact that his three "persons" in no way invalidate his oneness.
>
> As presented here by Jesus, the Holy Spirit is not a vague, ethereal life force. He is not impersonal or unthinking. The Holy Spirit is a "person" equal in every way with the Father and the Son. These Scriptures tell us that all the characteristics of God apparent in the Father and the Son are equally apparent in the Holy Spirit. However, we'll also see that the Holy Spirit has specific roles and functions in our lives. He is the Spirit of Truth—our guide. He's also our counselor, teacher, comforter, and friend.

---

"You've heard me tell you, 'I'm going away, and I'm coming back.' If you loved me, you would be glad that I'm on my way to the Father because the Father is the goal and purpose of my life.

"I've told you this ahead of time, before it happens, so that when it does happen, the confirmation will deepen your belief in me. I'll not be talking with you much more like this because the chief of this godless world is about to attack. But don't worry — he has nothing on me, no claim on me. But so the world might know how thoroughly I love the Father, I am carrying out my Father's instructions right down to the last detail.

"Get up. Let's go. It's time to leave here."

### The Vine and the Branches

**15.** "I am the Real Vine and my Father is the Farmer. He cuts off every branch of me that doesn't bear grapes. And every branch that is grape-bearing he prunes back so it will bear even more. You are already pruned back by the message I have spoken.

"Live in me. Make your home in me just as I do in you. In the same way that a branch can't bear grapes by itself but only by being joined to the vine, you can't bear fruit unless you are joined with me.

"I am the Vine, you are the branches. When you're joined with me and I with you, the relation intimate and organic, the harvest is sure to be abundant. Separated, you can't produce a thing. Anyone who separates from me is deadwood, gathered up and thrown on the bonfire. But if you make yourselves at home with me and my words are at home in you, you can be sure that whatever you ask will be listened to and acted upon. This is how my Father shows who he is — when you produce grapes, when you mature as my disciples.

"I've loved you the way my Father has loved me. Make yourselves at home in my love. If you keep my commands, you'll remain intimately at home in my love. That's what I've done — kept my Father's commands and made myself at home in his love.

"I've told you these things for a purpose: that my joy might be your joy, and your joy wholly mature. This is my command: Love one another the way I loved you. This is the very best way to love. Put your life on the line for your friends. You are my friends when you do the things I command you. I'm no longer calling you servants because servants don't understand what their master is thinking and planning.

No, I've named you friends because I've let you in on everything I've heard from the Father.

"You didn't choose me, remember; I chose you, and put you in the world to bear fruit, fruit that won't spoil. As fruit bearers, whatever you ask the Father in relation to me, he gives you.

"But remember the root command: Love one another.

### Hated by the World

"If you find the godless world is hating you, remember it got its start hating me. If you lived on the world's terms, the world would love you as one of its own. But since I picked you to live on God's terms and no longer on the world's terms, the world is going to hate you.

"When that happens, remember this: Servants don't get better treatment than their masters. If they beat on me, they will certainly beat on you. If they did what I told them, they will do what you tell them.

"They are going to do all these things to you because of the way they treated me, because they don't know the One who sent me. If I hadn't come and told them all this in plain language, it wouldn't be so bad. As it is, they have no excuse. Hate me, hate my Father — it's all the same. If I hadn't done what I have done among them, works no one has *ever* done, they wouldn't be to blame. But they saw the God-signs and hated anyway, both me and my Father. Interesting — they have verified the truth of their own Scriptures where it is written, 'They hated me for no good reason.'

"When the Friend I plan to send you from the Father comes — the Spirit of Truth issuing from the Father — he will confirm everything about me. You, too, from your side must give your confirming evidence, since you are in this with me from the start."

**16.** "I've told you these things to prepare you for rough times ahead. They are going to throw you out of the meeting places. There will even come a time when anyone who kills you will think he's doing God a favor. They will do these things because they never really understood the Father. I've told you these things so that when the time comes and they start in on you, you'll be well-warned and ready for them.

## The Friend Will Come

"I didn't tell you this earlier because I was with you every day. But now I am on my way to the One who sent me. Not one of you has asked, 'Where are you going?' Instead, the longer I've talked, the sadder you've become. So let me say it again, this truth: It's better for you that I leave. If I don't leave, the Friend won't come. But if I go, I'll send him to you.

"When he comes, he'll expose the error of the godless world's view of sin, righteousness, and judgment: He'll show them that their refusal to believe in me is their basic sin; that righteousness comes from above, where I am with the Father, out of their sight and control; that judgment takes place as the ruler of this godless world is brought to trial and convicted.

"I still have many things to tell you, but you can't handle them now. But when the Friend comes, the Spirit of the Truth, he will take you by the hand and guide you into all the truth there is. He won't draw attention to himself, but will make sense out of what is about to happen and, indeed, out of all that I have done and said. He will honor me; he will take from me and deliver it to you. Everything the Father has is also mine. That is why I've said, 'He takes from me and delivers to you.'

"In a day or so you're not going to see me, but then in another day or so you will see me."

## Joy Like a River Overflowing

That stirred up a hornet's nest of questions among the disciples: "What's he talking about: 'In a day or so you're not going to see me, but then in another day or so you will see me'? And, 'Because I'm on my way to the Father'? What is this 'day or so'? We don't know what he's talking about."

Jesus knew they were dying to ask him what he meant, so he said, "Are you trying to figure out among yourselves what I meant when I said, 'In a day or so you're not going to see me, but then in another day or so you will see me'? Then fix this firmly in your minds: You're going to be in deep mourning while the godless world throws a party. You'll be sad, very sad, but your sadness will develop into gladness.

"When a woman gives birth, she has a hard time, there's no getting around it. But when the baby is born, there is joy in the birth. This new life in the world wipes out memory of the pain. The sadness you have right now is similar to that pain, but the coming joy is also similar. When I see you again, you'll be full of joy, and it will be a joy no one can rob from you. You'll no longer be so full of questions.

"This is what I want you to do: Ask the Father for whatever is in keeping with the things I've revealed to you. Ask in my name, according to my will, and he'll most certainly give it to you. Your joy will be a river overflowing its banks!

"I've used figures of speech in telling you these things. Soon I'll drop the figures and tell you about the Father in plain language. Then you can make your requests directly to him in relation to this life I've revealed to you. I won't continue making requests of the Father on your behalf. I won't need to. Because you've gone out on a limb, committed yourselves to love and trust in me, believing I came directly from the Father, the Father loves you directly. First, I left the Father and arrived in the world; now I leave the world and travel to the Father."

His disciples said, "Finally! You're giving it to us straight, in plain talk — no more figures of speech. Now we know that you know everything — it all comes together in you. You won't have to put up with our questions anymore. We're convinced you came from God."

Jesus answered them, "Do you finally believe? In fact, you're about to make a run for it — saving your own skins and abandoning me. But I'm not abandoned. The Father is with me. I've told you all this so that trusting me, you will be unshakable and assured, deeply at peace. In this godless world you will continue to experience difficulties. But take heart! I've conquered the world."

### Jesus' Prayer for His Followers

**17.** Jesus said these things. Then, raising his eyes in prayer, he said:

Father, it's time.
Display the bright splendor of your Son
So the Son in turn may show your bright splendor.
You put him in charge of everything human
So he might give real and eternal life to all in his charge.
And this is the real and eternal life:
That they know you,
The one and only true God,
And Jesus Christ, whom you sent.
I glorified you on earth
By completing down to the last detail
What you assigned me to do.
And now, Father, glorify me with your very own splendor,
The very splendor I had in your presence
Before there was a world.

———

I spelled out your character in detail
To the men and women you gave me.
They were yours in the first place;
Then you gave them to me,
And they have now done what you said.

They know now, beyond the shadow of a doubt,
That everything you gave me is firsthand from you,
For the message you gave me, I gave them;
And they took it, and were convinced
That I came from you.
They believed that you sent me.
I pray for them.
I'm not praying for the God-rejecting world
But for those you gave me,
For they are yours by right.
Everything mine is yours, and yours mine,
And my life is on display in them.
For I'm no longer going to be visible in the world;
They'll continue in the world
While I return to you.
Holy Father, guard them as they pursue this life
That you conferred as a gift through me,
So they can be one heart and mind
As we are one heart and mind.
As long as I was with them, I guarded them
In the pursuit of the life you gave through me;
I even posted a night watch.
And not one of them got away,
Except for the rebel bent on destruction
(the exception that proved the rule of Scripture).

———

Now I'm returning to you.
I'm saying these things in the world's hearing
So my people can experience
My joy completed in them.
I gave them your word;
The godless world hated them because of it,
Because they didn't join the world's ways,

Just as I didn't join the world's ways.
I'm not asking that you take them out of the world
But that you guard them from the Evil One.
They are no more defined by the world
Than I am defined by the world.
Make them holy — consecrated — with the truth;
Your word is consecrating truth.
In the same way that you gave me a mission in the world,
I give them a mission in the world.
I'm consecrating myself for their sakes
So they'll be truth-consecrated in their mission.

————

I'm praying not only for them
But also for those who will believe in me
Because of them and their witness about me.
The goal is for all of them to become one heart and mind —
Just as you, Father, are in me and I in you,
So they might be one heart and mind with us.
Then the world might believe that you, in fact, sent me.
The same glory you gave me, I gave them,
So they'll be as unified and together as we are —
I in them and you in me.
Then they'll be mature in this oneness,
And give the godless world evidence
That you've sent me and loved them
In the same way you've loved me.

————

Father, I want those you gave me
To be with me, right where I am,
So they can see my glory, the splendor you gave me,
Having loved me
Long before there ever was a world.

Righteous Father, the world has never known you,
But I have known you, and these disciples know
That you sent me on this mission.
I have made your very being known to them —
Who you are and what you do —
And continue to make it known,
So that your love for me
Might be in them
Exactly as I am in them.

## SEARCHER ON THE WAY

*From the Head to the Heart*

Blaise Pascal, born in 1623, was a brilliant scientist, mathematician, and philosopher. Although he lived to be only thirty-nine, he created mathematical theorems that are still used today. He was known for his mastery of logic, reason, and probability, writing volumes of theory, rhetoric, and prose that remain foundational in contemporary education. Whether it was designing a mechanical calculator, discovering the properties of a vacuum, or debating the existence of God with the finest minds in Europe, Pascal was known as a truly special intellect.

Although Pascal had a genius mind, he struggled with questions of the soul. Beginning with the unbearable loss of his mother to a mysterious illness when he was three, he later developed his own illness that sapped his life. Ultimately, Pascal's intellect couldn't provide all the answers.

On November 23, 1654, Blaise Pascal was reading chapter 17 of John when he had a life-changing encounter with God. He wrote the following:

From about half past ten at night to about half an hour after midnight,
FIRE
"God of Abraham, God of Isaac, God of Jacob," not of philosophers and scholars
Certitude, heartfelt joy, peace.
God of Jesus Christ.
God of Jesus Christ.
The world forgotten, everything except God.
"O righteous Father, the world has not known You, but I have known You" (John 17:25).
Joy, joy, joy, tears of joy.

It was at this moment that Pascal knew it wasn't enough to know about God or debate his existence with the finest thinkers in the world. Rather, it was essential to meet God personally.

Pascal was an intellectual giant who wrote about God for years. However, it was this emotional event that shook Pascal into the truth that you can't know God through intellect alone. He later wrote, "The heart has its reasons; that reason knows not of."

### Seized in the Garden at Night

**18.** Jesus, having prayed this prayer, left with his disciples and crossed over the brook Kidron at a place where there was a garden. He and his disciples entered it.

Judas, his betrayer, knew the place because Jesus and his disciples went there often. So Judas led the way to the garden, and the Roman soldiers and police sent by the high priests and Pharisees followed. They arrived there with lanterns and torches and swords. Jesus, knowing by now everything that was coming down on him, went out and met them. He said, "Who are you after?"

They answered, "Jesus the Nazarene."

He said, "That's me." The soldiers recoiled, totally taken aback. Judas, his betrayer, stood out like a sore thumb.

Jesus asked again, "Who are you after?"

They answered, "Jesus the Nazarene."

"I told you," said Jesus, "that's me. I'm the one. So if it's me you're after, let these others go." (This validated the words in his prayer, "I didn't lose one of those you gave.")

Just then Simon Peter, who was carrying a sword, pulled it from its sheath and struck the Chief Priest's servant, cutting off his right ear. Malchus was the servant's name.

Jesus ordered Peter, "Put back your sword. Do you think for a minute I'm not going to drink this cup the Father gave me?"

Then the Roman soldiers under their commander, joined by the Jewish police, seized Jesus and tied him up. They took him first to Annas, father-in-law of Caiaphas. Caiaphas was the Chief Priest that year. It was Caiaphas who had advised the Jews that it was to their advantage that one man die for the people.

Simon Peter and another disciple followed Jesus. That other disciple was known to the Chief Priest, and so he went in with Jesus to the Chief Priest's courtyard. Peter had to stay outside. Then the other disciple went out, spoke to the doorkeeper, and got Peter in.

The young woman who was the doorkeeper said to Peter, "Aren't you one of this man's disciples?"

He said, "No, I'm not."

The servants and police had made a fire because of the cold and were huddled there warming themselves. Peter stood with them, trying to get warm.


## The Interrogation

Annas interrogated Jesus regarding his disciples and his teaching. Jesus answered, "I've spoken openly in public. I've taught regularly in meeting places and the Temple, where the Jews all come together. Everything has been out in the open. I've said nothing in secret. So why are you treating me like a conspirator? Question those who have been listening to me. They know well what I have said. My teachings have all been aboveboard."

When he said this, one of the policemen standing there slapped Jesus across the face, saying, "How dare you speak to the Chief Priest like that!"

Jesus replied, "If I've said something wrong, prove it. But if I've spoken the plain truth, why this slapping around?"

Then Annas sent him, still tied up, to the Chief Priest Caiaphas.

Meanwhile, Simon Peter was back at the fire, still trying to get warm. The others there said to him, "Aren't you one of his disciples?"

He denied it, "Not me."

One of the Chief Priest's servants, a relative of the man whose ear Peter had cut off, said, "Didn't I see you in the garden with him?"

Again, Peter denied it. Just then a rooster crowed.

## The King of the Jews

They led Jesus then from Caiaphas to the Roman governor's palace. It was early morning. They themselves didn't enter the palace because they didn't want to be disqualified from eating the Passover. So Pilate came out to them and spoke. "What charge do you bring against this man?"

They said, "If he hadn't been doing something evil, do you think we'd be here bothering you?"

Pilate said, "You take him. Judge him by *your* law."

The Jews said, "We're not allowed to kill anyone." (This would confirm Jesus' word indicating the way he would die.)

Pilate went back into the palace and called for Jesus. He said, "Are you the 'King of the Jews'?"

Jesus answered, "Are you saying this on your own, or did others tell you this about me?"

Pilate said, "Do I look like a Jew? Your people and your high priests turned you over to me. What did you do?"

"My kingdom," said Jesus, "doesn't consist of what you see around you. If it did, my followers would fight so that I wouldn't be handed over to the Jews. But I'm not that kind of king, not the world's kind of king."

Then Pilate said, "So, are you a king or not?"

Jesus answered, "You tell me. Because I am King, I was born and entered the world so that I could witness to the truth. Everyone who cares for truth, who has any feeling for the truth, recognizes my voice."

Pilate said, "What is truth?"

Then he went back out to the Jews and told them, "I find nothing wrong in this man. It's your custom that I pardon one prisoner at Passover. Do you want me to pardon the 'King of the Jews'?"

They shouted back, "Not this one, but Barabbas!" Barabbas was a Jewish freedom fighter.

## The Thorn Crown of the King

**19.** So Pilate took Jesus and had him whipped. The soldiers, having braided a crown from thorns, set it on his head, threw a purple robe over him, and approached him with, "Hail, King of the Jews!" Then they greeted him with slaps in the face.

Pilate went back out again and said to them, "I present him to you, but I want you to know that I do not find him guilty of any crime." Just then Jesus came out wearing the thorn crown and purple robe.

Pilate announced, "Here he is: the Man."

When the high priests and police saw him, they shouted in a frenzy, "Crucify! Crucify!"

Pilate told them, "You take him. You crucify him. I find nothing wrong with him."

The Jews answered, "We have a law, and by that law he must die because he claimed to be the Son of God."

When Pilate heard this, he became even more scared. He went back into the palace and said to Jesus, "Where did you come from?"

Jesus gave no answer.

Pilate said, "You won't talk? Don't you know that I have the authority to pardon you, and the authority to — crucify you?"

Jesus said, "You haven't a shred of authority over me except what has been given you from heaven. That's why the one who betrayed me to you has committed a far greater fault."

At this, Pilate tried his best to pardon him, but the Jews shouted him down: "If you pardon this man, you're no friend of Caesar's. Anyone setting himself up as 'king' defies Caesar."

When Pilate heard those words, he led Jesus outside. He sat down at the judgment seat in the area designated Stone Court (in Hebrew, *Gabbatha*). It was the preparation day for Passover. The hour was noon. Pilate said to the Jews, "Here is your king."

They shouted back, "Kill him! Kill him! Crucify him!"

Pilate said, "I am to crucify your king?"

The high priests answered, "We have no king except Caesar."

Pilate caved in to their demand. He turned him over to be crucified.

## The Crucifixion

They took Jesus away. Carrying his cross, Jesus went out to the place called Skull Hill (the name in Hebrew is *Golgotha*), where they crucified him, and with him two others, one on each side, Jesus in the middle. Pilate wrote a sign and had it placed on the cross. It read:

JESUS THE NAZARENE
THE KING OF THE JEWS.

Many of the Jews read the sign because the place where Jesus was crucified was right next to the city. It was written in Hebrew, Latin, and Greek. The Jewish high priests objected. "Don't write," they said to Pilate, "'The King of the Jews.' Make it, 'This man said, "I am the King of the Jews."'"

Pilate said, "What I've written, I've written."

When they crucified him, the Roman soldiers took his clothes and divided them up four ways, to each soldier a fourth. But his robe was seamless, a single piece of weaving, so they said to each other, "Let's not tear it up. Let's throw dice to see who gets it." This confirmed the Scripture that said, "They divided up my clothes among them and threw dice for my coat." (The soldiers validated the Scriptures!)

While the soldiers were looking after themselves, Jesus' mother, his aunt, Mary the wife of Clopas, and Mary Magdalene stood at the foot of the cross. Jesus saw his mother and the disciple he loved standing near her. He said to his mother, "Woman, here is your son." Then to the disciple, "Here is your mother." From that moment the disciple accepted her as his own mother.

Jesus, seeing that everything had been completed so that the Scripture record might also be complete, then said, "I'm thirsty."

A jug of sour wine was standing by. Someone put a sponge soaked with the wine on a javelin and lifted it to his mouth. After he took the wine, Jesus said, "It's done . . . complete." Bowing his head, he offered up his spirit.

Then the Jews, since it was the day of Sabbath preparation, and so the bodies wouldn't stay on the crosses over the Sabbath (it was a high holy day that year), petitioned Pilate that their legs be broken to speed death, and the bodies taken down. So the soldiers came and broke the legs of the first man crucified with Jesus, and then the other. When they got to Jesus, they saw that he was already dead, so they didn't break his legs. One of the soldiers stabbed him in the side with his spear. Blood and water gushed out.

The eyewitness to these things has presented an accurate report. He saw it himself and is telling the truth so that you, also, will believe.

These things that happened confirmed the Scripture, "Not a bone in his body was broken," and the other Scripture that reads, "They will stare at the one they pierced."

The crucifixion account of Jesus Christ agrees with the first-century customs and practices of the Romans. The evidence for Christ's horrible and painful death is unquestioned by today's scholars. Crucifixion typically began with a scourging of the victim's back. The Romans used a whip called a flagrum, which consisted of small pieces of bone and metal attached to a number of leather strands. The number of blows was typically thirty-nine (one less than the forty called for in the Jewish Law, to prevent a counting error). During the scourging, the skin was ripped from the back, exposing a bloody mass of tissue and bone.

After the flogging, the victim was often forced to carry his own 100-pound crossbar, or patibulum, to the execution site. Once there, the patibulum was put on the ground and the victim was forced to lie upon it. Spikes about 7 inches long and 3/8 of an inch in diameter were driven into the wrists. Already standing at the crucifixion site would be the 7-foot-tall post, called a stipes. The patibulum was lifted onto the stipes, and the victim's body was awkwardly turned so that the feet could be nailed to it. At this point, there was tremendous strain put on the wrists, arms, and shoulders, resulting in a dislocation of the shoulder and elbow joints.

Ultimately, the mechanism of death in crucifixion was suffocation. To breathe, the victim was forced to push up on his feet to allow for inflation of the lungs. As the body weakened and pain in the feet and legs became unbearable, the victim was forced to trade breathing for pain and exhaustion. Eventually (sometimes two or three days), the victim would succumb in this horrible way.

After all this, Joseph of Arimathea (he was a disciple of Jesus, but secretly, because he was intimidated by the Jews) petitioned Pilate to take the body of Jesus. Pilate gave permission. So Joseph came and took the body.

Nicodemus, who had first come to Jesus at night, came now in broad daylight carrying a mixture of myrrh and aloes, about seventy-five pounds. They took Jesus' body and, following the Jewish burial custom, wrapped it in linen with the spices. There was a garden near the place he was crucified, and in the garden a new tomb in which no one had yet been placed. So, because it was Sabbath preparation for the Jews and the tomb was convenient, they placed Jesus in it.

## Resurrection!

**20.** Early in the morning on the first day of the week, while it was still dark, Mary Magdalene came to the tomb and saw that the stone was moved away from the entrance. She ran at once to Simon Peter and the other disciple, the one Jesus loved, breathlessly panting, "They took the Master from the tomb. We don't know where they've put him."

Peter and the other disciple left immediately for the tomb. They ran, neck and neck. The other disciple got to the tomb first, outrunning Peter. Stooping to look in, he saw the pieces of linen cloth lying there, but he didn't go in. Simon Peter arrived after him, entered the tomb, observed the linen cloths lying there, and the kerchief used to cover his head not lying with the linen cloths but separate, neatly folded by itself. Then the other disciple, the one who had gotten there first, went into the tomb, took one look at the evidence, and believed. No one yet knew from the Scripture that he had to rise from the dead. The disciples then went back home.

But Mary stood outside the tomb weeping. As she wept, she knelt to look into the tomb and saw two angels sitting there, dressed in white, one at the head, the other at the foot of where Jesus' body had been laid. They said to her, "Woman, why do you weep?"

"They took my Master," she said, "and I don't know where they put him." After she said this, she turned away and saw Jesus standing there. But she didn't recognize him.

Jesus spoke to her, "Woman, why do you weep? Who are you looking for?"

She, thinking that he was the gardener, said, "Mister, if you took him, tell me where you put him so I can care for him."

Jesus said, "Mary."

Turning to face him, she said in Hebrew, "*Rabboni!*" meaning "Teacher!"

Jesus said, "Don't cling to me, for I have not yet ascended to the Father. Go to my brothers and tell them, 'I ascend to my Father and your Father, my God and your God.'"

Mary Magdalene went, telling the news to the disciples: "I saw the Master!" And she told them everything he said to her.

## SEARCHER ON THE WAY
*Testimony of the Gospels*

Simon Greenleaf was born in Massachusetts in 1783. He became an attorney and practiced law in Maine for a number of years. In 1833, Greenleaf joined the staff at Harvard University, where he is credited as one of the founders of Harvard Law School. In 1842, he authored the authoritative three-volume text *A Treatise on the Law of Evidence,* which is still considered "the greatest single authority on evidence in the entire literature of legal procedure."

Greenleaf literally wrote the rules of evidence for the U.S. legal system. He was certainly a man who knew how to weigh the facts. Greenleaf was also a religious skeptic until he accepted a challenge by his students to investigate the case for Christ's resurrection. He was certain that a careful examination of the biblical texts would prove all the myths at the heart of Christianity. Although biased, he tried to pursue his challenge with an open mind.

> In examining the evidence of the Christian religion,
> it is essential to the discovery of truth that we bring
> to the investigation a mind freed, as far as possible,
> from existing prejudice, and open to conviction.
> There should be a readiness, on our part, to
> investigate with candor to follow the truth wherever
> it may lead us.

After collecting and examining the evidence based on authoritative legal rules, Greenleaf concluded the exact opposite of his original premise. In the end, the evidence revealed that the Gospel writers were reliable witnesses and the resurrection of Jesus Christ really happened. Greenleaf gathered his findings in the classic *Testimony of the Evangelists*.

> Let [the Gospel's] testimony be sifted, as it were
> given in a court of justice on the side of the adverse

## To Believe

Later on that day, the disciples had gathered together, but, fearful of the Jews, had locked all the doors in the house. Jesus entered, stood among them, and said, "Peace to you." Then he showed them his hands and side.

The disciples, seeing the Master with their own eyes, were exuberant. Jesus repeated his greeting: "Peace to you. Just as the Father sent me, I send you."

Then he took a deep breath and breathed into them. "Receive the Holy Spirit," he said. "If you forgive someone's sins, they're gone for good. If you don't forgive sins, what are you going to do with them?"

But Thomas, sometimes called the Twin, one of the Twelve, was not with them when Jesus came. The other disciples told him, "We saw the Master."

But he said, "Unless I see the nail holes in his hands, put my finger in the nail holes, and stick my hand in his side, I won't believe it."

Eight days later, his disciples were again in the room. This time Thomas was with them. Jesus came through the locked doors, stood among them, and said, "Peace to you."

Then he focused his attention on Thomas. "Take your finger and examine my hands. Take your hand and stick it in my side. Don't be unbelieving. Believe."

Thomas said, "My Master! My God!"

Jesus said, "So, you believe because you've seen with your own eyes. Even better blessings are in store for those who believe without seeing."

Jesus provided far more God-revealing signs than are written down in this book. These are written down so you will believe that Jesus is the Messiah, the Son of God, and in the act of believing, have real and eternal life in the way he personally revealed it.

### Fishing

**21.** After this, Jesus appeared again to the disciples, this time at the Tiberias Sea (the Sea of Galilee). This is how he did it: Simon Peter, Thomas (nicknamed "Twin"), Nathanael from Cana in Galilee, the brothers Zebedee, and two other disciples were together. Simon Peter announced, "I'm going fishing."

The rest of them replied, "We're going with you." They went out and got in the boat. They caught nothing that night. When the sun came up, Jesus was standing on the beach, but they didn't recognize him.

Jesus spoke to them: "Good morning! Did you catch anything for breakfast?"

They answered, "No."

He said, "Throw the net off the right side of the boat and see what happens."

They did what he said. All of a sudden there were so many fish in it, they weren't strong enough to pull it in.

Then the disciple Jesus loved said to Peter, "It's the Master!"

When Simon Peter realized that it was the Master, he threw on some clothes, for he was stripped for work, and dove into the sea. The other disciples came in by boat for they weren't far from land, a hundred yards or so, pulling along the net full of fish. When they got out of the boat, they saw a fire laid, with fish and bread cooking on it.

Jesus said, "Bring some of the fish you've just caught." Simon Peter joined them and pulled the net to shore — 153 big fish! And even with all those fish, the net didn't rip.

Jesus said, "Breakfast is ready." Not one of the disciples dared ask, "Who are you?" They knew it was the Master.

Jesus then took the bread and gave it to them. He did the same with the fish. This was now the third time Jesus had shown himself alive to the disciples since being raised from the dead.

## Do You Love Me?

After breakfast, Jesus said to Simon Peter, "Simon, son of John, do you love me more than these?"

"Yes, Master, you know I love you."

Jesus said, "Feed my lambs."

He then asked a second time, "Simon, son of John, do you love me?"

"Yes, Master, you know I love you."

Jesus said, "Shepherd my sheep."

Then he said it a third time: "Simon, son of John, do you love me?"

Peter was upset that he asked for the third time, "Do you love me?" so he answered, "Master, you know everything there is to know. You've got to know that I love you."

Jesus said, "Feed my sheep. I'm telling you the very truth now: When you were young you dressed yourself and went wherever you wished, but when you get old you'll have to stretch out your hands while someone else dresses you and takes you where you don't want to go." He said this to hint at the kind of death by which Peter would glorify God. And then he commanded, "Follow me."

Turning his head, Peter noticed the disciple Jesus loved following right behind. When Peter noticed him, he asked Jesus, "Master, what's going to happen to *him*?"

Jesus said, "If I want him to live until I come again, what's that to you? You — follow me." That is how the rumor got out among the brothers that this disciple wouldn't die. But that is not what Jesus said. He simply said, "If I want him to live until I come again, what's that to you?"

This is the same disciple who was eyewitness to all these things and wrote them down. And we all know that his eyewitness account is reliable and accurate.

There are so many other things Jesus did. If they were all written down, each of them, one by one, I can't imagine a world big enough to hold such a library of books.

## SEARCHER ON THE WAY
*The Atoning Act of an Alaskan Chief*

John Muir, the famous nineteenth-century explorer and naturalist, traveled to Alaska in 1879. In his book *Travels in Alaska,* Muir tells an amazing story of the Thlinkit Indians.

Two Thlinkit tribes, the Stickeen and the Sitka, had been at war all summer. It was getting late in the year, and if they didn't stop battling to store up food for the winter, they would all starve to death. So the Stickeen chief went out alone to a clearing and called out the leaders of the Sitka tribe.

"We have fought long enough; let us make peace. You brave Sitka warriors go home, and we will go home, and we will all set out to dry salmon and berries before it is too late."

The Sitka chief replied, "You may well say let us stop fighting, when you have had the best of it. You have killed ten more of my tribe than we have killed of yours. Give us ten Stickeen men to balance our blood-account; then, and not till then, will we make peace and go home."

"Very well," replied the Stickeen chief, "you know my rank. You know that I am worth ten common men and more. Take me and make peace."

This noble offer was promptly accepted; the Stickeen chief stepped forward and was shot down in sight of the fighting bands. Peace was thus established, and all made haste to their homes and ordinary work. The chief literally gave himself as a sacrifice for his people. He died that they might live.

Thirty years later, John's account of Jesus was shared with the Thlinkit tribes. The chiefs immediately understood the message.

"Yes, your words are good," they said. "The Son of God, the Chief of chiefs, the Maker of all the world, must be worth more than all mankind put together; therefore, when His blood was shed, the salvation of the world was made sure."

# INTERMISSION

Yes, we all pursue something.

    Whether wealth and power—prestige and success . . .

    Whether purpose and meaning—joy and hope . . .

    At the heart of it all, humanity seeks.

    We are different from all the other creatures on earth. We reason, we ponder, we meditate on the unknown. However, since we don't settle for instinct, we struggle with life's questions. We wrestle with pain, suffering, and trial. We test our conscience. We weigh thoughts of fairness and justice. We discern right and wrong. We cherish good—we contemplate evil.

    In a nutshell, existence isn't enough for humankind. We're all driven to pursue more.

    Living the "true life" is hard work. Pondering the miracle of our origin and the mystery of our destiny is deep stuff. The quest has driven some to numbing fear, others to hedonistic escapism, and still others to vain philosophy. Some commit their lives to good works and charity, while others go insane.

    So, looking at the legacy of humanity over the last 5,000 years, what seems to be the *Greatest Pursuit* of all?

    Success?

    Happiness?

    Power?

    Love?

Maybe asked better, What *should* be the *Greatest Pursuit* of all?

As you reflect on the journeyers that have gone before us, spend some time with this question. Go to a quiet place and journal your thoughts and experiences. What have you pursued in your life? What are you pursuing today? In the deepest place of your heart, what's pursuing you?

# A LITTLE FURTHER

THE *GREAT PURSUIT* CONTINUES

If you're just starting your quest or you've just found new inspiration to go a different path, we encourage you to dig deeper and seek more. To that end, we went to our friends at www.AllAboutGOD.com and www.GotQuestions.org to pick their brains. They've been collecting questions, preparing answers, and delivering content on the Web for a number of years. They've archived thousands of e-mail questions and prepared thousands of e-mail responses in the area of spiritual journeys.

We discovered that people really are asking questions—normal questions, not questions with big theological words. So, we've tried to dump any "religion-speak" and give you some of the nitty-gritty. Italicization indicates words or phrases directly from *The Message* text.

## Is there any real right or wrong?

You might have heard someone say, "There's no right and there's no wrong," but you have to ask yourself, is this statement right or wrong? And I'm sure you've heard someone say, "It's wrong for you to impose your morals on me!" But if you think about it, by telling you that something is wrong, that person is imposing morals on you!

The fact is, we all inherently know right from wrong; we just have this weird tendency to disregard morality when it conflicts with our desire for pleasure or personal gain. Sure, you might justify having an affair, but you certainly wouldn't condone your spouse cheating on you! And you might justify taking something without permission, but if you were the one being robbed you wouldn't think it was okay! There isn't a person alive today who would come home from work to discover that the house has been robbed and say, "Oh, how wonderful that this burglar is able to enjoy all of my things without my permission. And who am I to impose my view of right and wrong on this poor burglar?"

Here's a good way to determine right from wrong: Turn the situation around on yourself. Jesus said it best: "Treat people the same way you want them to treat you." Simply, we all know that murder, rape, lying, stealing, torture, and injustice are absolutely wrong because we wouldn't want any of these things to happen to us!

## How can anyone claim a universal system of morality?

Everyone has a God-given conscience. Not everyone acknowledges it, but everyone has one.

The human tendency to justify ourselves is evidence of a healthy conscience. We know that wrong is bad, so we want it to be right! If there were no such thing as right and wrong, we wouldn't have the capacity to weigh actions on the scales of justice. Yet we obviously have that ability, because we feel the need to justify ourselves!

Simply, God gave us his moral law to serve as a standard external to our God-given conscience. The "Ten Commandments" are a universal sample of God's moral standard. For example, you know that it's wrong to lie. No one needs to tell you that lying is wrong; your heart tells you that it's wrong. The ninth Commandment ("You shall not lie") serves to give your conscience a standard external to itself. So when your heart tells you it's wrong to lie, you can look at God's Law and say, "My heart is right, I shouldn't lie."

Isn't this the universal basis for all law? What is justice without notions of right and wrong? How can we have an insanity defense if we don't have sanity as a standard?

## Why do I even exist?

The Scriptures we read tell us that God's ultimate purpose for the cosmos is to reveal his glory. Those texts also tell us that God's ultimate purpose for mankind is to reveal his love. These are simple truths not only found in Scripture but also proclaimed in everything we see. When we peer to the edge of the massive universe, delve into the intricate world of the microscopic cell, explore principles of quantum mechanics, and map the digital code of the human genome, we can't deny the glorious complexity and unity in everything around us. Remarkably, it's all there for God's pleasure!

Remember David's Psalms? In a nutshell, they reveal that everything comes from God, everything lives by his power, everything declares his glory, and everything exists for his purpose. Yes, God created mankind for his pleasure. He didn't need to create us, but he chose to create us for his own pure enjoyment. God is a loving Father and we were created to be his children. It's no different with us—parents simply choose to have children to love them and raise them. Well, because of his love, God decided to make us his children. This was his pleasure and purpose in all things—from the beginning.

## If God exists, why is there evil in the world?

How could God allow for love without the potential for evil? God could have created organic robots programmed to forever say, "I love you," but such creatures would be incapable of a real love relationship.

Love is a choice, and the Scriptures say God desires a real love relationship with his creation. Love is not real unless we have the ability to not love. God is all-knowing. God knew that in a world with choice, there would be much evil. However, there would also be the capacity for real love.

As we saw in the books we read, the potential for love outweighs the existence of evil, especially if evil can exist for only a time. Evil is a side effect of love. Suffering and death are side effects of evil. The Scriptures reveal that this side effect is only for a time. Evil serves the limited purpose of establishing real love relationships between creation and the Creator, and evil will be done away with after that purpose is achieved.

## Why doesn't God still perform miracles like he did in the Bible?

When God performed amazing and powerful miracles for the Israelites, did that cause them to obey him? No, the Israelites constantly disobeyed and rebelled against God even though they saw all the miracles. The same people who saw God rain fire on a mountain and produce water from a rock later doubted God's role in their lives.

Jesus performed countless miracles, yet the vast majority of people did not believe in him. If God performed miracles today as he did in the past, the same result would occur. People would be amazed and would believe in God for a short time, but that faith would be shallow and would disappear the moment something unexpected or frightening occurred.

Actually, look all around you. God still performs miracles—just many of them go unnoticed or are denied. However, history shows that we don't need more miracles. What we need is to believe in the greatest miracle of all—that God came to earth in the Man, Jesus Christ. What have we done with that miracle?

## What about all of the atrocities we find in the Bible?

You may have read through our chosen texts and thought to yourself, "If this is God's book, I don't want to have anything to do with him!" Why is there so much depravity in the Bible? Why didn't God just leave those parts out? Well, because that just wouldn't be reality. God tells it like it is. The Bible is God's book and it serves its purpose well—it illustrates mankind's fundamental brokenness.

When reading through the biblical Scriptures it's important to distinguish between what the Bible RECORDS and what the Bible APPROVES. The fact is we read about a bunch of human depravity, and a bunch of God's judgment upon that depravity. But that doesn't mean God is responsible for mankind's actions, and it doesn't mean he enjoys sending judgment.

A recurring theme throughout the texts is God asking, "Why? Why are you doing this? Why do you bring judgment upon yourself? You know I'm not going to just let you get away with this, so why do you persist?" The Bible warns us flat out, *"Don't be misled: No one makes a fool of God.*

*What a person plants, he will harvest."* And just because God is righteous and just, that doesn't mean he enjoys punishing us. *"I take no pleasure in anyone's death. . . . Make a clean break! Live!"*

Undoubtedly, the most depraved act recorded in the Bible was the crucifixion of Jesus Christ. Christ was the only perfect being to ever tread the face of the earth—and we nailed him to a cross for it. But as we see throughout the historical texts, God can use our evil for good. God took the murder of his Son and turned it into the redemption of mankind. Whoever is willing to denounce evil and put his or her faith in Christ can have a new beginning with God.

## Don't all religions lead to God?

There's an old saying, "All roads lead to Rome." Well, all roads must lead away from Rome, too. It all depends on which direction you're going.

*Jesus said, "I am the Road, also the Truth, also the Life. No one gets to the Father apart from me."* The Scriptures tell us that on the road to heaven there are only two directions: toward Christ or away from him. You can accept this or you can reject this. You can call Jesus Lord or you can call him a liar. . . . But that's what he said.

*Many people sincerely believe that even though they've broken God's rules, they can earn his forgiveness by doing good works—for example, by observing the* Five Pillars of Islam, *or the* Buddhist Eight-Fold Path, *or the* Hindu Doctrine of Karma. *But how will doing some good works that we should have done all our lives make up for the countless times we've failed? The Scriptures tell us that we can scrub and scrub—using the strongest soaps—but the sin-grease won't come out!*

The Scriptures also tell us that someone has to pay for our sins, for we have rebelled against a just God. The fantastic news is that Jesus willingly took God's righteous judgment upon himself, and those who accept his death as payment for their sins will be reconciled to the God whom they've offended. If we could ever earn God's forgiveness, why would Jesus die? *"If a living relationship with God could come by rule-keeping, then Christ died unnecessarily."*

## What about the "ignorant" person who hasn't heard about Jesus?

The Scriptures tell us that God is perfectly loving, perfectly holy, and perfectly just. Therefore, it's against his nature to "hide the ball" on salvation or condemn someone who is ignorant of his truth. In fact, Scripture declares that God is loving and patient—"restraining himself on account of you, holding back the End because he doesn't want anyone lost."

God is a perfectly righteous judge. Although we don't understand all of his ways, he somehow reveals the simple truth of Jesus Christ to everyone willing to listen. In Africa, missionaries often tell how Christ reveals himself in nature. In India, many people meet Jesus for the first time in a dream or vision. Whatever the form of revelation, God holds each of us accountable for what we know and what we've done with that knowledge.


## What about all the wars caused in the name of Christianity?

First, just because someone claims to be a Christian doesn't necessarily make him a true follower. Second, a title or label doesn't make someone an "official" representative. Therefore, it's crucial to distinguish between biblical Christianity and the actions of those who merely claim the name. Sadly, this world is full of hypocrites. And if a group of people claim to be followers of Christ, yet they live out their lives contrary to his teachings, we shouldn't label that group Christian, we should call them hypocrites. Jesus himself reserved his harshest criticism for religious hypocrisy.

The point is we don't identify Christianity by citing the actions of hypocrites; we identify hypocrites by citing the teachings of Christ in the Bible. So, rather than ask, "What about all the wars caused in the name of Christianity?" we should ask, "Were those wars caused by Christians acting in line with Christ's teachings from the Bible?"

Remember, accepting Jesus Christ as your sin-bearer doesn't turn you into a robot. You still have the capacity and the freedom to choose right from wrong. The sad fact is we have a tendency to abuse our free will by abusing each other. So yes, Christians are still perfectly capable of making mistakes, even serious ones like wars.

## How can an all-loving God send anyone to hell?

Does God send people to hell, or do we decide to send ourselves there? God does everything possible to keep us out of hell while maintaining our nature as free-will human beings. God made us in his image and after his likeness, giving each of us the ultimate power to say "yes" or "no." If we choose to reject God, we choose to spend eternity separated from him.

You ask, "Is that really loving?" Read Mark and John again. God demonstrated his love for us on the cross at Calvary. Jesus willingly took God's righteous indignation upon himself, and whoever accepts his death upon the cross as payment for their sins will be reconciled to God—no questions asked! Yeah, I'd say that's "super love"!

God is righteous and just. Therefore, someone has to pay for our wrongs. However, God is all-loving. Therefore, he paid for them in full! Christ endured hell on earth so that we don't have to. It seems perfectly fair to me; either Jesus paid for my sins, or I'll have to!

I'm no "sinner"—I'm a good person! So don't tell me I need a savior! Sorry for the ugly "religious" word. I said I wouldn't use those, didn't I?

Well, let's look at what the Bible says about sin. "Sin" is a biblical term that simply means "rebellion against God"—missing God's standard. Whether it's passive rebellion (not doing what God told you) or active rebellion (doing what God specifically told you not to do), rebellion is "sin." You see, God made us—God made everything. Therefore, God makes the rules.

So, what are the rules? God just wants us to be good—plain and simple. You know, don't lie, don't steal; love God and love your neighbor; do unto others as you would have them do unto you . . .

Wait. Before we profess our innocence again, let's each ask ourselves, "Has my God-given conscience ever clearly warned me against doing something, but I chose to do it anyway?" What about lying? No one needs to tell us that lying is wrong. Have you ever told a lie? Or how about this one: We wouldn't want anybody to habitually use our name as a curse word. Have you ever used God's name to curse? That's called blasphemy, and God doesn't appreciate that either.

Well, we know these things are wrong, because if I called you a "lying blasphemer," you'd be offended! So, think about it carefully and judge for yourself. If you were to stand before God to give an account, would you be innocent or guilty? Sorry, I won't use the "sin" word next time.

## Why can't I just believe in Jesus without being one of those "religious" people?

You can.

## Why are Christians so intolerant, close-minded, and unapproachable?

I wish I knew.

We're all damaged goods going through this crazy thing called life. Actually, if tolerance means "to put up with," I hope we're all doing better than that. Jesus didn't call us to put up with each other; he called us to love one another—a much higher standard!

## How can Christians say they have the only true religion?

They can't. That's truly absurd—ludicrous.

Christians don't have any special religious truth unavailable to Jews, Muslims, Hindus, Buddhists, New Agers—anyone truly seeking God. Simply, it's what you do with Jesus, regardless of your religious affiliation. A religious label has nothing to do with ultimate truth. Neither does church membership, good works, public service, charitable giving, mantras, creeds, or codes. Straight up—it's what you do with Jesus.

It's not about a "true religion" anyway. It's about a true relationship with God through the sacrifice of his Son, Jesus Christ.

**Well, I don't believe in God because religion has caused more dispute, despair, and death than anything else in history.**

Agreed—religion has issues. In fact, religion has probably kept more people from God than anything else in history. Interestingly, it seems Jesus hates religion too, probably for the same reason. When he saw what the career "religious" people did to his father's house—the Temple in Jerusalem—Jesus was truly angry. He took a bullwhip out and showed what he thought of religion.

Actually, a true relationship with God isn't about religion at all—it's about discovering and establishing a relationship with God. It's trusting in Jesus and what he did on the cross for us, not on what we can do for ourselves.

A true relationship with the God of the universe isn't about "organized religion." It's not about hierarchical structures, ornate buildings, flamboyant preachers, or traditional rules and rituals. In fact, let's just drop the religious labels all together. Simply, it's all about Jesus. He's either the Son of God who offers the only true hope for the world, or he's not. Case closed.

# SOURCES

## Ecclesiastes

### Poem/Lyrics Before 3:14

Pete Seeger's words and music were inspired by the book of
Ecclesiastes and later recorded as "Turn! Turn! Turn!" by The Byrds
in 1966. (See LyricsFreak.com—http://www.lyricsfreak.com/b/byrds/
turn+turn+turn_20026419.html.)

### Searcher on the Way—A King's Epic Tale

*Tablet 10, Column 3,* translated by Yanita Chen, 1994. http://www
.mythome.org/gilgamesh10.html.
See also, *The Epic of Gilgamesh*, translated by Maureen Gallery Kovacs
(Stanford University Press, 1989), 85.

## Job

### Searcher on the Way—Grappling with the God-Pain Paradox

Extracted quote from *On Order*, the first book of the newly converted
Augustine in AD 386.
Final quote comes from Augustine's famous doctrine of "blessed fault."

### Poem/Lyrics After 10:22

Jonathan Foreman of Switchfoot, "The Shadow Proves the Sunshine,"
© 2005 Meadowgreen Music Company/Sugar Pete Songs (mg)/
Switchfoot Co-pub Designee. All Rights Reserved. Used by permission.

### Searcher on the Way—From Suffering to Life in the Hoop

John Neihardt, *Black Elk Speaks* (Lincoln, NE: University of Nebraska Press, reissue edition, 1988).

Michael Steltenkamp, "Reflections of Black Elk's daughter, Lucy Looks Twice," in *Black Elk; Holy Man of the Oglala* (Norman, OK: University of Oklahoma Press, September 1997).

### Poem/Lyrics After 18

Mac Powell, David Carr, Tai Anderson, Brad Avery, Mark Lee, "How Do You Know?" © 2005 Consuming Fire Music (admin.). All Rights Reserved. Used by permission.

### Poem After 23:9

Alfred Tennyson, in C. Ricks, "Where Is the Wonderful," *The Poems of Tennyson* (Longmans, 1969), 1807.

### Poem After 33:30

Emily Brontë, "No Coward Soul Is Mine," *The Complete Poems of Emily Jane Brontë*, ed. Clement Shorter, collected by C. W. Hatfield (London: Hodder and Stoughton, 1923), 55-56. http://rpo.library.utoronto.ca/poem/223.html.

### Searcher on the Way—God's Great Sunrise

R. Ricks, *The Brownings: Letters and Poetry* (New York: Doubleday, 1970), 134-138.

### Searcher on the Way—Carp and the Theory of Everything

Dr. Michio Kaku, Theoretical Physicist, http://www.mkaku.org/.

## Habakkuk

### Searcher on the Way—A Lesson in Humility

Quotes taken from Daniel 4:30-37, *The Message*.

## Jonah

### Searcher on the Way—A Journey into Ancient Truth

http://www.archaeology.org/online/features/nineveh/.

http://en.wikipedia.org/wiki/Nineveh.

## Psalms of David

### Searcher on the Way—From Slave-Shepherd to Saint
Thomas Cahill, *How the Irish Saved Civilization* (New York: Doubleday, 1996). http://www.ccel.org/ccel/patrick/confession.html.

### Poem After 16
Stephen Crane, "The Black Riders and Other Lines," 1895. http://www.theotherpages.org/poems/crane02.html.

### Searcher on the Way—Pursuing the Evidence . . . Wherever It Leads
Interview of Antony Flew by Christian philosopher Gary Habermas for the Winter 2004 issue of *Philosophia Christi*, http://www.biola.edu/antonyflew/.

### Poem/Lyrics After 61
Mac Powell, Brad Avery, David Carr, Samuel Tai Anderson, Mark D. Lee, "Nothing Compares," © 2001 New Spring Publishing, Inc. (Administered by Brentwood-Benson Music Publishing, Inc.) Vandura 2500 Songs, (Administered by EMI Christian Music Group) (AScAp). Used by permission.

### Searcher on the Way—Fourteen Days
http://en.wikipedia.org/wiki/Abd-ar-rahman_III.
http://www.giga-usa.com/quotes/authors/abderrahmaniii_a001.htm.

### Searcher on the Way—A Legacy of Thanksgiving
This is the text of George Washington's October 3, 1789, National Thanksgiving proclamation, issued while he was president (as printed in the *Providence Gazette and Country Journal*, October 17, 1789). http://www.wallbuilders.com/resources/search/detail .php?ResourceID=111.

### Searcher on the Way—No Pit So Deep
http://www.corrietenboom.com/.

# Mark

## Searcher on the Way — A Record of History

*Antiquities,* book 18, chapter 3, paragraph 3 (translated from fourth-century Arabic manuscript).

Shlomo Pines, *An Arabic Version of the Testamonium Flavianum and Its Implications* (Jerusalem Academic Press, 1971), 69.

## Poem/Lyrics After 10:16

"Even in My Youth," Erin O'Donnell from the album *Scrapbook of Sorts.*

## Searcher on the Way — Karma vs. Grace

Transcript: Bono Remarks at the National Prayer Breakfast, February 2, 2006. http://lectiofaith.blogspot.com/2006/02/transcript-bono-remarks-at-national.html.

Michka Assayas, *Bono: In Conversation* (Riverhead, 2005).

# John

## Poem/Lyrics After 4:42

© 2003, 2004, Matt Maher. Published by SpiritandSong.com®, 5536 NE Hassalo, Portland, OR 97213. All rights reserved. Used with permission.

## Searcher on the Way — Amazing Grace

http://en.wikipedia.org/wiki/Amazing_Grace.

## Searcher on the Way — From the Head to the Heart

John Fischer, "Mind on Fire," February 16, 2006 (http://www.purposedrivenlife.com/devarchive.aspx?ARCHIVEID=1610) .http://www.probe.org/docs/pascal.html.

## Searcher on the Way — Testimony of the Gospels

Simon Greenleaf, *The Testimony of the Evangelists: The Gospels Examined by the Rules of Evidence* (Grand Rapids, MI: Kregel, 1995), 11, back cover.

**Searcher on the Way—The Atoning Act of an Alaskan Chief**
John Muir, *Travels in Alaska*, chapter XIII, "Alaska Indians," 1879,
http://www.sierraclub.org/john_muir_exhibit/frameindex.html?http://
www.sierraclub.org/john_muir_exhibit/writings/travels_in_alaska/
chapter_13.html.

# ABOUT THE AUTHORS

## EUGENE H. PETERSON

Eugene H. Peterson is a pastor, scholar, writer, and poet. After teaching at a seminary and then giving nearly thirty years to church ministry in the Baltimore area, he created *The Message*—a vibrant Bible paraphrase that connects with today's readers like no other.

It took Peterson a full ten years to complete. He worked from the original Greek and Hebrew tests to guarantee authenticity. At the same time, his ear was always tuned to the cadence and energy of contemporary English.

## RANDALL NILES

Randall Niles is a corporate attorney who now spends most of his time pursuing his passion: developing cutting-edge media to spark critical thinking and truth-seeking in a new generation. For the past five years, Randall has served as cofounder and director of operations at www.AllAboutGOD.com, where he's written and published hundreds of articles on comparative worldviews and Christian apologetics.

When he's not writing or speaking, Randall teaches college courses in the areas of business, law, and philosophy. In 2004, Randall published his "great pursuit," *What Happened to Me: Reflections of a Journey*, which now travels the virtual world via blogs and social networks as www.AllAboutTheJourney.org. Randall's education includes Georgetown, Oxford, and Berkeley. He lives in Colorado with his wife and three kids and can be reached at Randall@RandallNiles.com.